Passport Please
Epic of the Kingdom III

By Pete Nielsen

Passport Please – Epic of the Kingdom – Volume 3

Copyright © 2007-2020 by Peter S. Nielsen

Passport Please - Epic of the Kingdom III
by Pete Nielsen

Printed in the United States of America

ISBN 978-0-578-64708-1

Scriptures quoted in the end notes are either from:
THE HOLY BIBLE, NEW INTERNATIONAL VERSION®
NIV® Copyright © 1973, 1978, 1984, 2011 by Biblica, Inc.™
Used by permission. All rights reserved worldwide.

Or from:
THE HOLY BIBLE, NEW INTERNATIONAL VERSION®.
NIV1984® Copyright © 1973, 1978, 1984 Biblica.
Used by permission of Zondervan. All rights reserved.

All rights are reserved solely by the author.

The author guarantees all contents are original and do not infringe upon the legal rights of any other person or work.

No part of this book may be reproduced in any form without the permission of the author.

Views expressed in this book are not necessarily those of the publisher.

www.epicofthekingdom.com

Applause for
Passport Please

"A remarkably engaging novel.
A grand adventure and one heck of a fun read!"

> John Debney, Composer
> Iron Man, Spider Man
> The Passion of the Christ

"*Passport Please* takes an enormous number of seemingly unrelated Biblical events and weaves them into a highly readable adventure."

> Bobb Biehl, Founding Director
> Focus on the Family

"An entertaining and thought-provoking rendition of the most influential book in history."

> Quinn Mills, Professor Emeritus
> Harvard Business School

Amazon.com reviewers said:

"Remarkably accurate to the Bible"

"Some parts I laughed out loud"

"A cohesive, flowing tale"

"A big, big picture"

"It's not preachy"

PASSPORT PLEASE
Epic of the Kingdom III
Table of Contents

ം‍ൟ

Introduction		1
Previously, in Epic of the Kingdom I: Beginnings		5
Previously, in Epic of the Kingdom II: Betrayal		9
1:	End of the Age	11
2:	Transition	17
3:	A New Beginning	23
4:	Rebel's Dare	27
5:	Rule 1 - Family First	31
6:	Betrayal	39
7:	Consequences	45
8:	Into the Wild	53
9:	Intimate Assault	61
10:	Three Prongs	67
11:	National IDs	73
12:	Loyalty Lessons	79
13:	Escape from Tyranny	87
14:	Law School	93
15:	Freedom Ahead	99

16:	School of Government	105
17:	King's Crossing	113
18:	Summit Meeting	121
19:	Hidden in Plain Sight	125
20:	Challenging Authority	131
21:	The Set-Up	139
22:	Blood Matters	145
23:	Legal Matters	151
24:	Transfer of Authority	155
25:	Free Will	161
26:	Competing Offers	165
27:	Punch - Counterpunch	171
28:	Media Blitz	179
29:	Out of Harm's Way	183
30:	Commence Firing	189
31:	The Take-Down	197
32:	Last Gasp	203
33:	Immigration Hearing	209
34:	Moving Day	215
35:	Another Age Begins	219

Appendix 1: Time Zones and Time Lines *221*
Appendix 2: Endnotes *225*

*notes for this chapter
start on page 226*

Introduction

❦

Passport Please is an Allegory

Passport Please says, "I'll tell you a story about *this*, to show how *that* works, because both of those things operate in a similar way."

Written in the style of a novel, *Passport Please* tells a story about relations and travel between neighboring countries, earth and the Kingdom of Heaven. If you have ever travelled from one country to another, and crossed through passport control when you arrive, you will have no trouble seeing the big picture of the Bible as told in *Passport Please*.

Is *Passport Please* fiction? That is for you to decide. This book simply tells the big picture of the Bible, as if it is true.

All the plot elements in this story are detailed in hundreds of end-notes, showing where to find their basis in the Bible.[a]

The author's goal is not to prove that this story, or the Bible, is true, but rather to show that *Passport Please* is true-to-the-Bible. It may be helpful to have a Bible handy when you read *Passport Please*, and check this out for yourself.

---

[a] Endnotes for each chapter start on the page noted at the top of the first page of each chapter.

A Story of Wartime Immigration

The Bible uses language describing the interactions between heaven and earth as if they were nations with rulers, citizens, ambassadors, armies, borders, legal systems and entry requirements – and it turns out these nations are at war.

Jesus said, to cross into heaven one must be naturalized or, in his words, be "born again."[1] Naturalization gives a person the same status as a "natural-born" citizen, including the issuance of a passport, which is required to enjoy access to their new country, in this case, the Kingdom of Heaven.

A Multi-Dimensional Story

String theory is a relatively new field of physics. It tells us there are many overlapping dimensions in our universe, most of which are undetectable by humans.[2]

Since Jesus told Roman governor Pilate, "My kingdom is not of this world," *Passport Please* takes the position that Jesus' kingdom is above, located in higher dimensions that are invisible to humans, yet still very real.[3]

Passport Please is Episode III of an Epic Story

In 1977, *Star Wars* was just a great movie. No sequels, no prequels... but everyone knew there had to be more. In 1981, that same movie was retitled: *Star Wars – Episode IV – A New Hope*. Only then did the really big picture start to emerge, and it all started in the middle, with *Episode IV*.

So it is with *Epic of the Kingdom III*. The Bible story is usually told starting with Adam and Eve, but references throughout the Bible point to dramatic events from much earlier, giving context to the world that they, and we, were brought into. Starting on page 5, summaries of *Epic of the Kingdom I & II* provide a Bible-based glimpse into the origins of *Passport Please - Epic of the Kingdom III*.[4]

Introduction

Background: Citizenship

Citizens are always allowed to cross the border into their home country. Citizenship of a country can come to a person in one of three ways:

by Birth: Anyone born in a particular country has historically been guaranteed full citizenship in that nation.

by Bloodline: A child can always be a citizen of the country where either one of their parents is a citizen.

by Naturalization: A citizen of one country can become the legal equivalent of a natural-born citizen of another through naturalization, usually by giving up citizenship and allegiance and swearing allegiance to the new nation.

Background: Diplomatic Positions

Prime Minister: the King's senior government minister, who oversees and directs their country's diplomatic corps of ambassadors and consuls. The PM speaks for the King.

Ambassador: a citizen of one country, posted in another, who represents the head of state of their home country. The ambassador's words carry the same weight as if the head of their home country has spoken.

Consul: a citizen of one country, posted in another, who promotes good relations between the countries.

Honorary Consul: a citizen of the country they live in, (i.e. an American living in the USA) who works voluntarily to support the Ambassador of a foreign country (like Uganda), to promote good relations between those countries.

Passport Please - Epic of the Kingdom III

Our Story: The Characters

The King is the patriarch of the Kingdom of Heaven. He is also known as the Royal Father. The King sets the vision for the nation, and he is the final authority of the kingdom.

The Prince is the King's son, who has the same passion for the Kingdom as his father. He commands the kingdom's armed forces and has a reputation as a builder and creator.

The Prime Minister communicates the vision, the work and the words of the Royal family, and is in constant touch with kingdom patriots on the earth. He steps in to support them whenever necessary.

Michael and Gabriel are generals in the kingdom army. Each commands a legion of troops, providing security for the kingdom and carrying out kingdom missions.

Lucifer, the third general in the kingdom army, a peer of Michael and Gabriel. He is confident, ambitious and well loved by the Royal family. At least, that is the case when our story begins...

notes for this chapter start on page 227

PREVIOUSLY, IN

Epic of the Kingdom I
Beginnings

☙❧

Before the beginning, before the earth, the stars and the galaxies were formed, even before time itself began, there was a King whose domain spanned dimensions that human words cannot adequately describe.[1]

The King lived in a mansion with his son the Prince and the Prime Minister; the Royal family of the Kingdom. They were attended by a company of servants and were protected by Generals Lucifer, Michael and Gabriel, who led the Kingdom's armed forces.[2]

While he lacked nothing, the King often expressed a desire to have a bigger family.[3] Today he would take the first steps toward fulfilling that desire. He summoned everyone, from every corner of the realm, to the Great Kingdom Hall for a big announcement.

The room was packed. The Royals smiled and waved to friends in the crowd. The King rose and the room fell silent. "Today, the Kingdom of Heaven will establish a frontier colony outside our current borders. It will include a garden paradise filled with a multitude of biological life forms, under an enormous light-filled canopy."

Whispers could be heard throughout the room.

Before the pause became too awkward, General Lucifer asked what everyone was wondering, "Your majesty, what exactly is a garden... and what are biological life forms?"

The King chuckled and motioned to the Prince.

"It will be better just to show you," the Prince said. "But first, we need to create a few things, including physical matter and a three-dimensional space to put it in."

"Only three dimensions?" Lucifer enquired." [4]

"Three and a half, actually," the Prime Minister clarified. "In the Frontier, time will only move in one direction – forward - so that after a word is spoken, a decision is made or an event occurs, it will be final, unchangeable, and recorded in the Kingdom archives." [5]

Lucifer asked, "So you are saying that in the Frontier, one cannot move back and forth in time?"

"That is correct," the PM responded. "Only into the future, one day at a time... but not at the same rate as here in the Kingdom. Frontier Standard Time will run about a thousand years for every day in KST." [6]

Lucifer looked toward Michael and Gabriel to see if they understood it any better. It was obvious that everyone in the room was confused.

The King stood up. "As my son indicated, it will become clear once we get started. Some of you will travel to the Frontier to establish and protect our kingdom colony." He nodded to the Prince, "...and we're about ready."

The Prince motioned toward the main doorway, "Please, if everyone will make your way to the viewing platform by the Crystal Sea, you'll have a front-row seat!"

The generals followed the last of the crowd, closing the big doors behind them as they exited, leaving the Royals to themselves. The Prime Minister turned to the King and Prince and said, "So it begins."

The King nodded. "Raising up this family of ours will not be easy."

"And it will require sacrifice," the Prime Minister said, turning to the Prince, "that we cannot even speak of, until it is done." [7]

"But it will be well worth the price," the Prince said confidently.

The three Royals enjoyed the moment. Taking a deep breath, the Prince winked at the others. "Let's do it." He pulled a shiny sphere the size of a marble out of his pocket and walked toward the balcony doors. All three stepped out into the crisp air. The Crystal Sea, surrounded by majestic mountains, was a breathtaking sight. Throngs of kingdom citizens gathered below, with all eyes on the Royals.

Like a centerfielder making the long throw to home plate, the Prince threw the marble out over the crowd into the water, which started to swirl around the spot where the marble had plunked.

The marble descended through the water, first glowing, then illuminating the surface of the Crystal Sea from below. Suddenly, the sphere erupted, throwing off white-hot burning stars which lit up the Crystal Sea, to the amazement of the spectators.[8] They watched through the surface of the water, as galaxies roared into existence one after another, shooting away toward some far-off destination below and beyond the kingdom. Finally, as the eruptions slowed, the onlookers could see the earth, rotating slowly in the warm glow of the sun, against a backdrop of countless shining stars. Earth was beautiful and ready to be inhabited.[9]

"Behold the heavens and the earth!" the King declared from the balcony, to the crowd below. "Planet earth is the kingdom's crown jewel of the lower frontier." The crowd erupted in sustained cheers, which grew into a chorus of voices singing the anthem of the kingdom. [10]

The joy of the Royals was evident. They stood, arms wrapped over each other's shoulders, with radiant smiles.

Finally, the Royals made their last waves and returned inside the Great Kingdom Hall, where General Lucifer was now waiting for them. "Lucifer!" the King said with affection. "My trusted General." Placing his hands on Lucifer's shoulders, the King said, "Be governor over our earth, the steward of all life on it and the protector of our new kingdom colony." [11]

Lucifer bowed low, "I am your humble servant."

"Go my faithful friend," the King commanded. "Go in the name of the Kingdom!"

Lucifer smiled proudly as he walked from the room, ready to take on his new assignment. An exciting new era of expansion had begun for the Kingdom of Heaven.

It was clear the Kingdom had spared no expense in crafting the earth and populating it with exotic and beautiful plants and animals, large and small.

Countless years passed...
  Life on earth was good...
    Both the Royals and Lucifer were pleased.

Lucifer knew he was doing well as governor of the colony. Often, he dreamt of the honors sure to be bestowed on him by a grateful King.

One day, a Lieutenant on Lucifer's staff delivered a hand-written note. He read it and re-read it, dumbfounded.

He looked to the sky, crumpled the note, and snarled, "You have betrayed me..."

*notes for this chapter
start on page 230*

PREVIOUSLY, IN

Epic of the Kingdom II
Betrayal

~~~~

The note had been written by an officer on Lucifer's staff, regarding a conversation he had overheard outside the throne room of the Great Kingdom Hall, between members of the Royal family.

In essence, the King appeared to be making plans to install a new governor over the earth. This was Lucifer's worst nightmare. The King was going to replace him with a human – a human who would rank higher than Lucifer and the other Generals![1]

Lucifer was incredulous. "Those creatures can't manage their own lives, much less rule a planet like this one!"[2] Lucifer screamed, "and the humans will outrank me? They've never even seen the throne room or even spoken to a member of the Royal family!" Despondent, Lucifer felt he was getting pushed farther and farther from the throne. The Lieutenant who had handed him the note was slowly backing up, trying to stay out of harm's way.

Lucifer was not about to leave his future to chance. He needed to protect his position. Obsessed with holding onto power, he began making his own plans.

He became increasingly convinced that he should be the one to rule - not just the earth, but the entire Kingdom of Heaven![3] He was sure that, given the chance, Michael and Gabriel would join him. Lucifer let his troops know that a showdown with the Royal family was coming.

Lucifer fired the first shot by sending a message of his own, curtly stating that he had no intention of giving up the earth. He invited Michael and Gabriel and their armies to join in to "Free the Frontier" from Royal family domination.

Michael and Gabriel were appalled. Their comrade's act of treason would bring full-scale war into the Kingdom. Furious at Lucifer's rebellion, the King ordered Michael and Gabriel to use every means necessary to bring the rebels to justice. The Generals were more than ready.

The Kingdom's armed forces descended and violently shook the earth.[4] After a fierce struggle, they captured Lucifer and his army, bound them and whisked them back into the Kingdom to face justice.

Then, at the King's command, floodgates beneath the Kingdom's Crystal Sea were opened, unleashing a torrent of water that destroyed the earth and spread through the lower frontier, extinguishing light from the sun and the stars. The flood engulfed the earth and terminated all life on the planet.[5] Darkness reigned.

Lucifer and his army were marched in shackles before crowds of kingdom citizens who lined the main street of Heaven. Most just stared at Lucifer, shaking their heads, not wanting to believe what they were seeing.[6]

General Lucifer would be locked-up until it was time for him to stand before a court martial in the Kingdom.[7]

The earth had become a graveyard. The planet was ruined... frozen, formless and void.[8]

Next: Passport Please - Epic of the Kingdom III

*notes for this chapter
start on page 234*

1: End of the Age

The main courtroom in the kingdom Justice Center was silent. Sitting forward in his chair behind the judicial bench, the Prince used both hands to close the massive book of evidence.

The balconies were jammed with celestial beings, straining to see and hear. The book closed with a thump of finality that echoed off the high arched ceilings.

Four heavily-armed kingdom deputies surrounded Lucifer, the accused, who sat in silence. His eyes were fixed on his two former comrades in arms in the front row of the courtroom. Both Gabriel and Michael, the two ranking generals in the army of the kingdom, had been prosecution witnesses against him. Their eyes were fixed on the Prince.

"The Prince's poodles," Lucifer thought. "How did I ever see them as brothers? They command armies, but they are completely in the Prince's pocket. I don't think they have an ounce of free will between them."

Lucifer's mind drifted to an earlier time when the three of them led armies into battle, protecting the kingdom and bringing honor to the Royal family. He shook his head thinking how things changed since the Royals decided to replace him as earth's governor, with a human, no less!

"Michael and Gabriel never said a single word in support of their comrade-in-arms. Those poodles!"

"The accused shall stand!" thundered the stern-faced bailiff. One deputy on each side grabbed Lucifer's elbows and jolted him to his feet. Lucifer set his icy gaze upon the Prince.

The Prince returned his gaze. Lucifer felt it burn into the heart of his being, and he winced.

"Lucifer! General of the army of the kingdom and pre-eminent among the citizens of heaven, I have reviewed the evidence against you. You are accused of willful violation of the prime directive of the kingdom, which is: 'Total allegiance to the King,' and you have shown absolutely no remorse. Reliable witnesses have testified that you conspired against the Royal family, personally inciting rebellion amongst those in your charge, encouraging them to turn against the kingdom and follow you in insurrection against the King. It is the judgment of this court that you are guilty of treason. Does the accused have anything to say to the court before I pronounce sentence?"

Lucifer looked over his shoulder to see his troops, thousands of warriors all wearing the dark capes of Lucifer's regiment in the kingdom army. They were a disciplined, lethal fighting force that had followed their general to the end. Gathered behind the invisible but impenetrable force field in the defendant's arena, they had cast their fate with Lucifer. All of their eyes were fixed on him.

Lucifer's gaze returned to the Prince. He knew he was about to lose his rank and perhaps even be thrown out of the army. Lucifer was determined, however, that no matter what, *he* would have the final word.

Clearing his throat, Lucifer lifted his head and turned away from the Prince and toward the public gallery. He spoke in a loud voice, so he could be heard throughout the courtroom. "Citizens of the kingdom! You know that I have

1: End of the Age

always been a kingdom patriot.[1] The Royals themselves have commended me many times for my commitment and service to the kingdom. Now they call me a terrorist and have accused me of treason. My crime? They call it rebellion; I call it fighting for our freedom. Watch now how the Royals reward anyone who refuses to be a puppet on the string of this self-absorbed Royal family."

A murmur swept through the crowd. The tension between Lucifer and the Royals was well known, but Lucifer's statement was a provocative public slap in their faces. The bailiff hammered his staff on the floor to restore order. "Silence in the courtroom!"

"Indeed, you are no puppet," the Prince said coolly. "And as of this moment, you are no longer a general, either. As is the right of a citizen of the kingdom, you have been duly tried and found guilty of treason. You are hereby stripped of your rank and are dishonorably removed from the King's army, permanently."

Even though he had expected this humiliation, Lucifer still boiled inside. He thought, "Have they forgotten everything I have ever done for them ... and who I am?" Furious, Lucifer spun around to face the royal section of the courtroom gallery. His eyes burning, he focused intensely on the Prime Minister. "Take your damned kingdom citizenship as well!" he bellowed. "I don't want it!"

A collective gasp could be heard in the courtroom as all eyes went from Lucifer to the Prime Minister. The PM closed his eyes at what amounted to a total renunciation of the kingdom and the Royals.

After a moment of silence, the Prince, the King, and the Prime Minister exchanged glances. The King, sitting next to the Prime Minister, nodded silently. The Prime Minister looked at the Prince and said, almost inaudibly, "So be it."

"So be it!" the Prince repeated, loud enough for everyone to hear. "Lucifer, you have publicly and willfully renounced your citizenship in the kingdom of heaven. Your renunciation has been recognized by the Prime Minister. As of this moment, you are no longer a citizen of the kingdom.[2] Accordingly, you are to be deported and confined to the earth, which has been destroyed as a result of your actions."[3]

Burning with rage, Lucifer began to process the consequences of his sentence. In his mind, he rationalized, "At least we'll be across the border and away from these overbearing Royals. The frontier is not like heaven, that's for sure, but the royal garden down there used to be pretty nice.[4] It's a mess now, but it's a start, and I will be in charge again, free from the stench of that Royal family.[5] Yes," Lucifer concluded, "I can deal with this."

Turning to the defendant's arena, the Prince addressed the captive army.

"Army of the kingdom under Lucifer! You were misled by the one who is now about to be exiled. He has brought you to the brink of condemnation, but not yet into it. Your leader has fallen and you shall be deported with him, but hear this! You need not be exiled forever."

"You were trained well and you have been loyal to the authority placed over you, however corrupt that authority may have become. Choose your destiny while you are in exile! A final judgment awaits you." [6]

To no one's surprise, the faces of Lucifer's soldiers showed only contempt. Disciplined to the end, they drew strength from their leader's defiance of the Prince. Lucifer stood silent and proud.

"So be it," said the Prince. "Lucifer, your pride has led you into darkness. Bailiff! Carry out the sentence. Escort the prisoners to the portal!" The Prince hammered his gavel, stood, and turned to exit the courtroom.

A company of heavily armed kingdom deputies surrounded Lucifer and his soldiers. They moved the

1: End of the Age

condemned army out of the courtroom, toward the edge of the Crystal Sea, the portal to the lower frontier.[7]

The lower frontier spans far fewer dimensions than the kingdom proper, so Lucifer knew that when he and his army returned to earth, they would be constrained, able to move only in the dimensions of the lower frontier, and kept from reentry into the kingdom by means of a secure border.

Lucifer and his soldiers were led down a road leading to the portal. In a final act of bravado, Lucifer stopped suddenly and turned to his army. He raised his clenched fist and shouted, "Follow me to freedom from the King!" He turned toward the portal and together, the entire condemned army let out a shout, "FREEDOM!" With thousands of defiant fists shaking in the air, they ran down the steep hillside, over the edge of the cliff, and into the Crystal Sea, disappearing from the kingdom of heaven.

Lightning crashed across the sky as the portal swallowed them up, and its glassy surface closed behind them. The condemned leader and his army fell, as if tumbling down a dimensional staircase, into the lower frontier.[8]

*notes for this chapter
start on page 236*

2: Transition

B etween the marble floors and high arched ceilings of the great kingdom hall, the atmosphere was one of eager anticipation. The tiered walkways lining the walls and crossing over the hall were filled with thousands of kingdom officials and staff bustling back and forth, attending to the business of heaven, and making last-minute preparations for the resurrection of earth.

Light poured through the tall windows, brightly illuminating thousands of flags hanging along the walls,[1] representing dominions and regions in every corner of the kingdom.

The great kingdom hall is the preeminent building of the kingdom and can be seen from the far reaches of heaven. Behind the king's throne, floor-to-ceiling windows looked out over the Crystal Sea, through which Lucifer and his army had been deported. From this waterfront vantage point, the King had an unobstructed view through the sea and into the lower frontier. Often, he had swiveled his throne around,[2] slid the massive windows open and rested his feet on the edge of the balcony while he pondered the future of his lower frontier.[3] Today, the pondering was over, and the plan was about to unfold.

Passport Please - Epic of the Kingdom III

The King sat on his throne, overlooking all the bustle in the throne room, waiting expectantly for his son.

The Prince strode confidently into the great kingdom hall, excited and prepared for the challenge ahead. It was to be an adventure that would change everything. He and his father had been planning to restore the earth for a long time. Expanding the borders of the kingdom around the lower frontier had been their favorite topic of conversation since Lucifer's rebellion had been put down.

The outline of the earth can be viewed from the observation deck above the Crystal Sea portal, but ever since the rebellion, there hasn't been much to see. The earth was covered with water and ice, and since the lights in the sky were extinguished in the flood, it had been completely dark.

The citizens of heaven looked forward to restoration of the heavens and the earth. It was widely understood that after it was cleaned up, the Royals planned to move the Kingdom headquarters to earth, and most everyone looked forward to visiting earth themselves.

One question was still on everyone's mind... what about Lucifer? Everyone knew he was still on the earth.

On and above the dark, cold and wet earth, Lucifer wandered bitterly in the company of his soldiers. He barely recognized the planet but was resigned to his new situation. "I'd rather be in charge of this wasteland than groveling in heaven," he told his army, outwardly defiant. Lucifer was fully aware of the strength of heaven's border security, and the hopelessness of attempting a forced reentry. Confined to the dimensions below the kingdom gates, the lower frontier was their prison.

"Damn you, Prince!" he shouted at the invisible kingdom when none of his troops were looking, shaking his fist in no particular direction.

As if skating on ice, the Prime Minister of the kingdom slid across the surface of the Crystal Sea, toward the great

2: Transition

kingdom hall and throne room. He was squinting, looking down at the dark earth below the sea, and thinking about the kingdom expansion into the frontier and all that it would mean.

It would mean a lot of humans immigrating into the kingdom, for one thing. Then, at the end of the age, moving the entire Kingdom and all its new citizens back to earth.[4] The PM shook his head just thinking about it.

He glided into the crowded Kingdom Hall. He greeted the King and the Prince. Together, the ruling family of the kingdom was about to launch something big.

The King waved his hand for quiet in the room and said, "It's time." The noise level in the great hall dropped, but the activity around them continued as a thousand conversations transitioned to whispers. The King motioned for the Prime Minister and the Prince to come closer. "Over the coming week, we will restore the lower frontier. We'll re-ignite the stars and populate the earth with living beings — not just plants, fish, animals and birds like the kind we had before – but human members of our Royal family.[5] And when we extend the kingdom borders around the earth, we'll go there and live with them. It'll be heaven on earth!"

"Son, this project is under your authority. You are going to make it happen. These humans will be your people, your nation. In the end, heaven and the earth will become a united kingdom."[6] The King gripped the back of his son's neck with a fatherly squeeze, as the Prince beamed.

As a general, one of Michael's primary jobs was security and protection for the kingdom and for the Royals. Stepping forward, he hesitated a moment, not wanting to dampen the mood. Then he spoke, "You know that Lucifer will consider your colony on earth to be an invasion of his territory."

"He knows the lower frontier was never his to begin with," the King responded.

"Correct," The Prime Minister added, "But the facts don't matter to him. He'll claim squatter's rights, or whatever legal maneuver he can come up with to assert his authority."

"He will try anything he can to humiliate us and to derail our family plans," the Prince agreed in a somber voice.

"So be it," the King said with authority. "We are expanding the borders of the kingdom around the lower frontier, whether Lucifer likes it or not. How he responds to our presence there is for him to decide, but he will live with the consequences of whatever actions he takes."

Michael nodded slightly, satisfied that he had done his job by raising the issue, and secure in the knowledge that the Royals had taken these matters into account long ago.

The Royals stood quietly for a moment and the King broke the silence, "You know, son, preparing the earth and building our colony will be the easy part. Raising up a family of patriots who love our kingdom will be the hardest thing you have ever done."

The Prince nodded. He was ready.

The Royal Father looked at the Prince and said, "It's all yours, son."

The restoration of earth was the top priority in the kingdom, and all of heaven's resources stood ready to take the next step.

The Crystal Sea Operations Center, the CSOC, located below the surface of the Crystal Sea, overlooked the lower frontier. Though the earth was right below them, at this point there was only blackness outside the windows.

The Prince entered the CSOC, joining Generals Michael and Gabriel and the commander of the Kingdom Corps of Engineers. After confirming the plan, the Prince said to his friends, "Next week, you'll hardly recognize the view." With that, he turned, stepped into the CSOC dimension-lock and the door closed behind him.

2: Transition

When the higher dimensions of the Kingdom meet the lower dimensions of the lower frontier, it's like high and low-pressure weather fronts colliding... it's a recipe for lightning. When someone "from above" carries those higher dimensions on their person, into the frontier, they carry that lightning with them. So it was with the Prince.

As the outer door opened into the frontier, a shower of light shot into the cold, wet darkness and the Prince of the Kingdom stepped out to resurrect his creation.

The door closed behind him. The Prince shined brightly as he approached the earth from above. Since the sun and stars had been extinguished when Lucifer's rebellion was crushed, light emanating from the Prince was the only light in the frontier. The Prince circled around the back of the planet. To those in the CSOC the backlit outline of the earth looked like the corona of a total solar eclipse. As the Prince came into view again, his brightness was like the first dawn breaking through the darkness.[7]

The Prince looked around the wasted earth, smiling as he anticipated what was about to happen.

Looking up to the CSOC, he addressed the Commander of the Kingdom Corps of Engineers in a loud voice, "It's time – come down and let's reboot the frontier!" [8]

*notes for this chapter
start on page 240*

3: A New Beginning

~~~

At the Prince's command, wave after wave of kingdom engineers scrambled down through the surface of the Crystal Sea. The portal swallowed them up as they shot through into the lower frontier for a week of hard work, executing the King's plan.[1]

"Let's get some of this water away from the planet. I want a big open sky between the earth's oceans and the Crystal Sea," the Prince shouted to his team. Looking up at his father, he added with a wink, "That should give the King a better view of what's going on down here, from that big old throne of his." [2]

The earth began to slowly move away from the Crystal Sea portal. As it moved, an open sky filled the space between the water on the earth's surface and the Crystal Sea in the kingdom above.[3] Looking up from the surface of the earth, the bright sky was a beautiful light blue.

The Prince liked what he saw and looked up at his father, who nodded in approval. There was still plenty of water covering two-thirds of the earth, so the Prince tasked some of the engineers with pooling the oceans, others with shaping the continents, and carving the rivers. The Prince's detailed plans even included a global plumbing system for irrigating the land with clean, fresh water. That was critical, given the unimaginable number and variety of plants and trees that were being planted just about anywhere there was dry land.

The earth was shaping up well. The Prince tasked teams to set the planets and moons in precise orbits to light up night sky. A team of kingdom engineers re-ignited the stars and configured the SPS (Starlight Positioning System) to provide reliable signs for humans who would soon be travelling the globe.[4]

It was a lot of work, for sure, but the Prince reassured them that it all would be complete within a few days, on Frontier Standard Time, that is. All the kingdom engineers knew what Einstein later discovered, "time flows at different rates, depending on whose watch you are using!"[5] They knew that the Prince always kept to his schedule.

Birds, wild animals, livestock were all being brought back to the earth, each with the same design as their species had before the devastating flood which ended the rebellion and destroyed everything.[6] It was all coming together.

Lucifer was astonished. He watched from the shadows while the Prince refurbished the once-formless and flooded earth. "He's turning my prison into a paradise again," he thought. "Is the King extending an offer of peace and reconciliation? Has he finally realized the mistake he has made? It took a while for him to admit it, but I think the King may be coming around!"

Lucifer did not know that a survey team of kingdom engineers was busy redrawing their maps to include the earth as a colony of heaven. Their maps included the part of the frontier where invisible higher dimensions spilled across the border from the Kingdom. This border region is called, "the heavenlies," which benefitted heavenly beings, but was unseen by and inaccessible to the residents of earth.

Lucifer had discovered this border region and had set up camp in the heavenlies, out of sight from the earth and just below the border with the Kingdom.[7]

3: A New Beginning

Redrawing the kingdom maps was the first step in formally extending the kingdom borders around the entire lower frontier – but Lucifer was not yet aware of the kingdom expansion plan. As the surveyors moved closer to the earth, Lucifer moved closer to losing his status as the freewheeling frontier warlord on this dismal swamp. He was on his way to becoming an undesirable alien in a colony of the Kingdom of Heaven.

The frontier was ready. The time had come for the centerpiece of restoration of earth, the creation of a completely new kind of human being.

The Prince wanted to create this human personally, with his own hands. They would be unlike anything that had ever walked the earth before.[8] Later, the PM would come alongside, and even enter into, these newest members of the Royal family, to teach them everything they needed to know.

With a nod to his father and the PM, the Prince once again stepped down through the Crystal Sea portal and entered the lower frontier.

The Prince knelt in the dirt of his newly renovated earth. He plunged his hands into the moist clay and carefully, artfully formed the first man. It was a marvelous, complex creation. Bending over, the Prince drew a breath and breathed into the man, the breath of life. Royal blood started circulating in the man and he was alive.[9] The Prince called the man Adam.

The Prince called Michael, Gabriel and their squad leaders over to show them the first human member of the Royal family.

Those in the crowd that had gathered around the portal in heaven were amazed. They watched as the Prince looked upon the newest member of the Royal family, asleep in the grass.

The Prince flashed a huge smile, looked up through the portal, and said to the crowd, "This is very good." The crowd erupted into applause.

The Royal Father nodded in agreement and added, "But not so good if he is going to be alone down there!"

The Prince knew exactly what his father meant; Adam needed a wife, but as it turns out, that would have to wait.

On the edge of the meadow, just beyond the tree line, Lucifer had been watching...

*notes for this chapter
start on page 244*

4: *Rebel's Dare*

~~~~

Lucifer was curious, frightened and angered all at once. He could not just stand by any longer. Taking a deep breath, he walked toward the Prince and the soldiers. As Lucifer approached, the kingdom warriors instinctively snapped their hands to the hilts of their swords. The Prince turned toward Lucifer, and with a slight move of his hand, motioned to Michael to keep their weapons sheathed.

The Prince and Lucifer had not been face-to-face since that day in the kingdom Justice Center when the Prince handed down his verdict, hammered the gavel, and deported Lucifer and his army from the kingdom into the lower frontier.

They stood and looked at each other. Finally, the Prince broke the silence. "So, where have you been?"

Lucifer bowed slightly. "Roaming through the earth. I must say, you have restored it far beyond its original beauty."

The Prince nodded to acknowledge the compliment. "Have you seen my greatest creation?" he asked gesturing toward the sleeping Adam. "A human being." [1]

"I've seen humans before," Lucifer said, unimpressed.

"But not like Adam. He is intelligent and creative, *and* he is the first full-blooded human member of the Royal family." [2]

That struck Lucifer like a hammer. He thought, "Just what I don't need on my earth—another stinking Royal!" Knowing he had to respond, Lucifer collected himself and smoothly floated his response.

"He'll be everything you expect, my Prince," he said with a patronizing smile. "He has no choice."

Michael and Gabriel stiffened as the tension mounted. The Prince looked Lucifer in the eye and let him continue.

"Is there anything off limits for this human? Why not draw a line in the sand? You can tell him all the reasons why he absolutely must not cross it. And let's see what the he does when given a real choice."

Michael and Gabriel looked at each other, aghast at their former comrade's brashness. The Prince did not blink.

"You said he is intelligent." Lucifer paused. "Intelligent enough to choose between your truth and mine ...?"

The Prince looked down, shook his head and responded, "Lucifer, you don't even know what truth is. Lies are your native language." [3] He sighed deeply. "Very well, Adam will choose. You may speak to him, but you may not lay a hand on him or any other human."

"Understood," Lucifer responded, almost unable to contain his excitement. "And if he chooses to turn his back on you, will you hand him over to me?"

The Prince did not answer right away. Glancing up, he saw his father watching. Their eyes met for a moment. The Prince looked down at Adam and said slowly, "If the man chooses to turn his back on us and follow you, I will hand him, and all that he has, over to you." [4]

Michael and Gabriel could hardly believe what they were hearing.

"This man and the entire human family are free to make their own choices," the Prince spoke in a strong, steady voice. "But understand this, Lucifer. Every detail of my father's plan will come to pass. I guarantee it." [5]

4: Rebel's Dare

Lucifer bowed with feigned respect while stepping backwards, withdrawing from the meeting. He turned quickly and bolted.

The Prince watched Lucifer disappear into the forest, then he looked at the sleeping human. "And so it begins, Adam. The enemies of the Royals are now the enemies of man." [6]

*notes for this chapter
start on page 245*

5: Rule 1 - Family First

∽∾

Adam and the Prince became close friends. They enjoyed exploring together, walking through the earth, marveling at the newly created creatures and enjoying the abundant food. The earth was full of plant life, including an outstanding garden of fruit trees—pears, nectarines, passion fruit, kiwi, bananas, cherries, apples, lemons—to name a few. "Delicious and nutritious!" the Prince said to Adam, as he sank his teeth into one of them, juice dripping down his chin. "It's not that I don't enjoy the other trees, it's just that if a tree doesn't produce good fruit, it isn't nearly as useful. You can always tell a good tree by its fruit." [1]

It was a great experience for both of them, wilderness camping and hiking amongst the wildlife in the virgin forest. They would sit around a fire in the evening and just talk. The Prince was eager for a close relationship with Adam. Their conversations lasted late into the night.

"You say there's even more to the universe than all of this?" Adam asked, poking his stick at a smoldering log while gesturing with his head toward the star-filled sky.

"Oh yes," responded the Prince. "There are several dimensions, each separate and distinct, and they all occupy the same physical space. So far, you have only seen a few of them."

Adam pondered his place in the universe, not really knowing where to begin. "How can all the dimensions occupy the same space?" he asked.

"Remember the flocks of birds we saw today?"

Adam nodded. The Prince continued, "Well, a bird can move in the up-down dimension, no matter where it is in the east-west or north-south dimensions. All three of those dimensions, length, width and height, overlap each other, and occupy the same space. Time is like that as well. No matter where the bird flies, the dimension of time overlaps its physical position."

They sat silently for a while as Adam thought about living in multiple dimensions simultaneously. He poked the log again and it broke, exposing a glowing core.

Adam asked, looking directly into the Prince's eyes, "So there are more? You can sit here with me, then get up and move into a dimension where I can't follow you, or even see you?" He half expected the Prince to get up and disappear.

"I can, and I do, often," smiled the Prince, not moving from his seat on the log.[2] Adam nodded and looked back at the log's glowing center and jabbed it, sending up a shower of sparks into the shower of stars above.

"Here, take a look at this." The Prince pulled out a map of the kingdom and the lower frontier. "It's not to scale, but I think you'll get the picture...."

(see map on next page)

Running his finger over the map, the Prince explained, "As a human, Adam, you can move freely in the three physical dimensions of the lower frontier—length and width and height. Time runs through all of them, and there are a few invisible dimensions which you can't see. We call those "the heavenlies." There is still a lot to explore here in the garden, but all these dimensions? They're nothing compared to what is up here," he pointed out on the map, "in the kingdom proper."

5: Rule 1 – Family First

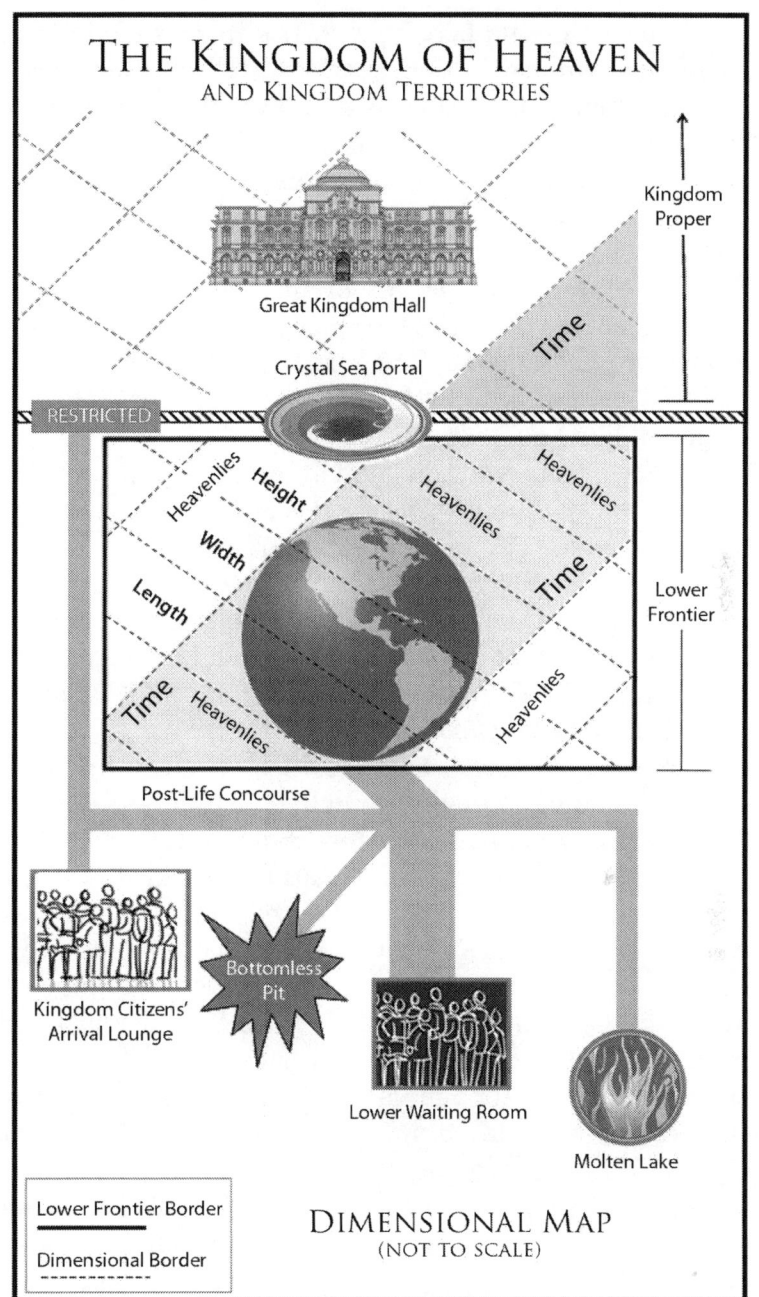

"I came from up here," the Prince said, pointing to the great kingdom hall. "Long ago my father established a barrier, actually more like a moat, on the border of the kingdom proper, separating it from the lower frontier." [3]

Adam thought that was interesting. "He did that because...?"

That is a story for another day, my friend," smiled the Prince, deciding that the tale of Lucifer's rebellion could wait until later. "But when the kingdom proper and the lower frontier are finally united, the barrier will be removed. Then you will be able to move in *all* of the dimensions of the kingdom, like I do."

"So why are we here now?" Adam asked, not fully understanding the importance of this question, or the answer he was about to hear.

The Prince lifted his eyes from the map and looked at his friend. "This is not just about expanding the borders of the kingdom. It's about us, Adam. About you being part of the Royal family." [4]

Adam looked down and smiled, not sure what to say. On the other side of their campfire, a pair of furry ring-tailed animals waddled through the firelight and disappeared into the darkness. Adam asked, "How about them?"

"No, they're not family," the Prince chuckled. "Not like you are anyway. They have bodies, and their own mind, will and emotions, but that is where the similarity between you and them ends. They are part of the kingdom, but they will never be kingdom royalty." The Prince looked off into the woods. "So," he asked, "what do you call those things?"

Adam thought for a moment. "Uh, raccoons, of course."

"Raccoons," the Prince nodded thoughtfully, "of course." They both laughed.[5]

After a while, Adam looked back at the map and tried to grasp what the Prince had told him. "You said that *time* is one of the overlapping dimensions here in the lower

5: *Rule 1 – Family First*

frontier." The Prince nodded. Adam pressed-in, "Are you saying I can walk back and forth in time? It feels like right now I am just being pulled along by time, at its own pace, not mine."

"You can't walk back and forth through time, yet... Here in the frontier, time runs like a river and you are being pulled along by it. When you are ready, you will be able to walk freely in every dimension, including time, just like I do," replied the Prince. "That's what we call eternal life. Time never runs out, any more than east or west runs out."

"When will that be?" Adam asked, ready to be an eleven-dimensional man.[6]

The Prince laughed, "You just got here, man! What's your hurry?"

Adam tried to keep from smiling but did anyway.

"My father and I have high expectations for you, Adam," the Prince explained. "You will learn about kingdom law and justice, and about the authority and responsibilities you will have as a kingdom citizen, and as a Royal. The Prime Minister and I will teach you all these things."

Adam was out of questions for the night. He already had a lot to process. It had been a long day and he was ready to get some sleep. The heat of the day had turned comfortably cool. The embers of the fire flickered in the gentle breezes, and a choir of crickets provided background music.

"I'm sure it will all make sense in the morning," Adam said as he lay back on the grass and looked straight up at the stars. "G'night Prince."

"I'm sure," smiled the Prince. "Good night, Adam."

That night as Adam slept, the Prince planted two special fruit trees in the middle of the garden. He called the first one the "Tree of Life" and the other he called "the Tree of Knowledge of Good and Evil." [7]

Eating fruit from the Tree of Life would allow Adam to walk back and forth in time, as easily as one might walk back and forth through a field of grass... time would never run out, but the Prince knew Adam wasn't ready for immortality. He still had things to learn about the world and about being a human member of the Royal family.

The other tree, the knowledge of good and evil tree, was the "line in the sand" which the Prince had discussed with Lucifer. In the morning, the Prince looked Adam in the eye, pointed at it and said, "Do not eat from this tree. If you do, you will die." [8]

For Adam, this new world was full of mysteries and the Prince's command not to eat from that tree was only one of them. He didn't give the tree a second thought. He was more interested in his next safari with the Prince.

That night, the King's words echoed in the Prince's heart. "It is not good for the man to remain alone on the earth." It was time for the Prince to let his human friend begin the Royal family line on earth.

Once again, the Prince personally created a human being with his own hands. He wanted a real "oneness" between the man and the woman, so this time he didn't use the dirt of the earth, but rather, he surgically removed a bone and tissue sample from Adam. Beginning with those, the Prince constructed a woman. She had dark, beautiful eyes, delicate hands, long thick hair and a shape that made Adam's heart pound. She was stunning.

The Prince was pleased. She was a perfect mate for his friend Adam.

Adam was, of course, delighted. He called her Eve. The Prince joined them together by presiding over the first marriage ceremony, right there in the garden. Now they were one, not only physically, but legally as well. The Prince pulled Adam aside for a bit of advice, "Adam, you need to love this woman more than you love your own life." [9]

5: Rule 1 – Family First

As a wedding gift, the Prince gave Adam and his bride authority over the earth and everything on it—all the animals, birds, fish, plants, and trees on the whole planet.[10]

"Everything on the earth now belongs to you, and you belong to our family," the Prince told these first Royal colonists in the lower frontier.

Adam took his bride on long walks through the meadows of the garden, showing her the places where he and the Prince had explored. She particularly enjoyed being introduced by Adam to the sheep, the horses, and other animals which roamed the garden, with no fear of the humans.

"They're all ours?" she asked as she stroked the wooly head of a lamb that had come up and nuzzled her.

"All ours," smiled her husband.

Unbeknownst to Adam and Eve, they were not alone in the garden. Besides the animals and fish that filled the forests and waters, they were sharing the lower frontier with Lucifer and his army of followers, and Lucifer had been watching them...

*notes for this chapter
start on page 247*

6: Betrayal

※

Lucifer commented to his two lieutenants, "The Prince thinks these creatures made from dirt are going to rule my earth," he said, breaking into an evil smile. "He banished us from the kingdom for violating his prime directive. Now, isn't it ironic—these humans are about to go down the same way."

His lieutenants nodded, not sure what their leader had in mind, but confident in his leadership, nonetheless.

"The Prince is so proud of his so-called kingdom justice," Lucifer continued. "Watch how I get these stupid humans to spit in his face and follow me. If the Prince wants to maintain justice, he will have no choice but to keep them out of heaven, just like he kicked us out of the kingdom. If he doesn't, he has only two options; he can either go home and leave the lower frontier to me, or he can declare amnesty and let us *all* back into the kingdom. Anything else and he will be exposed as the hypocrite he truly is!"

Wanting to be sure he could not be accused of "touching" the humans, Lucifer found a snake in the garden. Lucifer's body shimmered, became transparent, and he slid into the reptile. He blinked snake-eyes at his lieutenant, who was speechless. Lucifer chuckled as he slid off, "No hands, no foul." [1]

The former general moved toward his objective—the woman. She had heard the command about the tree, not from the Prince, but second-hand from her husband. Lucifer slithered into the garden when neither the Prince nor the man was in sight. Eve was delighted to talk with one of the animals. They entered into a friendly conversation. When he asked her about the Tree of Knowledge of Good and Evil, Eve responded by reciting the Prince's command, just as Adam had told her, "We will die if we eat from that tree—or even if we touch it!"

"Eve, I think you've misunderstood what the Prince meant when he spoke with your husband," Lucifer blinked, intrigued by her embellishment regarding "touching" the tree.[2] "The Prince isn't always as clear as he ought to be. You won't literally *die*. He was saying that when you eat from that tree, your *ignorance* will die, and you'll be as wise as he is. That's why it is called the Tree of Knowledge."[3]

He had her attention. She wanted to be seen as wise.

"The Prince knows that you will be like him when you eat that fruit. You really could be like him. You *should* be like him. Trust me." He motioned toward the tree with his head.

Eve looked at the fruit. "The Prince will appreciate us more when we are as wise as he is," she rationalized.

"Of course he will. You seem to be getting smarter already," Lucifer nodded his snake head, smiling inside.

She took a bite. The juice gushed out as her teeth broke through the skin of the fruit into the sweet soft flesh, which melted in her mouth.

Adam saw what Eve was doing. She looked at him and held out a fruit. "These are really good, Adam," she said with juice dripping from her lips, "I've got to believe that this is really okay. You know, getting knowledge and all. Here, have one."[4]

Lucifer held his breath in anticipation.

6: Betrayal

Watching from the edge of the Crystal Sea above, thousands of collective breaths were being held as one.

Adam's mind was racing. There was no mistaking what the Prince had told him. The consequences had been made terribly clear. If the Prince had spoken the truth, Eve had just crossed the line and she was as good as dead already! Adam realized that meant he'd never be with his wife again! He began to panic.

He thought, "What if the Prince's warning was really just a figure of speech? No! Why wouldn't he mean just what he said? Is the Prince a liar? Of course not!" Adam knew the Prince. He had lived and walked and talked with the Prince. The Prince was no deceiver. "If I eat what she is offering," he thought, "we'll both die. If I don't eat it, my wife will die alone—and the Prince just told me that I need to love her more than I love my own life."

As if standing on the edge of a rushing river watching a loved one being swept away to their death, Adam came face-to-face with the hardest decision of his short life. Overcome with love for his wife but knowing full well that he had no hope to offer her, Adam made his choice. Taking the fruit from the hand of his beautiful yet condemned bride, he took a bite, knowing it was all wrong.[5]

He had effectively jumped into the raging river and grabbed hold of his wife, all the while thinking, "What have we done?" The safety of shore receded swiftly.

The snake shimmered as Lucifer stepped out of it, into the garden. He smiled sympathetically at the humans, "Tough times require tough choices. Welcome to my world, humans."

As promised by the name of the tree, both Adam and Eve began to gain knowledge immediately—knowledge of fear, fear of Lucifer, fear of the Prince, fear of the Prince finding out what they had just done.[6] They had chosen to follow this snake in the garden instead of the one who had given them life. They were now both as good as dead, according to the Prince. Adam grabbed his wife's hand and they both ran into the bushes.

Adam explained their dilemma to Eve. She responded, "What kind of crazy rule is that anyway? Knowledge will make us more like him. What's so bad about being like the great builder of the kingdom? Hey, we can build things as well!"

Eve reached for a nearby fig tree and pulled down a few giant leaves. With the help of some thin vines, she created a coat for her husband and one for herself. "Now, there you go," she said, adjusting his new outfit. "That's much better than running around naked. You'll see. The Prince should be quite impressed. He'll see our ability to improve our situation, and he will respect us for it. Trust me."

Adam saw some logic in his wife's statement, and he *was* impressed with the clothing she had created. Suddenly he remembered what the Prince had said, and his heart skipped a beat. Adam knew the Prince was a man of his word.

At sunset, they heard the Prince call out, "Adam! Hey Adam! Where are you?" Adam and Eve hid for a while, then finally stepped out from the bushes, both suddenly embarrassed at the coverings they had fashioned for themselves. The Prince stood before them, taking in the moment. He shook his head slightly at the sight of their ridiculous wardrobe.

"OK Adam, what happened?" the Prince said. "Did you disobey my command and eat fruit from that tree?"

"This wife you gave me offered me the fruit. She had eaten some already, so I had no choice but to eat it with her."

"Sounds like you had a choice and you made it," said the Prince. He turned to Eve, "And your story?"

"He lied to me," she said, pointing at Lucifer, "and I believed him."

6: Betrayal

"Let me rephrase that for you," the Prince said, "you trusted him instead of me." Eve looked down at the ground in silence.

The Prince turned to Lucifer. They both knew the terms of the deal.

"I never laid a hand on them, I swear!" Lucifer wanted to crack a defiant smile but couldn't bring himself to do it. In spite of his apparent victory, Lucifer was still very intimidated by the Prince.

The Prince looked at Lucifer with eyes of steel. "You think with one lie you can drag them down into the dust with you? Take a good look at this woman you tricked; one of her descendants is going to crush your head.[7] Lucifer, you have no *idea* who these humans really are."

Looking again at Adam, the Prince said, "I told you not to eat fruit from that tree. I know exactly what you did and why you did it. Regardless of your reasons, your actions have consequences. The laws of the kingdom apply here in the frontier. Otherwise, there would be no order in the territory. Here's what you need to understand about kingdom law out here in the frontier: "Willful disobedience to kingdom authority is treason, and treason is punishable by death." [8]

"If the judge finds anyone guilty of treason, they will have to pay with their own life. That is, unless their debt, their sentence of death, is paid for by someone else."

"Treason?" Adam stuttered. "All we did was eat some fruit. That's treason?"

*notes for this chapter
start on page 249*

7:   Consequences

୬୦ଏ

"You're right," replied the Prince. "All you did was eat some fruit. You did the *only* thing I told you not to do on the whole planet. Sorry Adam, kingdom law does not recognize big or little acts of treason, only treason."

"We get the death penalty for eating fruit?" Adam asked, incredulous.

"You didn't listen to what I said," the Prince responded. "Yes, all treason merits the death penalty here in the frontier, but under kingdom law, someone else may take your punishment for you, if they are qualified. To be your substitute under kingdom law, they must meet three qualifications. First, they must be innocent under kingdom law, not under condemnation themselves. Second, they must willingly accept your punishment, the death penalty. And third, they must be a member of your household, not a random stranger."

Adam and Eve were trying hard to follow what the Prince was saying, but kingdom law was all new to them.

"OK," Adam said slowly. "Who will do that for me?"

"Don't worry," responded the Prince. "I will provide the One you need."

Lucifer was fully aware of this provision in kingdom law, but he was not sure how it applied to this situation. His mind began to race ...who could qualify as their substitute? Under kingdom law, it had to be from the human's family.

"Who could be in their family and be *the One*?" Lucifer wondered. Then it hit him, "Crusher! The Prince promised that the woman's descendant would crush my head! The Royals want to crush me, and free the humans from death row in one shot!"

Lucifer reflected on that for a moment and concluded to himself, "I don't have a plan to deal with this yet, but understanding the problem is half the challenge."

"You establish a death penalty for treason, but you show traitors how to avoid the penalty?" Adam asked, trying to understand the logic behind kingdom justice.

"Exactly. Admit your guilt and when it is offered, accept the pardon. But until we start issuing kingdom pardons," he explained, "you need to do your part."

"Which is ...?"

"Like I said, first, admit you are guilty of breaking Kingdom law. Then find a substitute who will willingly take the punishment in your place."

Adam was really trying to follow, but ...

"Here," said the Prince, "Let me show you."

The Prince turned his head slightly and listened. Through the bushes, they all heard the rustling sound of the lambs ripping up grass and munching on it. "Are those your lambs?" the Prince asked Adam, already knowing the answer. Adam nodded, feeling sure that he was not going to like what was coming next.

The Prince turned and strode into the bushes. A few minutes later he returned with blood on his hands, carrying two robes made from sheepskins.[1]

"Now," said the Prince, "take off those fig leaf creations of yours. They can't cover what you have done. Cover yourselves with these." He held out the robes to the man and the woman.

7: Consequences

Adam and Eve stood in silence, aghast at what they were witnessing.

"Awful, isn't it?" said the Prince.

"But what *you* did is awful ..." Eve blurted. Adam put his arm around her, hoping she would hold back, but she couldn't. "Those beautiful sheep—they didn't do anything wrong. They're dead! Because of *us*?"

"You are right, Eve, on all counts," the Prince responded. "These sheep were innocent, willing substitutes that took your punishment for you. If you will accept that their lives satisfied the death penalty which hung over your head, then you will be free. If you don't, then their deaths will have been for nothing and *you* will face the death penalty."

"We recognize that offering up the lifeblood of these animals is the closest you can get to satisfying kingdom law until I provide the One, the perfect substitute, who can take your punishment. These animals resemble the One in each of the three requirements, but they don't *quite* qualify.

First, the animals *are* innocent, not under condemnation, *but* they lack the human sense of right and wrong.

Second, the animals *are* willing, as beasts of burden, to carry even this burden for you, *but* they don't comprehend the significance of their sacrifice.

Third, the animals *are* from your household, since I gave all the animals to you, *but* they are only animals, not humans from your family."

"So they don't *exactly* qualify as a substitute, but it's the best you've got until I provide the One to take your punishment for all time," said the Prince, "Do you understand?" [2]

Eve wasn't really listening to the Prince. She blurted, "But they're dead! How could you be so cruel?"

The Prince responded like a father addressing a child who cannot possibly understand the magnitude of a problem or its solution. He asked, "Eve, do you know what happens to animals when they die?"[3]

"No," Eve responded.

"Well, I do," responded the Prince. "I made them, and I know exactly what happens when they die, but the explanation involves things that your human mind simply cannot comprehend while you live on the earth." He paused. "Look around at everything I've made and everything I've given you. Can you trust me on this?"

"I suppose," she said quietly, realizing more than ever how much she didn't know.

The Prime Minister, seeing what was unfolding in his colony, stepped down through the Crystal Sea with a large envelope under his arm. He walked through the garden and whispered in the Prince's ear, "It's time to get them out of the garden and away from the Tree of Life." [4]

The Prince nodded.

Looking at Adam and Eve, the Prince said, "I told you that you would eventually walk freely in all dimensions of the lower frontier, including time. I planted the Tree of Life so when you ate its fruit, you could live forever. Well, you have chosen a different path."

"Today," the Prince said somberly, "you must leave the garden and live on the earth. You will walk freely in the three physical dimensions of the earth, but not in the dimension of time. Until the judgment you will be a prisoner of time. It will sweep you along and carry you to the kingdom courtroom where you will face the judge." [5]

Not knowing exactly what that meant, the man and his wife pulled their lambskin coats a little more tightly, as the evening had begun to turn noticeably cooler.

Lucifer was taking it all in, trying to put the pieces together in his mind.

The Prime Minister tapped Lucifer on the shoulder and signaled for him to step to the edge of the garden. The PM

7: Consequences

spoke softly to him, showing Lucifer the envelope, and discussing it.

The Prince continued to speak with Adam and Eve, "You were the first residents of the kingdom's colony on earth. I appointed you as rulers over the earth, under my authority." There was a note of sadness in his voice. "But you turned your back on me and followed a new leader. By disobeying the only directive I ever gave you, you aligned yourselves with ..." he paused as his eyes moved to Lucifer, "...with that snake."

They looked over at the Prime Minister and Lucifer, who were concluding their discussion.

"By your choice," he hesitated, "this earth I gave to you is now under the legal authority of the warlord Lucifer, and you are both now citizens of his earth. But remember," the Prince continued, "a Royal never takes back a promise. Trust me, everything ultimately still belongs to me, including you. Even though you have chosen to follow that traitor, in the end I will get back what is mine." [6]

Adam and Eve waited in stunned silence, as their entire world turned inside out.

Lucifer and the Prime Minister finished their discussion. Quivering with excitement, Lucifer could hardly contain himself. He looked for a moment at the humans and smirked, then bolted from the garden. As he retreated, Lucifer was ecstatic, thinking, "These humans will be locked in the three physical dimensions of earth and we will be all over them in all the heavenlies! They'll never even see us coming. That's what I call authority! Back in the saddle again!" [7]

The PM could now speak privately with the Prince. "The humans can't stay here in the Garden after rebelling against your authority. If they eat from the Tree of Life before they can be taught right from wrong, we'll have a race of immortal humans in the Royal family, who make up their own rules for living without any regard to what the King says." [8]

The Prince nodded sadly and asked the Prime Minister, "Is everything you discussed written down?" He was referring to the terms of the transaction handing authority over earth from Adam to Lucifer.

"Signed and sealed. You will need it later when we implement the Immigration Project and allow humans to return across the border into the kingdom," the Prime Minister responded confidently.[9] "We will hold up our end, but Lucifer will certainly try to find a loophole."

The Prince shook his head, "It was the only kingdom directive I ever gave them, and such a small one!"

"It's time," said the PM. "Send them out of the Garden, away from the Tree of Life."

The Prince looked at Adam and his wife. "Go now, down to Lucifer's earth. You'll live and work there until your bodies wear out and die."

"Our bodies will die? What happens then?" asked the man, still unclear about most of what had just transpired.

"When your life has run its course, your bodies will return to the dirt it came from. Then, you will both stand before the judge to explain why you chose to break kingdom law." [10]

In what seemed like a moment, they went from an adventurous, exciting life with the Prince in the garden, to an uncertain future in a strange place, under the authority of the Prince's enemy... and then they'll be tried like criminals? This was almost too much for Adam and Eve to bear.

"Take heart," the Prince said. "You are still my family. Remember what I told you about the One who can clear your kingdom record? Until he comes, remember what I showed you. You need to regularly offer back some of the animals I gave you, so you will be in good graces with the judge when you stand before him."

7: Consequences

They stood in silence, looking at the Prince, not really wanting to leave.

Like a parent disciplining a child, yet suffering with them, the Prince finally said, "Leave the garden, now."

*notes for this chapter
start on page 253*

8: Into the Wild

~~~

Adam and Eve walked down the path, away from the garden. They glanced back as a mist closed in behind them. Their minds raced with uncertainty and fear. They had no concept of what lay ahead. At the bottom of the path, they walked out into a dusty field. Looking back, they saw a kingdom guard brandishing a sword at the entrance of the path, but that too was fading away.[1] Soon, they couldn't even see the entrance to the garden path, just the dust and dirt in the three dimensions of earth.

The Prince and the Prime Minister returned to the kingdom proper.

The polished wooden table dominated the glass-enclosed conference room just off the throne room in the great kingdom hall. The King presided over the meeting from the head of the table, flanked by his son the Prince, and the Prime Minister. Generals Michael and Gabriel sat opposite each other, further down the table.

"Permission to speak freely?" General Michael asked.

"Absolutely," nodded the King.

"What you are doing is amazing," Michael began. "These humans will receive an incredible gift, the opportunity to have their record wiped clean, and to become citizens of the kingdom again. But it is clear that they don't appreciate or even understand what you are doing for them. To them, Prince, you look—forgive me—like an ogre."

"Some might view it that way," replied the Prince. "But having them understand my plan completely, or even for them to *like* me is not an immediate goal of the Immigration Project. In time, that can come, but for now, I'll settle for respect, even if they think I'm being too harsh. Eventually they will realize that there is nothing I wouldn't do for them—*nothing*."

"There is no other way to bring them back into the kingdom," said the King. "If we don't treat kingdom violations with the deadly seriousness they deserve, the humans will never take them seriously either."

"I know," said the Prince, gazing thoughtfully out the window, down at the earth through the Crystal Sea. "I know."

Adam and Eve settled in their new domain. It was nothing like the garden; that was for sure. They couldn't put their finger on it exactly, but everything just seemed so flat and gray after the richness and vibrant colors of the garden, which was quickly becoming a distant memory.

They worked hard for their food, but the Prince had personally instructed them on the art of plowing, planting and threshing their grain so they could now enjoy bread.[2] They began to raise a family, and in time, their family farm prospered.

Lucifer was quite pleased at the way things had developed. From here on out, everyone born on his earth was, by birth, a citizen of earth and subject to him. "The Prince isn't the only one who can be a nation builder," he said to himself. "These humans may be the Prince's family by blood, but from now on, they'll be citizens of *my* earth, by birth."

The Prince regularly left the kingdom, crossed the border to visit with Adam and Eve and their little family, *his*

8: Into the Wild

family. He was anxious to strengthen the relationship which had been strained in the garden.

Adam and Eve appreciated the Prince's visits and they had come to recognize that despite the hardships of farm life, the prosperity they enjoyed was a direct result of the gifts which the Prince had given them: the land, the water, the flocks of animals. Their friendship grew, as together they established Adam and Eve's family on earth.

Adam, however, was still occasionally haunted by the words of the Prince in the garden, "You are guilty of treason and someone has to pay ..." Adam knew that he and his wife had foolishly crossed the line in the garden; there was no arguing with that. He knew that they still crossed the line on earth, and they could usually trace it back to their own selfish behavior. At least the Prince had shown them the way to getting right with kingdom law, offering back from what the Prince had freely given them.

Adam and Eve had two sons, Cain and Abel. Both young men understood from their parents about offering back the best of what the Prince had provided, as a substitute for when they crossed the line. They knew that the kingdom's prime directive was a line that they selfishly wandered across on a regular basis. Cain and Abel were glad to offer back to the Prince the best of what they had, to keep their kingdom records clean.

Cain, being a farmer, offered to the Prince the best of his farm, fresh-baked breads made from the grain he grew in his field. Abel, a shepherd, slaughtered the best lamb from his flock for the Prince. Both brothers offered the Prince the absolute best they had in their household. They were determined to do better than their parents did in the garden.

The Prince accepted Abel's sheep with appreciation. "Kingdom law is no threat to you Abel!" the Prince said approvingly.

Cain was absolutely speechless when the Prince told him that his offer of bread was inappropriate. He couldn't believe that the Prince was so ungracious and ungrateful.

"I worked hard to grow the grain," Cain protested. "I kept the birds away from it, harvested it, ground it, kneaded it, and baked it!" In his anger, he raised his voice at the Prince, "All my brother did was watch those stupid animals grow, and then he killed them! Don't I get even a little respect for my effort?"

"Son," the Prince said, "let me teach you something really basic. If you don't understand this, you won't understand the kingdom at all. No human on earth can live up to what is expected of a Royal. The consequence for treason is death, and that's why you need a qualified substitute to take your punishment, so you can live." [3]

Cain's eyes were down. He shook his head and mumbled, "Uh huh, I know. I brought you a substitute—a good one."

"Hey, look at me." The Prince put his hand on Cain's shoulder and gave him a fatherly look, straight in the eye. "Your bread doesn't qualify. It is the work of your hands, your planning, your time, your efforts. Understand this, Cain; your life-work doesn't cut it as an acceptable substitute, but what will, is the lifeblood of an innocent, willing substitute in your household. That is something only I can provide, and it will clear your record. You can't get right with the kingdom by your own efforts."

"That's all there is to it, Cain. Your bread smells great, but you need to get yourself an animal to offer back. Trade for it if you have to. Once you own it, kill it and bring it to me. That will be an acceptable substitute to take your death sentence, and kingdom justice will be satisfied. Clear your record or your record will eventually kill you. This isn't just a good idea, Cain, it's the law."

8: Into the Wild

The Prince stood quietly, allowing what he said to sink into the young man's consciousness. A long minute passed silently.

"What-*ever*," said Cain as he turned his back to the Prince and walked away, feeling totally rejected. "That Prince has no idea how hard I worked to provide that bread for him," he thought. "My bread ought to be good enough for him. He has no respect for me or what I can do. If he does, he certainly doesn't know how to show it."

Later that day, he found his brother Abel in the field, watching what Cain had called "his stupid animals." Cain's frustration turned to anger. Lucifer whispered, "Just do it," and Cain's anger turned to murder. Abel bled to death in his field as the sheep watched silently.

Lucifer and several of his soldiers sat and watched the entire scene from one dimension up, out of human sight. "I don't think this is exactly what the Royals had in mind when they fixed this place up and started their little family on earth," he cackled, "but I like the way this is shaping up."

Abel was a natural-born citizen of the earth, and Lucifer was eager to take custody of the first human to depart the planet. "Bring him on down," he said to his assistants.

Lucifer wanted to bring Abel's soul into the lower waiting room, which had been prepared for human citizens of earth whose earthly bodies have died.[4] They wait here for the judgment, which the Prince had spoken about. Since the lower waiting room is a facility for citizens of earth, Lucifer has management and administrative authority over it. The ambiance of the room reflects the warmth that Lucifer feels toward his human subjects; it is not comfortable at all. The lower waiting room is basic at best. There are thousands of rows of wooden benches, and there aren't many lights. The high, sealed windows let in a glow from the outside, but it never seems very bright, and the slowly turning ceiling fans only stirred the dusty air.

Lucifer's soldiers approached Abel's body and suddenly stopped dead in their tracks. Two tall, intimidating warriors of the kingdom had appeared out of a dimension above them all and was lifting Abel's soul out of his body.

"Hey! Leave him alone! He's ours!" Lucifer's troops shouted.

The larger of the warriors straightened up and looked down at the two, who were now wishing they hadn't used that tone of voice. "This one is ours," he replied. "He is an honorary citizen of the kingdom by his Royal bloodline. Besides, the Prime Minister has authorized me to bring him to the kingdom citizens' arrival lounge." He waved a paper at them.[5]

They didn't care to get close enough to read it.

"Don't worry. I'm sure you'll find some humans to take care of soon enough," the warrior said as he went back to his task. He lifted Abel's soul and they headed toward the kingdom citizens' arrival lounge.

"Where are we going?" Abel asked.

"Be there in just a minute," the first warrior said as the other opened the door for the new arrival.

They were met by the lead attendant of the Kingdom Arrivals lounge. "Welcome Mr. Abel!" the attendant greeted his first guest, "May I get you something to drink?"

The arrivals lounge is like a replica of the great kingdom hall, with light streaming in through the tall windows, plenty of comfortable seats, snacks and drinks, all managed by an attentive staff from the kingdom Department of Immigration. It was established for humans who, while on earth, had demonstrated a pro-kingdom lifestyle.

Abel settled into a comfy chair with his drink. He looked around at the nearly empty lounge. He was the only one there, except for the staff. An attendant noticed Abel was staring at the digital clock on the wall:

8: Into the Wild

Monday, 12:16 AM KST ⧖ 3861 BCE FST

The attendant smiled. "Takes a bit of getting used to, I imagine. We're empty now, but in another 6,000 earth years, it'll be Saturday night here, and this place will be hopping, so sit back and relax!" [6]

Abel took a sip and settled in for what promised to be an interesting week.

Back on earth, shortly after Abel's murder, the Prince confronted Cain in the field. "Don't think you can just walk away from this!" he shouted, "Listen to me![7] Do you have any idea whose blood you spilled today? That was Royal family blood! My family blood!"

"I showed you how to come out from under the condemnation of kingdom justice, but your pride wouldn't let you take what I offered you." The Prince made no attempt to hide his displeasure. "Cain, you are done with being a farmer. In fact, you're done with this land. Get out of here and wander through the earth for the rest of your life. You don't want to be subject to kingdom justice? Fine. It's your choice. You can try living life outside the law, but understand this—an outlaw finds no protection under kingdom law! Unless you first get right under the law, you'll find no sympathy from the kingdom judge." [8]

"But if I'm outside the law, anyone who finds me can murder me!" Cain pleaded. "You're sending me out to be killed!"

"Oh, I see. So now you think murder is a bad thing," the Prince said with more than a hint of sarcasm.[9] Reflecting for a moment on the fear he saw in Cain's eyes, the Prince said, "Don't worry, I will see to it that when people see you, they will know that I am protecting you. Anyone who kills you will bring a double helping of kingdom justice down on their own heads."[10] The Prince reluctantly sent the son of his friend Adam out into the wilderness. "Get moving, Cain."

The Prince saw Lucifer and his soldiers watching, but he didn't care. In fact, the Prince wanted Lucifer to hear his warning about staying away from Cain.

*notes for this chapter
start on page 257*

9: Intimate Assault

~~

As the years went by, Adam and Eve had other sons and daughters.¹ The population of humans on the earth grew. The men were strong, most lived hundreds of years, and the women were very easy on the eyes.

The humans spread across the face of the earth, as if they owned it. The rebel soldiers who had been ejected from the kingdom to earth with Lucifer were closely watching the Prince's family. The soldiers enjoyed watching the women. They *really* liked to watch the women.

A few of his troops approached Lucifer requesting that he would let them take up permanent residence in the lower three dimensions of earth. They wanted to introduce themselves to a few of these women, start up a friendly conversation, and see what developed.

Up until this point, Lucifer had wanted to keep his soldiers physically separated from the Prince's family, lest some in his army might be tempted to turn back to the kingdom. But he thought about what the Prince had said, "One of her descendants is going to crush your head."

"So, one of the descendants of the Royal family on earth is going to crush my head," Lucifer mused. "The Prince seems to be putting a lot of faith in the downstream potential of his Royal family here on earth. I think perhaps a little tinkering with the bloodline is just what this family needs. Who knows what could develop?"

"These humans are natural-born citizens of my earth," he mused. "Hmmm. If they become part of my bloodline, they will be citizens of my earth by their bloodline as well as by birth. So, if the Crusher comes from their household, there will be no question that he's my boy, not the Prince's."

Satisfied with his own logic, Lucifer turned to his troops and said with a grin, "Why not? Go for it!" Those of his soldiers who moved down to the earth had no trouble finding human women who eagerly embraced them and had children with them. With fathers who had been higher-dimensional beings, it came as no surprise that these offspring grew to be physically huge. They were known far and wide for their superhuman strength—and their cruelty to other humans. People called them "the Nephilim." [2]

Lucifer enjoyed watching this unfold. He was pleased that the Prince's Royal bloodline was now competing with his own.

"There's more than one way to deal with this Royal family," he thought. To Lucifer, the prospect of becoming a Royal in-law seemed just too hilarious.

Lucifer was riding high. The people of earth grew less interested in the kingdom, and more interested in getting ahead—bigger farms, more gold, more cattle—just *more*.

Thanks to the antics of Lucifer's soldiers, the humans were losing their Royal bloodline, removing them from any claim to being part of the Prince's kingdom family on earth.

The lower waiting room was filling up with a steady stream of deceased citizens of earth. Most of these guests had committed themselves to living successful lives, had minimal bloodline ties to the Royal family, and showed no interest in the kingdom.

"We are back in business!" Lucifer joked with his lieutenants. "The Prince may have grabbed Abel and a few

9: Intimate Assault

others, but don't worry. There will always be some kingdom loyalist fanatics we can't get our hands on, but everybody else? They are mine! Hah!"

Lucifer's humor was appreciated neither by the Prince nor his father. It became clear that humans were on a path to self-destruction and with Lucifer's encouragement, they made a mockery of kingdom law. The King looked at the clock...

Tuesday, 3:44 PM KST ⌛ 2344 BCE FST

He said sadly, "We only started yesterday and I am already fed-up enough to wipe the slate clean on earth and begin again. These humans are nothing but murder, violence, selfishness, and grief!" He sighed, "Let's let the floodwaters cover the earth again." [3]

"Wait," pleaded the Prince, reaching out for his father's arm. "Most of them are not in our family, but there's a man down there who is still one of us. Noah - he is loyal to the kingdom and is a pure, full-blooded Royal. None of his bloodline has been polluted by the enemy." [4]

"You are right about how despicable the humans have acted, Father," the Prince continued. "When left to themselves, they have always chosen a self-destructive path. Let's do as you say, Father. I will wipe the slate clean on earth, but let me begin again with this man Noah and his family. I will stay close to them and I'll form them into our own nation on earth. I will lead them and protect them, and the Prime Minister will educate them in the ways of the kingdom."

The King's Academy was the school that the Prime Minister had designed for the Prince's nation, to teach them what it means to be part of the Royal family. The academy had no buildings. The world was its campus. Here they would learn hands-on lessons in loyalty, justice, law, and government. It was all part of Adam and Eve's choice to gain knowledge of good and evil. It was also part of the Royal's plan to educate and raise their family on earth.

The King and Prime Minister acknowledged that the Prince's plan was the right thing to do, but they were all fully aware that the bad seed sown by Lucifer was going to be trouble for generations to come.

"OK son," the King said, "time to save the human race from destruction …"

"And the animal kingdom as well," chimed the PM.

"Of course," said the Prince with a grin. Excited about the fresh start, the Prince went to the earth and spoke directly to Noah, providing all the information and materials Noah needed to build the ship that would save his family from extinction.

When Noah and his family had completed preparations and loaded the animals, as the Prince had directed, Noah sent his wife up the ramp into the boat. He called to his three sons, "Boys! Time to go! Drop what you are doing and get your wives onboard."

Two of Noah's sons had married local girls, but his middle son, Ham, had chosen a beautiful, tall wife from a neighboring region. No one in Noah's family knew much about her background, but they loved her as if they had known her all their lives. That was good, because it was going to be close quarters for the next year.

Once all eight were on board, the Prince slammed the door shut behind them and said to the assembled team from the kingdom Corps of Engineers, "Pour it on."

At the Prince's command, the CSOC operations chief opened the floodgates above and below the earth, covering the planet with water. Everything and everyone on the earth who breathed air, died. Everyone that is, except the one man with the pure Royal blood in his veins, and his family.

9: Intimate Assault

As the tainted human bloodline on earth was being washed clean, the lower waiting room was dealing with a surge of human citizens from earth, but it was nowhere near capacity.

Already, several of the lights in the lower waiting room had burned out and none of the staff there seemed interested in replacing the bulbs. The brightest light came from the flickering screens with a video feed from the kingdom citizens' arrival lounge. Watching the comfortable, casual setting of the arrivals lounge, without being able to go there, only served to mute the atmosphere in this already drab and miserable place.

Newcomers would always ask, "How do we get to the arrivals lounge?"

If they could coax an answer from a waiting room staffer, it was always the same. "You can't get there from here." [5]

"It's a new day, Noah," the Prince said as they stood looking over the now dry earth. It had taken almost fourteen months for the floodwaters to rise, recede, and finally yield to dry land. It had been a long and frightening voyage, surrounded by death.

When they landed, Noah knew the first thing he needed to do was to recommit himself and his family to the kingdom on the newly cleaned up earth and claim it for the kingdom. He did it by offering back to the Prince some of the animals he had brought along, just for this purpose.

The Prince was impressed, "You really do get it, Noah. Right from the start, you are keeping your kingdom record clean with the blood of these animals from your household. That blood will make you honorary citizens of the kingdom. As your family spreads out across the earth, feel free to eat the meat of animals, but not their blood. Don't eat it, don't drink it, and don't take it for granted. Remember to use the blood only to get right with the kingdom."

Noah and his family unloaded the ship and got back to the business of tending the land and their flocks. Lucifer's attempt at hijacking the Royal bloodline had been thwarted, or so it seemed.

Noah enjoyed planting and tending his vineyard and became expert at making his own wines. One day, after Noah had sampled way too much of his own vintage, Ham found his dad, naked and unconscious on the floor of his tent.

"This is just too funny," Ham thought. He ran out and told his brothers—who didn't think it was funny at all. When Noah later awoke, he was furious with Ham and cursed him for having gossiped to his brothers about Noah's indiscretion. Ham packed up his wife and children and his family settled far away in Egypt, Gaza, Lebanon and more.[6]

Over the years, Ham's family grew, but not just in numbers. Like his wife, the children of Ham grew tall and strong—some of them were actually giants. This came as a surprise to Ham, but not to his wife, who told him she had brothers and cousins, before the flood, who were over seven feet tall.[7]

*notes for this chapter
start on page 260*

10: Three Prongs

୬୦∝

After some reflection, Lucifer decided he was impressed with the Prince's gutsy move of killing virtually everyone and everything on the planet. Recalling the Prince's burning gaze in the kingdom Justice Center so long ago, he thought, "This Prince is no softy. He is a certified fanatic." Lucifer was coming to the sobering realization that the Prince would never allow his conviction to be overturned. Groping for ideas, but coming up short, he thought, "I need to find a legal loophole."

Lucifer shook his head and let his anger keep him from sinking into depressive thoughts. "Dammit, this flood was an illegal act by the kingdom!" he shouted, hoping the Prince would hear. "This is my earth! We have a deal! You have no business meddling in the local affairs of my earth!"

Composing himself, Lucifer was determined to find an opportunity to strike back at the kingdom. He thought, "I can do this. I will take these humans down somehow and turn this entire lower frontier into a killing field. Either the humans will do the killing, or the Prince will do it again himself. Either way, no humans will get to be part of his family or his kingdom!"

Over time, the human population got big and got busy. If they even had time to think about it, the reasons for "that flood" long ago were totally irrelevant to their busy lives.

Passport Please - Epic of the Kingdom III

The earth's pioneers had a can-do attitude, relying on themselves to make things happen. In the city of Babel, for example, some of the more ambitious people launched a project to construct a massive skyscraper, just so they would be known throughout the world as the ones who designed and built the world's tallest tower.[1]

The Prince shook his head in dismay. "I was hoping they'd want to be known as the royalty of the kingdom on earth. It seems that for these people, 'What we do,' has replaced 'Who we are.'"

Lucifer was not dismayed in the least. "Self-respect," he thought, "will be the foundation of my plan! These humans are no different from the two in the garden. They just want to be recognized for their own wisdom, their accomplishments, and their ambitions."

Lucifer gathered his lieutenants around him and began to rehearse his marketing plan. He explained how they would win and hold onto the hearts and minds of the humans.

"They all want to be successful. I can help them get what they want. After all, I respect their wisdom and accomplishments, as a great leader should. I, for example, would never have turned Cain away like the Prince did. *My* earth is a "meritocracy." Here, humans earn respect from me and from other humans by what they do—for their beauty, their accomplishments, and their wisdom—not through some barbarous, bloody ritual."

Lucifer knew that his plan was a winner, and his lieutenants agreed. He aimed to keep the attention and the allegiance of most, if not all, of the Prince's humans.

Not surprisingly, the Prince had an altogether different view regarding his "meddling in local affairs" as Lucifer called it. He knew that the kingdom was the ultimate owner of the lower frontier, and Lucifer's authority would not last forever.

10: Three Prongs

Under kingdom law, when anything belonging to the Royal family is lost, whether through misfortune or mismanagement, it is not lost forever. The Prince knew that, under the terms of their deal with Lucifer, the earth would eventually revert back to the kingdom. At any time, the earth could be bought back by a member of the Royal household on earth who is qualified, willing, and able to pay the price.[2]

"I am really glad you wrote it all down," the Prince said to the PM. "Lucifer knows full well he is obligated to accommodate our right to buy back the earth. You can never trust a snake with just a handshake."

"We both know he is going to try to scam us," the PM said. "He thinks he can void everything by letting his soldiers have sexual relations with the women of your nation. Through their children, Lucifer will try to hijack the bloodline of our Royal family on earth."

The Prince nodded, "Lucifer thinks he can stop us from opening the gates of heaven. He wants to tie this whole deal up in a custody battle. He will claim that the One, the Crusher, is really from his household, not ours—so no one will be qualified to enforce the provisions of the mortgage."[3]

"For safekeeping, I had the mortgage sealed and stored in the kingdom archives," the PM said. "I have no doubt we will need to invoke the penalty clauses in another six thousand years or so." [4]

Lucifer was very well aware of kingdom law and the terms of his lease on the earth. He also knew he could scam just about any deal, written or not. He was the expert on "managing situations."

"Without having their kingdom records permanently wiped clean," he thought, "the humans won't survive their judgment any better than I survived mine. If I can disqualify the Prince's substitute, even those so-called honorary citizens in the arrival lounge will all be doomed." Lucifer concluded, "Then the Prince will have three choices—

destroy all his precious humans, go home and leave all the humans to me, or let us *all* back into the kingdom."

Lucifer pondered the facts as he knew them, "The Prince said that Crusher would be a descendant of the woman in the garden—a human. He'll also have to be completely innocent under kingdom law, living a life of total allegiance to the King; but I've never seen a human who could keep their record totally clean—not one."

He didn't know the answer yet, but he kept thinking of how he could cut off the Crusher. Lucifer knew that he had stepped on the Prince's nerves by allowing his soldiers to intermarry with the human women. The Prince had been so upset, that he was willing to wipe out almost the entire planet to put an end to their behavior.

"I am definitely on the right track here," Lucifer mused.

It was all coming together in Lucifer's mind, and he was very excited to see a way to unravel the Prince's plan. Lucifer smiled a smug grin. Calling his lieutenants together, he explained the situation. They were in awe of their leader, of how Lucifer had seen right through the Prince's plan.

"We've got a three-pronged attack strategy here," Lucifer began. "First of all, keep an eye out for a human baby, probably a boy, who will be born into the Prince's nation. The Prince told me he will send this One specifically to crush us all. We are the legal rulers of earth and the kingdom is trying to crush us! We have got to stop this terrorist."

He continued with instructions for his officers, "You all need to listen to what the humans are saying. If anyone gets wind of this boy's arrival, do whatever it takes to kill him. I don't care if we have to wipe out a whole generation of boys, just get him!"

His staff nodded with determination, ready to defend the earth from kingdom terrorism.

10: Three Prongs

"Second, every good plan has a Plan B. I trust you, but I also know what a sneak the Prince is. If somehow we miss our target and the boy slips through our net, we must make sure he has no weapons to use against us. Here's how we are going to take away his ammunition. We will continue to aggressively insert ourselves into the Royal bloodline. Then, if this boy does show up, *I* will be his daddy! We'll claim he's in *my* household, not the Prince's, and the DNA will back us up! Nobody will be able to buy back the earth and the agreement will be void. In the end, we'll see whose head gets crushed."

Once again, Lucifer authorized a number of his most trusted soldiers to aggressively pursue the women of the Royal family on earth. "And while you're at it, let them know that sex is a gift that is meant to be enjoyed *by* everybody, *with* everybody. Share the goodness!"[5]

"Third, while they are getting on with the ladies, the rest of us will be out and about, encouraging the humans to commit themselves totally to following their own dreams. These humans will be so consumed by their own busy lives, that even if little Crusher can somehow clear their kingdom record and get a pardon for them, they won't care one little bit. They will blow off the Prince exactly the same way my man Cain did ... 'What-*ever!*'"

Lucifer knew his plan was a winner. "The Prince may think he's got a deal, but he's got nothing!"

*notes for this chapter
start on page 261*

11: National IDs

〜〜

If the Prince is a builder at heart, the Prime Minister is a teacher through and through.

"At the King's Academy, we will teach your people the principles our kingdom rests upon," the Prime Minister explained to the Prince. "They'll learn by repetition, and they'll have a lot of field work. They will get firsthand knowledge of what is good and what is evil. They will find out what is acceptable and what is not, in the kingdom."

"It needs to be clear to them why kingdom immigration policy is as strict as it is," said the Prince. "and why we can only let kingdom citizens in."

"That's why we've got our national ID system, designed to help keep the King's Academy students in, and the troublemakers out!" said the PM. He looked at the clock and said to the Prince, "Time for you to go..."

Wednesday, 1:09 AM KST ⧖ 1952 BCE FST

Noah was still alive when his descendant Abram was born in present-day Iraq.[1] The Prince came to Abram in his home with a simple yet stunning message: "You have been chosen to be the founding father of the kingdom's nation on earth."

Though Abram wasn't perfect, the Prince knew he had found his man. The Prince shared his vision for the nation, "This is going to be a great nation, Abram, with more people than there are stars in the sky. Someday, everyone on the earth is going to reap the benefits of your nation's special relationship with the kingdom and with me." [2]

"But understand, it takes extreme pressure and extreme heat to make a diamond, Abram," the Prince continued. "I will send your people to the King's Academy, the most difficult of schools, but they will learn to trust me, and learn that I will always defend and rescue them. Your nation's enemies will be my enemies and your nation's friends will be my friends."

At the Princes direction, Abram packed up his entire household and moved to the land of Canaan, some five hundred miles to the west. He was ready and willing to start building this nation, but, "You *do* know that I am eighty-five years old," he said to the Prince, somewhat dubious about having a child, "and my wife is no youngster either. How is this going to work?"

"Just trust me," said the Prince. "I have you covered."

Lucifer was amused, thinking, "Perhaps Abram's wife Sarai can help him think through this little conundrum." He chuckled, remembering the incident in the garden, "Déjà vu!"

Sure enough, Sarai, just trying to be practical, suggested that Abram could start this nation by having a child with their lovely young au pair from Egypt. Without a moment's hesitation, Abram, man that he was, went along with his wife's suggestion. At eighty-six, he became the proud father of Ishmael.

The Prince was understandably disappointed. "This is *not* what I had in mind for you Abram. Ishmael is a fine boy, and from him will come the mighty nations of Arabia, but his descendants will be nothing but trouble for our nation for

11: National IDs

the next four thousand years." [3] The Prince implored, "Would you just trust me when I tell you something? I really do have you covered, Abram."

It took more than another ten years, but the Prince finally came to Abram and said, "It's time to start that nation we talked about. But first, from now on, you will be called Abraham and your wife will be called Sarah. I don't want anyone to say you made a name for yourself as the father of your country. I am the one who will make a name for you Abraham."

The Prince continued, "By this time next year you and Sarah will have a son." Sure enough, at the grand age of 100, Abraham had a baby, a son named Isaac.[4]

"It's absolutely amazing," Abraham said to the Prince, as they both looked at young Isaac in Sarah's arms.

"Abraham," explained the Prince, "you, Sarah, and Isaac are part of a 100% pure Royal bloodline, right from the kingdom of heaven. The warlord of this earth will try everything he can to hijack our Royal bloodline. As a matter of national security, we cannot let that happen."

Abraham and Sarah were surprised that the Prince's nation had just started and they already had attracted powerful enemies.

"This is how you will keep it pure—no one in this nation of mine shall have sexual relations with people from outside of my nation.[5] This is imperative. It is the only way you can protect my Royal bloodline."

"Little Isaac is only a few days old now. When he is eight days old, I want you to cut off his foreskin, circumcising him. Do this for every son born into my new nation," the Prince explained. "And do it for all the men who are now in your household." He paused, "Yes, Abraham, even yourself."

Abraham swallowed hard.

The Prince continued, "This circumcision is a man's proof of citizenship in the kingdom's nation on earth, our national identification system."

"When any woman in my nation gets married and is about to have intimate relations with her new husband, one look at his manhood and she will immediately know if that man is part of my Royal bloodline. If he is not circumcised, she will know he is not one of us, and if that is the case, she is not allowed to have sexual relations with him. No excuses! She can call out to her brothers and they will deal with the intruder.[6] My Royal bloodline in this nation must be protected from those who would pollute it."

Neither Abraham nor Sarah liked the idea of cutting part of their son's manhood for "national security," but Abraham remembered what grandpa Noah had told him about the Nephilim attacking their Royal bloodline.[7] As much as he hated the idea, circumcision did make sense.

"So outsider men are the only threat to the bloodline?" Sarah asked, "What about the outsider women?" thinking of Hagar, her servant-girl-turned-rival.

The Prince understood. He looked up and with a nod called down a squad of kingdom security agents who cordoned off a secure perimeter around them. What the Prince had to say to Abraham was not for Lucifer's ears.

The Prince leaned toward Abraham and Sarah. "I'm going to let you in on a little-known fact about the human body, which I personally designed," the Prince whispered. "A human baby in the womb is surrounded by the placenta, a membrane which keeps out all blood from the mother. The child is nourished by the mother's body, but not one drop of blood from the mother ever touches the developing baby."

"One thing that means is that the baby's blood begins to develop only after the father's contribution. Biologically, the bloodline of a human is determined by the father." [8]

11: National IDs

The Prince drove his point home, "The threat to our nation's bloodline is from men from outside our nation having intimate relations with our women. If that happens, their children will be in the bloodline of the outsiders. Circumcise your sons as a sign to our women. Protect our Royal bloodline!"

Abraham and Sarah nodded, understanding as well as they could. A few days later, Isaac was circumcised, as they had been instructed.

The Prince, his father and the Prime Minister met with Michael and Gabriel for a progress update in the great kingdom hall conference room.

"I could not have made it clearer," said the Prince. "Those who join themselves with enemies of the kingdom are essentially joining with prostitutes. Circumcision is their unmistakable reminder to marry only within our Royal nation." [9]

Gabriel spoke, "Point of clarification sir?"

"Of course," responded the Prince.

"You asked them to circumcise all the men in their household. You know that includes servants who are not from your Royal bloodline. Wouldn't that expose the bloodline to outside contamination, depending on where the servants came from?"

"Very observant, Gabriel," the Prince responded. "My instructions regarding circumcision did leave an apparent exposure, but that will not change the outcome."

The Prince glanced at the closed door and lowered his voice. "What I am about to say stays in this room. The success of the Immigration Project does not hinge on human efforts in keeping the Royal bloodline clean."[10]

Gabriel and Michael exchanged a glance.

The Prince continued. "Did you hear that little 'secret' I shared with Abraham and Sarah, about the father's part in the bloodline? That is key to the entire Immigration

Project—if a father's blood is pure Royal, then his child's blood is pure Royal, no matter what else may lurk in the mother's bloodline."

"And that is the key to the success of the Immigration Project because …?" Gabriel trailed off.

"Because the One, or the Crusher, as Lucifer likes to call him, will not have a human being for a father."

Gabriel looked at the Prince, then the PM, then back to the Prince.

"Gabriel," the Prince whispered, "Crusher's mother—she will be a virgin!"[11]

Gabriel whispered back, "But how …?

The Prince glanced at the Prime Minister, who winked but said nothing.

*notes for this chapter
start on page 264*

12: Loyalty Lessons

~~~

When Abraham circumcised Isaac and the rest of the men in his household, the King's Academy had effectively drew a line between their campus and the rest of the earth. The Prince was fully aware that this border would make his nation even more of a target than ever. He knew that to withstand Lucifer's attacks, his new nation needed strong leadership, leadership that was completely loyal to the kingdom.

"You have chosen these people for the most difficult task imaginable," the PM said to the Prince.

"They need to know that they are up to the challenge," the Prince responded, "and Abraham will demonstrate what it means to be loyal to the kingdom."

Abraham was the Prince's chosen leader, but his loyalty had never been tested to the limit. Even he didn't know for certain how total his allegiance was to the King.

"Humans are nothing more than self-centered animals that walk on two feet," Lucifer explained to his officers. "Loyalty to anything outside of themselves is beyond their comprehension. I have seen too many self-absorbed and foolish humans to think otherwise."

"Let's show everyone what my man Abraham is made of," the Prince said, as he stepped out to meet him.

"Abraham, as the founding father of my nation, I want you to offer up your son Isaac as your substitute for kingdom justice," the Prince announced. "He fits the criteria—he is innocent, he is willing to do whatever you ask of him, and he is from your household, your only son. Take him up on the hilltop and offer him up as your substitute, so your kingdom record will be clean."

"Game over," thought Lucifer. "There is no way he'll go through with this."

Abraham set out to do exactly what the Prince had commanded, exactly the way he was told to do it. On a hilltop in what would later be called Jerusalem, Abraham gripped the knife with both hands and raised it over his son. He closed his eyes, gritted his teeth, and suddenly the Prince called out, "Abraham, stop! Now everyone knows you are totally loyal to the kingdom. Let Isaac go."[1]

"Whoa!" Lucifer was seriously taken aback. "So, they really can use that free will of theirs to act for the kingdom, in spite of themselves. At least this one can."

"Don't worry," Lucifer said to his lieutenants, "we still have plenty of humans to work with. Let's just stick to the plan and in the end, the Prince may wind up with a handful of humans, but the rest will be mine."

"He didn't hold back anything from you, Father," the Prince said proudly. "He trusted you to the limit."

"Now that's what I'm talking about!" said the PM. "The man is an all-out kingdom patriot. You've chosen the right man to establish your nation!"

In time, the man who came to personify the Prince's nation was Abraham's grandson, Isaac's son, Jacob. He earned a reputation for being aggressive and contentious. Once, he even physically wrestled the Prince himself to the ground, demanding special kingdom privileges. Jacob was a handful, but the Prince respected him. The Prince told him, "You deserve a name to match your temperment, so I am

12: Loyalty Lessons

going to call you 'Israel,' meaning, 'he struggles with the King.'"

As a child struggles to accept a parent's authority, the Royal family on earth struggled with the authority of the Prince. Knowing they would struggle even more as they attended the King's Academy, the Prince decided that "Israel" was also an appropriate name for his nation.[2]

Up in the throne room, the Royal Father said to the Prince, "Nice wrestling match, son. It looks like that family of yours has a lot of spunk," he grinned.

"That she does," replied the Prince, as he brushed the dust of the earth from his smiling face.

The first aspect of Lucifer's plan was in full swing. All his soldiers were keeping an eye out for the arrival of the Crusher.

Secondly, a number of his soldiers were contributing to the human bloodline again, although circumcision was clearly slowing their direct assault on Israel.

To compensate for that, Lucifer's soldiers adjusted their tactics, focusing more on embracing women outside of Israel. There were a lot more of them, and this way, Lucifer could participate in the broadest segment of the human bloodline, worldwide.

Once Lucifer's soldiers made their DNA contributions, all they had to do was help mankind understand the benefits of promiscuity, multiple sexual partners, and the pleasure that these all bring. The worldview that they were promoting became the force multiplier of Lucifer's plan, making every lusty man and woman on earth his partner.

Within a few generations, virtually all the men in the nations surrounding Israel became prospective Royal bloodline hijackers. Lucifer was confident that given a little time, human nature would prevail, even in the kingdom's nation on earth.

Passport Please - Epic of the Kingdom III

The third aspect of Lucifer's plan was also going well. Most humans continued to focus on living well and being the best at what they did. They kept their primary attention on living the successful life, and consequently had little time to even think about the kingdom.

While all this was going on, Lucifer continued prowling the earth, always looking for ways to stay on top of the situation.[3]

The lower waiting room was servicing a steady influx of guests awaiting final judgment, and the kingdom citizens' arrival lounge was filling somewhat more slowly. The Prince wished all the citizens of earth would show interest in becoming kingdom citizens, but he had always maintained, "No one is going to be forced into the kingdom."

With twelve sons, Abraham's grandson Jacob (or Israel as he was known to many) did his part in expanding the Royal family on earth. However, Joseph, the youngest of Jacob's sons, was not well-liked by his brothers.

"I have this sense," Joseph would often tell his brothers, "that you will all bow down to me someday."

His brothers were sick of Joseph and his delusions of grandeur, but Jacob said nothing to correct his youngest son. One day, Jacob sent Joseph to bring lunch to his brothers in the field.

"This is our chance," the brothers agreed, "let's kill him and make it look like an accident." Fortunately for Joseph, a caravan approached from over the hill, loaded with goods to sell in Egypt. After a quick negotiation, the traders exchanged some coins for Jacob's son, who was now headed for the Egyptian slave market.

His brothers, at last rid of "the boy who would be king," told their father Jacob his youngest son had been killed by a wild animal. Jacob was devastated.

"This is just too easy," Lucifer thought. "A little jealousy amongst brothers and these humans will destroy

12: Loyalty Lessons

their would-be nation faster than I could do it myself. It's Cain and Abel all over again."

As he had promised his father, the Prince never lost sight of Joseph. The Prince orchestrated one unlikely event after another, and Joseph went from slave to prison inmate to Prime Minister of Egypt, reporting directly to Pharaoh.

When a famine hit their nation, Joseph's brothers and their families sought relief from starvation. They traveled to Egypt without any idea that Joseph was there. Joseph was surprised to see that the ones who had sold him into slavery didn't even recognize him. Keeping himself disguised, he had his brothers tell their life stories. He asked questions and his brothers shamefully admitted that long ago they had effectively murdered their little brother. Joseph saw their remorse and hopelessness and revealed himself. Their little brother was now effectively "back from the dead." With embraces and tears, Joseph welcomed them into Egypt and out of the famine. Using the authority of his position, Joseph provided food and shelter in Egypt for their entire nation.

"That was pure evil, what you did to me," Joseph told his brothers afterward. "But the Prince used it all for the good of his nation. He sent me ahead to prepare a place for you. That Prince certainly has got us covered." [4]

Centuries passed. Long after Joseph and his brothers had died, Egypt was swarming with Israelites. The new King of Egypt, who never knew Joseph, was feeling the pressure. There were so many ethnic Israelites who refused to assimilate by marrying Egyptian men and women.

"They are a threat to Egypt," whispered Lucifer, standing right next to Pharaoh, just out of sight, one dimension removed.

"The Israelites are a threat to Egypt," Pharaoh explained to his ministers, who were in complete agreement. "Round them all up and let's turn them from a threat to an asset. Let them serve Egypt as forced labor." [5]

Lucifer couldn't help but laugh, "The Prince's Royal family rounded up like cattle, and being worked like donkeys."

The Royals were not surprised at all by this turn of events. The lessons of good and evil were being learned by repetition, and they would continue to repeat throughout Israel's time at the King's Academy.

"I hope they'll pick up on the lesson," the Prime Minister said to the Prince, "When Cain murdered his brother, you drove him away to a place where Lucifer rules and where crops wouldn't grow.[6] Now, Jacob's sons practically murder their brother, and crop failure drove them into slavery under Pharaoh."

"However long it takes," the Prince said, "I'll be with them."

The Prince had told Abraham long ago that his nation would be slaves for 400 years. Now, after 430 years in the pressure cooker, Israel was about to see the Prince demonstrate his loyalty, buy back his people, and make them a free nation again.[7]

The nation of slaves grew until their numbers rivaled that of the Egyptians. Lucifer had gotten wind that the Prince planned to free his nation from Egypt by sending someone to rescue them. "Could this be the Crusher?" he wondered.

"Just look out your window," Lucifer whispered to Pharaoh, "You are about to lose control of your kingdom to those Israelite hordes."

"I have to stop this menace," Pharaoh thought. He called in his advisors and issued a decree that every boy born in an Israelite family in Egypt should be thrown in the Nile to drown.

"Whatever it takes to crush the Crusher," mused Lucifer. "Help for Israel is *not* on the way."

Under the protective hand of the Prince, an Israelite baby boy named Moses was spared from the infanticide. As with

12: Loyalty Lessons

Noah over a thousand years earlier, little Moses was carried to safety in a homemade boat and ultimately adopted by the daughter of the Pharaoh.[8]

As with Joseph, the Prince had plans for Moses to rescue Israel, but unfortunately, Moses took matters into his own hands, killing an Egyptian. Frightened, he fled across the border from Egypt into Arabia, to a land called Midian. Moses settled in, married a local girl and started a family. He thought he had escaped, but forty years later, the Prince caught up with him.

Wednesday, 6:00 PM KST ⏳ 1250 BCE FST

"There he is, tending his sheep in Midian." the PM said to the Prince as they looked down from the CSOC.

"My people have waited long enough," said the Prince. Turning to the engineer on duty, the Prince said, "Open up a dimensional wormhole down to earth, right there," he said, pointing to Moses. "I want to talk with him..."

*notes for this chapter
start on page 265*

13: Escape from Tyranny

~~~

Looking over the shoulder of the CSOC engineer, the Prince said, "Just behind that bush so we won't blind him, but he'll know it's us."

"Yessir," the engineer replied. "Right away."

Even though this wormhole burrowed through all the dimensions of the universe, the light coming from the Kingdom, into the desert, was blinding. The branches of the large bush scattered most of the throbbing light.

The Prince spoke from the CSOC in heaven, down through the bush.[1] "Moses! For your own safety, don't come any closer! I am the Prince of the Royal family in the kingdom of heaven. I am the one who was with Abraham, Isaac, and Jacob hundreds of years ago. I have heard the urgent calls for help from my people, and I will rescue them, Moses, through you. You will be the one to bring Israel out of Egypt into freedom."

Moses was understandably skeptical. He responded with a litany of questions and reasons why he was not the right man for the job. The Prince addressed each one, never wavering; "Moses, you are going to lead Israel to freedom. All the resources of my kingdom are available to support you. Kingdom soldiers will stand behind you, giving power and authority to words you will speak to Pharaoh."

"That is exactly the problem," explained Moses. "I am not a very good speaker. You really want someone who is eloquent, someone who ..."

"Moses, stop!" The Prince, clearly frustrated, turned for a moment and saw the Prime Minister and the King each suppressing a smile, but they immediately looked very serious when the Prince looked at them. The Prince took a deep breath, turned, and with the patience of a parent addressing a toddler, said slowly, "Moses, I will send your brother Aaron with you, and I will teach you both what to say and do."

Finally agreeing, Moses sent his wife and sons to stay with her father in Midian and he left for Egypt. He met with Aaron, and together they met with the leaders of Israel to discuss what the Prince had planned.

Pharaoh refused to yield to Moses and Aaron's demand of freedom for the people of the kingdom. This was in spite of several displays of shock and awe from the kingdom's armed forces, which Moses called down on Egypt—death and destruction with pinpoint accuracy, killing Egyptians and destroying their infrastructure. The Israelites were unharmed by the carnage, which somehow made Pharaoh's resolve stronger.

"I told your fathers that these people would be trouble," Lucifer whispered to Pharaoh. "Was I right or what? If you let them go, your legacy will be one of capitulation and shame. Think what people will say about you. Tighten your grip, man!"

The Prince told Moses, "Time to pull out all the stops. I will send The Destroyer from the kingdom's Special Forces tonight to kill the firstborn male in every household, Israelite and Egyptian. Remember, Moses," the Prince instructed, "it's all about finding the willing and acceptable substitute from your household to take your place. This time is no different. Go tell the Israelites how the Prince had already

13: Escape from Tyranny

provided their substitute and it is in their animal pen. Tell the people in every household to kill a young animal from their flock and paint the door of their homes with its blood. That will prove to the destroyer that the death sentence has already been carried out, and he will pass over their house."

There was a mad scramble by the Israelites to get their families together and safely locked indoors. The animals were slaughtered, and their blood was painted on the door of every home where the Prince's people lived.

That evening at midnight, the gates along the border of the kingdom swung silently as the kingdom Special Forces deployed The Destroyer across the border into the lower frontier. He visited every house in Egypt and executed every firstborn male. The kingdom expatriates of Israel huddled in their homes, hearing one scream after another from the houses of the Egyptians, as The Destroyer did his work. Whenever he saw the blood painted on the door, he passed over and the household was spared.[2]

The next morning, Pharaoh, with his country still reeling from the assault, practically threw the Israelites out of Egypt.

The nation of Israel, two million strong, followed the Prince out of Egypt. He led them personally from within a gigantic towering cloud. As they marched into the night, following the Prince, the cloud switched modes and became a towering torch, providing light for the road ahead, so they could travel by day or night.[3]

The Prince looked up to the CSOC and grinned. As promised, he was setting the captive nation free. Smiling broadly, the King and the Prime Minister each gave him a salute.

Lucifer saw the wilderness where the Prince's nation was heading and said, "This will be a good place for them to die." After giving Pharaoh a few days to reflect on his failures, Lucifer went to him, offering a suggestion on how he might salvage his dignity...

As if it was his own idea, Pharaoh realized what he had just allowed to happen. Almost every farm and public works project in Egypt had ground to a halt for lack of slave labor. On top of their devastating death toll, Pharaoh now had a political crisis. He couldn't live with the Israelites, and he couldn't live without them.

Pharaoh knew that nothing could bring back the firstborn of Egypt who had died, but he could certainly bring back those slaves. He reversed his position and sent the army of Egypt to round up the Israelites and bring them back into slavery.[4]

Egyptian horses and chariots thundered through the wilderness, ready to capture or crush the Prince's people. As Lucifer was fond of saying, "Whatever it takes."

The nation of Israel huddled on a wide beach on the Gulf of Aqaba, a northern extension of the Red Sea. Water to the east, steep mountains to the north and south, and a narrow pass through the rocky wilderness on the west—and the Egyptians were about to pour through that pass onto the beach. Israel was trapped. Ten miles to the east, across the water, Moses could see the mountains of Midian in Arabia, where his wife and children waited for his return; so close yet so out of reach. He looked up at the towering cloud as if to say, "Well?"

The windows in the great kingdom hall were jammed with heavenly beings peering down, and it was elbow-to-elbow on the Crystal Sea observation deck as well. They were all watching intently as Pharoah's war machine threw itself against the kingdom forces. Except for the Royals themselves, none of those watching from above were sure of the Prince's next steps, but none of them had any doubts about the outcome.

"Moses!" the Prince commanded from the cloud. "Lead my nation through the sea, into freedom!"

13: Escape from Tyranny

Moses turned to the sea as a team from the kingdom Corps of Engineers scrambled across the border into the lower frontier. They fired up an east wind and let it rip all night across the Gulf of Aqaba, creating two walls of water with a dry path down the middle. All the while, the Prince's tower of fire held back the Egyptian army.[5]

The besieged nation moved forward on the new path beneath the surface of the sea, and came up above the water, a free nation. As the last of the nation of Israel was coming up onto the shore of the Arabian wilderness, the Prince removed the tower of fire, allowing a hot pursuit by the Egyptian army.

As the Egyptians charged down the path through the sea, a kingdom engineer flipped off the wind allowing the waters to close over the army of Egypt, who marched on into Lucifer's lower waiting room, to wait for the final judgment.

Above the surface of the Crystal Sea of heaven, spontaneous applause and cheering erupted. The King and the Prime Minister had big smiles on their faces as they watched from the CSOC. "That is just awesome!" said the Prime Minister. "Going under the water as slaves, and coming up into freedom."

"Awesome indeed," said the King.

Watching as the waters of the Red Sea swallowed up the Egyptian army, Lucifer remembered his own exit from heaven through the Crystal Sea, and thought, "How I hate those Royals."

A messenger approached and handed Lucifer a note about the crush of soggy human beings from Pharaoh's army jamming the entrance to the lower waiting room. His lips curled into an evil smile.

*notes for this chapter
start on page 268*

14: Law School

With all the excitement of their escape through the sea behind them, the days in the desert were mundane by comparison. The needs and concerns of everyday life took center stage. The Prince knew exactly what his nation needed.

He showed Moses where to find water, then, calling on the logistics branch of the kingdom army, the Prince ordered up "meals for a million," a pre-dawn airdrop onto their camp, six days a week, with a double delivery on Fridays.

The kingdom army dropped tons and tons of what looked like bread flakes, onto the camp every day. By coincidence, the Israelites gave it the same name as the kingdom army had given it. They called it *manna*, which was the Israelite word for "What is this stuff?" [1]

For three long months after crossing the sea, the Prince led Moses and the nation through a barren land. Without the airdrops of manna, they would have undoubtedly starved. Finally, the nation set up camp at the base of Mount Sinai, in the rugged Arabian wilderness.[2]

The King rose from his throne. Stepping out and down into the Crystal Sea, he personally descended to the top of Mount Sinai, covering himself, and the top of the mountain, with thick dark clouds, smoke and thunder. It was terrifying, yet the people couldn't take their eyes off it.

His voice boomed out, "Moses! Come up here!"

Moses headed up the mountainside alone and was soon surrounded by thick smoke, which got brighter with each step. Surprisingly, it did not cause him to choke.

"That's far enough Moses," the King said, still hidden from view.

"I can't see you," Moses called out.

"No you can't. It would kill you to see me as I am.[3] Sit down Moses, we have a lot to talk about, my friend."

For forty days, the patriarch of the Royal family of the kingdom met with the patriarch of the Royal family on earth. They talked. They laughed. They wept. The King shared with Moses like he had never shared with any human before. In a way, it was like the time the Prince spent in the garden with Adam, getting to know one another, camping out together, bonding with each other.[4]

"Moses, I want these people to know and remember that they are my Royal family on earth," the King explained. "These people are my treasure." [5]

After forty days together, the King handed Moses two thick flat stones, which he had inscribed himself. "Moses," the King said, "these are the ten foundational laws of the kingdom.[6] You already know the prime directive; Total allegiance to the King. These laws provide a bit more detail, like a guide for daily living. If you find yourself disregarding any of these, you'll know you are disregarding the prime directive."

Moses brought the ten laws down the mountain to find that the people of Israel had been busy breaking most of them for the forty days he was up on the mountain with the King.[7]

14: Law School

> **The Ten Foundational Laws of the Kingdom**
> 1. Give total allegiance to the King
> 2. Put nothing ahead of your relationship with the King
> 3. When you take the King's name, bring honor to it
> 4. Set aside one day each week to spend with the King
> 5. Honor and respect your parents
> 6. Do not murder
> 7. Do not have sex outside of marriage
> 8. Do not steal
> 9. Do not lie
> 10. Do not set your heart on things that belong to others

"This is perfect," thought Lucifer. "With these statutes in place, we'll have all the proof we need that these people are constantly violating the prime directive. They'll know for a fact that they can *never* be good enough to be part of the Royal family!"

The Prince and Gabriel had been watching from the throne room as the King met on the mountaintop with Moses. "If the people follow those laws, it will be really good for your nation," Gabriel noted.

The Prince nodded but said nothing.

"Of course, you know that not one of your people will be able to keep all of those laws," he added. "Not even close."

"Precisely," the Prince responded. "The humans know it too. With these statutes in place, it will be obvious to them that they are constantly violating the kingdom's prime directive. They'll know for a fact that they can never be good enough to become citizens and enter the kingdom." [8]

"Unless ...?" Gabriel guessed something was coming.

"Unless," the Prince declared, "they can get their kingdom records cleared by the qualified substitute!"

"Knew it," Gabriel smiled as he thought, "The Immigration Project just continues to unfold."

For centuries, most of the Israelites had known the principle of kingdom justice that allowed their punishment to be absorbed by their animals. So, the laws which Moses brought them really did turn out to be a helpful guide for living, and not just a depressing list of unattainable values.

Even in the desert, families in Israel kept their kingdom record clean as best they could. They regularly offered up the lifeblood of a goat or lamb from their household in place of their own lives, keeping ahead of kingdom justice.

The Prince saw that of the two million people in the nation, there were thousands of households, each understanding kingdom justice in their own way, and not always getting it right. Petty arguments developed between families over the minutia of the right way to offer up the substitute, and how best to follow the laws which had been given to Moses. It was time for the kingdom Department of Justice to open a branch office at the King's Academy.

"We are going to provide my nation with a clear and consistent approach on how to clear their kingdom record of all the charges against them," the Prince explained to Moses. "I don't want anyone to be consumed with questions like, 'Is my kingdom record really cleared? Am I really free from the death penalty?'"

Moses didn't know exactly what the Prince was planning, but he knew a solution was desperately needed. He told the Prince, "Too many people have simply given up, saying, 'We can't know exactly what the Prince wants, so why bother? We'll deal with it on the judgment day.'"

"I know," said the Prince. "I will make it clear how to get right with kingdom law. The only ones who won't be cleared of their condemnation are the ones who simply don't care."

"Here are the plans for your new 'portable Justice Center,'" the Prince said to Moses, handing him a detailed list of specifications. "This Justice Center will move with you until you are established in your national homeland." [9]

"I don't think I need to tell you, Moses, how busy this portable Justice Center will be. With over a million people in Israel, the Justice Center will need to be staffed by a judiciary that is hard working and well educated in the laws of the kingdom."

"Who do you have in mind for that?" Moses asked, not wanting to be assigned even one more task.

"Remember, Moses, that night in Egypt, when I spared all the firstborn sons of Israel from the destroyer?"

Moses nodded, not sure where the Prince was going.

"I spared Israel's firstborn sons, and they literally owe their lives to me. In effect, I bought them for the kingdom. Today I am trading those I have bought, for the entire clan of Levi, your brother Aaron's family, all twenty thousand of them. These "Levites" will be Israel's judiciary, the staff of the kingdom Justice Center." [10]

The Prince went on, sounding a bit like an accountant. "I've got 273 more firstborn than you've got Levites, so you can make up the difference to me in silver, five shekels for each of the extra firstborns. Aaron will take that money to fund the startup of the Justice Center."

"No rounding it off and just calling it even?" Moses half joked at the Prince's attention to detail.

The Prince looked at Moses and responded, "No one gets rounded off or falls through the cracks in kingdom justice. Everyone is accounted for."

"Sounds good to me," Moses said.

"Me too," replied the Prince with a teacher's smile.

The deal was done. The team of Levites constructed the Justice Center in accordance with the detailed instructions the Prince had given Moses, and put it into operation. Now the kingdom Justice Center was the one place the nation of Israel could come to have their kingdom records cleared.

"You are going to have to do better than that!" Lucifer said, in an imaginary conversation with the Prince. "Thirty seconds after one of those people gets their record cleared at the Justice Center, they are back in the real world. Out there, every one of them violates one or another of your laws almost constantly."

Lucifer went through the logic for himself. "These people forget that their exoneration at the Justice Center is only for their past violations, not for what they do right after their record gets cleared. Kingdom justice doesn't care if it's a million violations or just that one which they committed since having their record cleared — they still get death."

Thinking about it, Lucifer was convinced there was more to the puzzle. "I'm sure the King plans to get around the issue of 'future violations' by ensuring that Crusher is somehow above the dimension of time, making his substitution valid for all time. But he's still got to be a descendant of the woman in the garden, a human in the Prince's Royal bloodline."

"I just need to stick to the plan," Lucifer concluded. "If we can dominate the human bloodline, Crusher will be disqualified from clearing anybody's kingdom record. Nice try, Prince! All your people are still doomed!"

The Prince was one dimension above, but only a few feet away from Lucifer, so he heard the entire one-sided rant. The Prince said to himself, "If you only knew the power of the kingdom, you little snake." [11]

The nation had been at the foot of Mount Sinai for almost eleven months. Add to that the three months since they passed through the Red Sea and they had spent as much time in the wilderness as Noah and his family spent with the animals in the Ark.

"Time to pack up and head out," the Prince told Moses. "I've prepared a place you..."

*notes for this chapter
start on page 271*

15: Freedom Ahead

❦

As fast as two million people and all their belongings can move, the nation of Israel headed north.

With their new homeland only a few short weeks away, the people still found things to complain about. They were tired of the snake and scorpion-infested wilderness and eating the same food every day. Moses sometimes felt he had only one nerve left, and these people were stepping on it. Frustrated, he told the Prince, "I'd rather be dead than have this job." [1]

Lucifer grinned broadly when he heard that. "These people have gone from being slaves of Pharaoh to being slaves of the Prince," he said to his lieutenant. "Moses is dragging them through the desert and the Prince only provides enough food to keep them from rioting. That Prince is as close to losing the people as he is to losing their leader, and that's fine with me."

The Prince worked with Moses and held the nation together until they approached Canaan (roughly twenty-first century Israel), the land that the Prince had promised to them.

Moses sent scouts ahead into Canaan. They reported that before Israel could settle into the land, they would first have to evict the current residents—giants—descendants of the Nephilim! [2]

Even though the Prince had assured Moses that the current inhabitants were not to be feared, everybody seemed to have their own opinion. Ten out of the twelve scouts warned that Israel would be massacred if they went forward into Canaan. Joshua and Caleb were the lone dissenters, encouraging Israel to follow Moses and the Prince, but they were shouted down by the crowds.[3] The nation refused to budge and even got ready to pelt Moses with rocks.

The Prince was livid. He pulled Moses aside. "Are these people blind as well as stupid? Since they left Egypt, I've proven that I can deliver them through anything, but they believe the lies of the warlord instead of my promises. I'm ready to kill them all now and start over again with you!" [4]

Moses, exhibiting an uncharacteristic calm said, "Now Prince, if you do that, you know that word will get back to Egypt, and you will be known as the Prince who couldn't lead his people out of a sandbox, so he killed them." [5]

"Fine," said the Prince, "I won't force anyone into a life of prosperity. You can all wander around in the desert until every one of the adults in your nation is dead! Joshua and Caleb are the only exceptions, since they stood for me and my kingdom. When every other adult is dead, then we can try again."[6]

"This is not so bad," Moses thought, having just influenced the Prince to spare his people.

"This is not so bad," the Prince thought, "Moses is really maturing as a leader. He is beginning to act as if he cares for these people, even when they are contentious beyond reason."

"This is not so bad," Lucifer thought, pleased at seeing how easily the people chose his advice over the Prince's.

"Looks like the Kings Academy will be extending into extra sessions," the Prince said to the Prime Minister.

"Sometimes the only lessons these humans really learn are the hard ones," the PM responded. "A few more years in

15: Freedom Ahead

the desert and perhaps the lessons of kingdom loyalty will really sink in."

Once again, Israel picked up and marched into the desert. This time, however, it was away from the land that the Prince had promised to give them.

For the next forty years, the nation wandered through the desert, being led and fed under the direction of the Prince. The portable Justice Center was in full operation and the people made a regular practice of getting their kingdom records cleared. Israel finally reached the Jordan River, across from Canaan, the same land into which the Prince had tried to lead them before.

The Prince and the Prime Minister came to Moses. The Prince told him, "Moses! You're 120 years old. Your time as Israel's leader is up. You were the right man for the job of getting the people out of slavery and taking them through law school, but no further."

"You must be joking," Moses stammered. "I've led these people for more than forty years. I've followed all your laws..." The Prince listened with genuine compassion to his friend who began to choke up. "I worked so hard—doesn't that count for anything? At least let me bring them across the border."

"I can't, my friend," the Prince spoke softly. "In the desert, remember?" Moses was silent. "Two million people, dying from thirst—they had their eyes glued on you. Aaron called them together to see for themselves how I would provide for them. They knew what was going to happen. All you had to do was command the rock like I told you, and I would make water pour from it—more than enough for everybody. They were straining to hear you speak those words—but instead you bashed the rock with your staff." [7]

"Yes, and water came out!" Moses pleaded. "Please, let me lead them across the border."

"Enough![8] You're not getting it, are you? Yes, water came out. My people were thirsty, Moses—of course I gave them water. The point is, you disrespected me in front of my people. Two million of my own family watched as you consciously ignored what I told you to do. No, you're not going to lead them in—and no, we're not going to discuss this anymore. Turn over your leadership to Joshua." [9]

An old man, Moses died within sight of the land that the Prince had selected for his family's homeland.

General Michael led a kingdom military honor guard to carry Moses out of his body to the kingdom citizens' arrival lounge. A group of Lucifer's soldiers watched from a safe distance. They were frustrated after years of watching Moses hide behind the Prince's protection. Just as the kingdom honor guard was leaving, Lucifer's soldiers stepped quietly toward the lifeless human body of Moses and were about to bring it to their General as a trophy. Michael turned and swung his massive sword, clipping but not killing the vandals. He shouted, "Back off! Don't you ever touch the body of an honorary kingdom citizen. Especially this one!" They jumped back and scurried away.[10]

Moses was met at the entrance of the lounge by Abraham, as well as a number of his friends from the past forty years in the desert. The welcome was heartwarming, but Moses still thought about not being able to lead his people across the border to freedom.

As he settled in, a lounge attendant approached him carrying a small tray with a sealed envelope on it. He said, "Message for you sir." Moses opened the envelope to find a hand-written note on Royal letterhead ...

15: Freedom Ahead

Moses ~

Meet me later on the mountaintop with Elijah. I want to talk with you about bringing many more people across the border ~ more than just Israel.

- Prince

Moses had no idea what the note meant. He exchanged a glance with Abraham who smiled but had nothing to say about it.[11]

notes for this chapter
start on page 273

16: *School of Government*

Moses's longtime assistant Joshua assumed leadership and was ready to take Israel into the homeland which the Prince had chosen. They were certain to face opposition, but along the way, Joshua had learned one thing: when the Prince says go, you go!

The Prince stood with Joshua and went over the instructions one more time. Waving his hand over the map, the Prince said, "From here to the Mediterranean, up to Lebanon and east to the Euphrates River in Iraq, it's all ours, just as I promised Moses.[1] OK Joshua, let's go…"

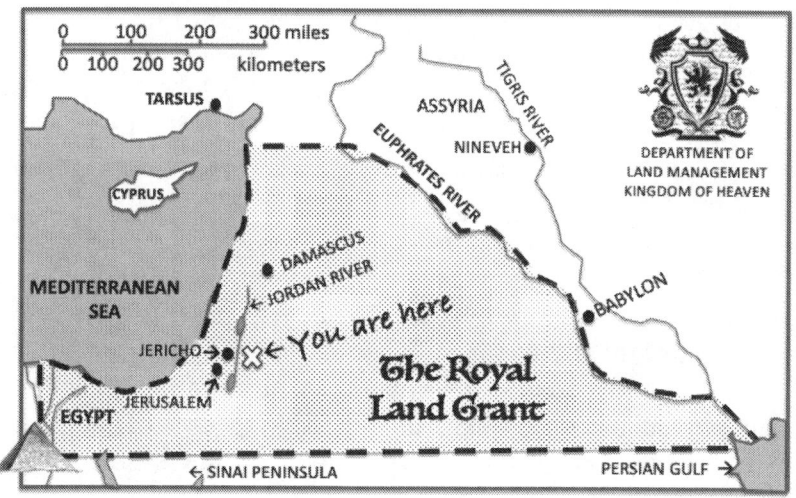

"Start packing up!" Joshua shouted to his leaders. The command echoed throughout the nation.

This time there were no arguments, no talk of the fearsome natives. They were heading west toward the Jordan River, toward their new homeland in Canaan, led by Joshua who was led by the Prince.

The influence of Lucifer and his soldiers had been felt in Canaan for years by the time Joshua and the Israelites arrived. As in many other parts of the world, freewheeling sex had become socially acceptable. Prostitution had become just another way to make a living.

On their first night at camp in the new land, the Prince came to Joshua in his tent. "There is something you need to do before we go any further. While you were in the desert, a lot of the people didn't circumcise their sons as they had been instructed. You know the reason for circumcision— for a woman to know for sure if the man she marries is one of us. While you were in the desert, it was a moot point, and I let it go. You were all alone out there, but Canaan is a very different place."

Joshua could tell where this conversation was going, and he wasn't looking forward to hearing the rest of it.

"You know what needs to be done, Joshua. Protect my family."

The next day, Joshua gathered his leaders and told them what the Prince had said. They were not excited about the assignment either, but agreed it had to be done.

That week, every man that had been born during their forty years in the desert was circumcised, over 400,000 of them. From that time on, the place they had camped was known as "the hill of foreskins." [2]

After a few weeks of recovery, Joshua and the nation he led moved across Canaan to the fortified city of Jericho. Spies were sent ahead to assess the city's defenses. They befriended a local woman named Rahab, who was well

16: School of Government

known throughout Jericho as a prostitute. She made no attempt to hide this as she met in secret with the men from Israel. Word traveled fast about the visiting spies, and when the King of Jericho heard, he sent word to Rahab for her to turn them in.[3]

The King's messenger banged on the door and Rahab bought a few moments to consider her situation. "Just a minute while I get decent!" she called.

"Rahab... decent," the messenger smirked as he waited.

"These men of Israel are the first ones to speak with me in *years* who weren't undressing me first with their eyes and then with their filthy hands," she thought.

Rahab quickly made her decision and confided in the men, "The King of Jericho is scared to death of you. Everybody in the city has heard that the Prince is with Israel, and about how he took you through the sea out of Egypt. Here's the deal—I'll help you escape, but when you take this city, you've got to spare me and my family."

"Deal," said the spies. "Just be ready when we come back."

"Rahab!" came the shout along with a pounding on her door. "Bring out the spies!" called the King's messenger.

Rahab composed herself, opened the door and flashed her professional smile. "Tell the King I'm sorry," she lied to the man at the door, "The men he is looking for left town just before the city gates closed last evening."

"Well then, why don't you invite me in and we'll talk about it over a glass of wine?" the messenger asked, jingling his coin purse. His eyes were drawn to Rahab's cleavage.

"Get out of here, you pig!" Rahab spit as she slammed the door. They were both surprised at her reaction, given her well-earned reputation.

Rahab helped the spies hide on the roof of her house that night, and the following day, the spies made their getaway. Within a few days, Israel marched on Jericho. The Prince told Joshua exactly what to do. The walls of the city collapsed before their eyes and what was left of the city was burned. True to their word, the Israelites whisked Rahab and her family out of the danger zone and they were welcomed into the Prince's nation.

"Welcome Rahab!" Lucifer shouted with glee. "I *love* it when a prostitute joins the Royal family! Descendants of my human children have been living it up in Canaan for a long time, so Rahab is certainly no Royal. She will carry on *my* family line inside the Prince's nation, and little baby Crusher will be *my* pride and joy—*my* legacy—*my* son!"

For decades, the Prince led his nation on a program of territorial expansion throughout Canaan. All that the Prince required was that the people give full allegiance to him, keep his laws and commands as best they could, and get their offenses cleared at the Justice Center regularly.

As needed, the Prince provided resources from the army of heaven to fight their battles for them. More than once, however, the people disregarded the Prince's instructions, and then the Prince would stand-down. Usually that meant Israel would get crushed for lack of kingdom air support.[4]

Two steps forward, one step back. Slowly, the nation of Israel spread out and settled throughout Canaan.

No matter how often the nation turned its back on the Prince, and went their own way, the Levites kept the fires burning at the Justice Center, day in, day out. Anyone who wanted to get right with the kingdom knew that was the one place to do it.

With the passing of Joshua, the Prince appointed one man after another to act as his representative to the people. But on the whole, the nation's attention seemed to be sliding away from the kingdom. The people told Samuel, the Prince's current representative, that they wanted the Prince to give them a real king, a human king, like the other countries had.

16: School of Government

Lucifer understood. "They want a real leader, not some being from another dimension who they seldom, if ever, see. Even the Prince's nation is coming around," he thought.

The Prince listened quietly as Samuel explained the people's demands for a human king. Finally, the Prince responded with a note of sorrow in his voice, "These people do not even remember why I made them separate from the rest of the nations, or why I told them over and over to protect their bloodline! They circumcise their own sons, and they don't even know why. They think it's about hygiene, or that it protects them from diseases or something! They've forgotten they are royalty. They have forgotten every provision of mine, and every battle I have fought and won for them!"

Samuel said, "They just want a strong man to look up to, one who will tell them what they need to do ..." His voice trailed off, realizing the rejection that the Prince must be feeling. Samuel felt he had let down both the Prince and the people.

"Samuel," the Prince said quietly, "don't take this on yourself. These people are not rejecting your leadership. They are rejecting mine.[5] They don't understand what human government is really like. It is time for our nation to attend the kingdom school of government."

Samuel sighed. He knew that there were no easy classes at the King's Academy.

The Prince said, "Tell them that their request will be granted. In the King's Academy school of government, they will learn from firsthand experience, exactly what it means to have a human king over them." He went into detail, "Tell them a human king will draft their sons into his army and force them to run into enemy fire. He'll conscript their sons and daughters to work in his own personal businesses and munitions factories. He and his friends will take the best of the people's personal production and on top of that, you can all expect a 10% tax on everything you have.[6]

"Samuel," said the Prince, "every single human government is like this, to one extent or another, not just the king I will give them. The one thing I want my people to learn in the school of government is the difference between a kingdom government and a human government. You've seen how *I* rule and protect my nation. Now you'll learn by experience that human governments wind up crushing their own people to one extent or another." [7]

"Samuel, remind them that I *want* to be their King, but they rejected me.[8] But so they don't despair, also remind them that I will continue to protect this rebellious, forgetful, and ungrateful nation, all the way through King's Academy graduation, and beyond."

Lucifer was quite satisfied that things were going his way. These people certainly weren't acting like they were the Royal family on earth. They acted exactly like everyone else. And now that the Prince had granted their request to be under a human king, they were back in slavery.

With his officers surrounding him, Lucifer gloated, "The Prince's whole protect-the-bloodline thing is dead, too. They just can't resist those foreign women. None of them can claim to be a Royal anymore! And circumcision...! Nice try, Prince! It didn't work. You can put that ritual in the museum!" [9]

"Even the prostitute Rahab from Jericho is now a matriarch in the Prince's human family, and that makes me a patriarch![10] Talk about a mixed-up family tree!" Lucifer cackled. "I say, put 'em all to death, let us all into the kingdom, or be a hypocrite!"

Lucifer was content, sure that the Prince's plan was a feeble, doomed attempt to win the affection and loyalty of these spineless, stupid, and self-centered humans. "And if

16: School of Government

that glorious substitute of his ever shows up, the Prince is going to be the one to get crushed, not me." [11]

Lucifer was confident that the Prince had misplaced his eggs in the flimsy basket of a pure Royal bloodline. Delighted at how his plan was falling into place, he shouted, "That bloodline isn't Royal anymore, Prince, and it certainly isn't pure, unless my boys and I are pure royalty!"

*notes for this chapter
start on page 276*

17: King's Crossing

~·~

On the top floor conference room, the King, the Prime Minister, and the Prince spoke excitedly about the Prince's upcoming trip across the border to earth.

This trip was not going to be a down-and-back hop through the Crystal Sea into some pasture of earth. This was to be total immersion into a world full of good and evil not unlike what Adam and Eve experienced when they stepped out of the garden.

The Prince was going human.

General Gabriel knocked and entered the room. He bowed slightly and then said, "Is it time?"

The Prince checked the clock...

Thursday, 11:58 PM KST ⌛ 6 BCE FST [1]

"Let's go," said the Prince. He and the Prime Minister followed Gabriel into the Crystal Sea, stepping down to the lower frontier. In a small town called Nazareth, in northern Israel, they found the one they were looking for.

In heaven, General Gabriel has a very impressive appearance, even amongst the fiercest squadrons in the kingdom army. When he enters the three dimensions of earth, visible to humans, he is incredibly intimidating.

As gently as he could, this giant of a warrior stepped into the presence of a fourteen-year-old girl and whispered, "Greetings, Mary." Not surprisingly, the general's unexpected entrance caused her to jump, then shake with fear. "Don't be afraid!" he said gently, "I have great news for you from the King of heaven. You know about the One who has been promised by the founding fathers of Israel for centuries—the One who will free the nation of Israel from the demands of kingdom justice? That One is your son, Mary."

"B-but, I have no son! Joseph, my fiancé—we are not yet married—I have never slept with a man!" she stammered.

"I know," said Gabriel, "the Prime Minister himself, from the kingdom of heaven is here. He will deposit the life of the long-awaited One into you, Mary—and don't worry about Joseph—I will talk with him tonight. He will be your husband, and Jesus will be your son." [2]

From a dimension unseen by Mary, the Prime Minister and the Prince of heaven stepped toward her. Both of them seemed to dissolve as they approached the young girl and disappeared into her body, but only the Prime Minister emerged on the other side. The Prince of heaven had entered a human, to become a human.

The long-promised One was born in an animal pen in the small town of Bethlehem, just south of Jerusalem.

Some foreign dignitaries who had studied the writings of Israel's founding fathers, journeyed almost 700 miles to welcome the promised One.[3] On the night of his birth, however, not many were on hand to greet the Prince. Other than Mary and Joseph, Jesus was surrounded by barnyard animals and a few local shepherds.

Everyone in the kingdom, however, knew of the big event. Thousands of kingdom soldiers paraded through the sky over Bethlehem, cheering and shouting to celebrate the Royal birth. As quickly as they had appeared, they slipped

17: King's Crossing

back into the kingdom, as if exiting through unseen doorways.[4]

Word of the birth of the One reached Lucifer quickly, and he almost choked. "What!?" he bellowed. "Tell me that again!"

The messenger stood nervously before him saying, "Bethlehem—in a stable—last night. The parents are a couple from Nazareth. I don't even think they are married. Kingdom security was tight; we could hardly get close enough to see. But we know it was him. It had to be."

It was clear that the Crusher had arrived, and his name was Jesus.

Enraged, Lucifer tore the head off the messenger, then composed himself and sat down to consider his next move.

Even after a period of reflection, Lucifer, though he appeared calm, was livid. "This One thinks he can just waltz onto my planet without consequence. The earth is still mine. Those humans gave it to me. The Prime Minister confirmed it. *I am* the legal authority here."

Lucifer knew the Royals were up to something, since one of the founding fathers of Israel had written that the Crusher's mother would be a virgin,[5] but at the end of the day, Lucifer knew this baby Jesus could not be part of the Royal family. "Virgin or not, his mother is still a human, and I own the human bloodline! It doesn't matter who his father is or isn't, Crusher will be at least half in my family!"

Lucifer tucked this ace in his pocket and he actually looked forward to seeing the great judge's face when he dropped that card on the table.

For now, however, he kept his eye on the ball that was in play. "I will crush this human king, and anyone who tries to follow him—this is war!"

Lucifer commanded his lieutenants, "Get word to the local king, Herod, that a competitor for his throne has arrived in Bethlehem. Let him know he needs to crush the Crusher.

Remember last time we missed Moses in the slaughter of the newborns, so make sure Herod casts a wider net this time!"

By the time King Herod commanded the execution of all male children in the region two years old and younger, the Prime Minister had already led Joseph and his family into Egypt.[6] They stayed there until Herod and his fury had died. Then the PM led them, under the wings of a heavily armed contingent of kingdom military guards, to the backwater town of Nazareth in northern Galilee, where young Jesus learned carpentry from his father Joseph.[7]

Though Israel was under Roman occupation, Joseph, Mary and Jesus led a relatively quiet life in the sleepy town of Nazareth. A battalion of heaven's soldiers stood watch from above and did battle with Lucifer's henchmen as needed, ensuring that, at least to the humans, the Prince's early days on earth were quiet.

When Jesus was about thirty years old, he traded in the life of a carpenter and set out to do what he had come to do—become the leader of the kingdom of heaven on earth. When he started his public life, the former carpenter hammered home one message more than any other, to anyone who would listen: "The kingdom of heaven is near."

Jesus' cousin John was known to Lucifer and his underlings as a radical, a troublemaker who stirred up the people against the status quo of earth, pointing them to the Prince's kingdom. Jesus sought John out and found him down at the Jordan River.[8] John announced, as he did every day to all who would listen: "The Prince of heaven is coming! Get ready!"

He told them that in order to gain kingdom citizenship, they need to publicly renounce their old life and renounce any loyalty to Lucifer, the ruler of the earth. If they did that, John would submerge them beneath the surface of the river and a moment later, lift them up. "Your life as a citizen of

17: King's Crossing

earth is about to be over! You are now pre-qualified for a new life as a citizen of the kingdom of heaven!"⁹

Kingdom-minded people came from all over, seeking kingdom citizenship. They were not sure how it would all work out, but they didn't want to miss the opportunity to become part of the kingdom which had been promised for centuries.

As each person was brought under the water and up again by John, there was cheering that rocked the gathered crowd around the Crystal Sea outside the great kingdom hall.[10]

Jesus approached his cousin John at the Jordan River. John had already suspected his Jesus's true identity. He had heard the stories from his mom and Aunt Mary, and somehow, he thought that Jesus might just be "the One." When Jesus asked John to bring him through the water, John was puzzled. Why would Jesus ask him to do that? If he was really the One, he was a kingdom citizen already. He didn't need to be pre-qualified. "What is going on here?" John wondered.

It wasn't about becoming a kingdom citizen for Jesus. John's suspicions were correct. He already was one. Jesus' father was a Royal from the kingdom itself, making Jesus a kingdom citizen by virtue of his bloodline. It was actually about renouncing his citizenship of earth.

Jesus was born in Bethlehem, making him a natural-born citizen of the earth. By birth, Jesus was legally a subject of Lucifer, the ruler of the earth. He was eligible for citizenship in both the earth *and* the kingdom of heaven. He was fully human by birth and fully Royal by blood.

Jesus explained this to his cousin, "Entry into the kingdom is restricted to citizens of the kingdom who carry kingdom passports, but dual citizenship is not recognized or tolerated in the kingdom.[11] If someone publicly gives up their citizenship on earth, renounces its ruler, and commits themselves fully to the kingdom and the Royals, they are eligible for citizenship and a kingdom passport."

John just stood looking at Jesus, hip deep in the flowing water, not saying a word.

"John," Jesus whispered in his cousin's ear, "anyone who wants to be admitted to heaven must take a stand for the kingdom and against its enemies. It is absolutely necessary for me to publicly renounce my citizenship of earth, and along with it any authority which the warlord Lucifer wants to exercise over me because I was born here."

John didn't move.

"I have to do this, John," Jesus said with a quiet urgency. "I cannot take on the mantle of leadership of my Royal nation on earth, until I publicly renounce the ruler of the land of my birth." [12]

It was a lot for John to process all at once, though he knew that it had to be true. Jesus broke the tension, "Just do it, John," he winked at his cousin, "or I'll tell your mother."

In a loud voice, John led Jesus in publicly renouncing Lucifer, the ruler of the land of his birth. John lowered him under the water and Jesus came up. There was an eruption of cheering on the Crystal Sea observation deck as Jesus burst through the surface of the Jordan River, with a huge smile on his face!

Clearly excited, the Royal Father reached down and literally tore a temporary wormhole from the border of heaven right down to that stretch of the Jordan River.[13] The Father called down, and everyone gathered around Jesus and John heard it.

"My son! I can't tell you how pleased I am with you!"

With his mouth open in awe, John watched. The Prime Minister stepped down through the new opening, and with the grace of a bird, landed on Jesus.[14] As he would do again many times for others in the coming years, the PM deposited a kingdom passport and full diplomatic credentials into the

17: King's Crossing

Prince's human body, authorizing access and authority in all dimensions through the top floor of heaven.

Prior to becoming human, the Prince had enjoyed unrestricted kingdom access, and more. Laying down that authority for the previous thirty years, and now getting it back, was exhilarating. However, as Jesus, he was about to have that authority tested and stretched by the warlord who was not about to let the kingdom muscle-in on his territory.

Unlike in the kingdom, the ruler of the earth has absolutely no problem with dual citizenship. "It's this intolerant renunciation that I can't stand," Lucifer would tell his troops. "Divided loyalties are just fine with me," Lucifer would say. "Can't we all just get along?"

Lucifer was even OK with having the Justice Center in the midst of his territory, as long as the people kept their loyalties divided. The new kingdom Justice Center in Jerusalem was so impressive that the justices in charge were more focused on maintaining their high-level jobs and social schedules, than they were on upholding the prime directive of the kingdom.

"Good for you!" Lucifer would cheer them on. "There are a lot of things going on in your life and they're all very important!" [15]

Despite some such apparent victories, Lucifer knew that John and Jesus had to be dealt with. "These renunciations of me personally need to stop before things get out of hand," he thought. "I need to talk sense to Jesus."

Lucifer wouldn't have long to wait.

The Prime Minister whispered to Jesus, "It's time to tune out the distractions.[16] Your father wants to prepare you for the battle ahead. Let's head out into the desert."

For forty days, Jesus walked alone in the desert, without food, without shelter. Near the end of that time, when his human body was running on empty, Jesus had a visitor.

*notes for this chapter
start on page 280*

18: Summit Meeting

～∾～

Lucifer considered what he would say to Jesus and decided to take the cooperative approach. He would not bring up the matter of Jesus' sketchy bloodline, saving that gem for later.

"We could be partners, even friends. The Prince wants the earth and its people; I've got the earth and its people. It's my earth and I can give it to the Prince if I want. We'll work together. It's a win-win. Yeah."

Lucifer found Jesus in the desert, blistered, tired, and hungry. He certainly didn't look like kingdom royalty.[1]

"Jesus," Lucifer said with convincing sincerity, "you need to eat something. I cannot believe the Prime Minister led you out here in the desert to starve like this. Let me get you some, uh …" He looked around. "Here, Jesus," he held out a rock. "Just say the word and turn this into a loaf of bread. If you really are the Prince of heaven, we both know that will not be a problem."

"Bread is not enough to keep a man alive." Jesus replied. "Humans are not simply animals that eat, sleep, and die on this earth of yours."

"Of course, Jesus, of course," Lucifer said, quickly dropping the rock. "But you are right. The entire planet is mine, as a matter of fact." Lucifer led Jesus through a dimensional doorway, to a vantage point high up in the heavenlies, where they could see the entire earth. "But in a lot of ways, it's a mess. It really does need you to straighten it out, Jesus, to rule over it. Tell you what—let me give it to you. Here, take it; it's yours. But first, let's just go back to the river and take back what you said about renouncing me and my sovereignty. We'll set the record straight for the people. Let them know that you are running the earth for me.[2] Let's—"

"Stop!" Jesus interrupted. "You know the prime directive of the kingdom, 'total allegiance to the King!'"

Lucifer paused. "Yes, of course. Forgive me, Jesus. What was I thinking? The King. Yes, everyone needs, first and foremost, to know and honor the King." He took Jesus through another dimensional doorway to the top of the tallest tower of the kingdom Justice Center in Jerusalem.[3] They looked down on the people milling about at the foot of the building. "You can point these people to the Royal Father in a very powerful way, Jesus. Jump down from here, right now, in front of all these people. You know that the King would never let you get hurt. Everyone would see the kingdom soldiers save you and they would know that the Royal Father sent you. You will be the talk of Israel, and you will point them to your Father!"

"You know what happens to those who force the hand of the King, don't you? *Don't you?*" Jesus repeated, knowing full well that Lucifer knew. "It never ends well."

They stood silently looking at each other.

This meeting had not gone as Lucifer had hoped. He now knew for certain what he had suspected earlier. This was no courtesy visit from a ruler of heaven to Lucifer's earth. This was definitely an illegal invasion of his sovereign territory. He realized that the Prince had come to crush him.

Furious, Lucifer vanished through an invisible door, muttering, "You have not heard the last of me."

18: Summit Meeting

A platoon of kingdom soldiers rushed through that same door, surrounding and tending to the Prince.[4]

John's pre-qualifications continued, for a while.

Lucifer knew better than most, that the humans had free will. He knew he was powerless to physically prevent them from using their free will to defect to the kingdom.

"But we can convince them that their renunciation wasn't genuine," he explained to his henchmen. "It'll be easy! They actually prove it to themselves every time they put their own interests above the kingdom's or violate a kingdom law. When they do, we'll whisper a little reminder, 'That's why you are not pre-approved for citizenship in heaven. Application rejected! Hah!'"

Lucifer's staff joined in with other one-liners for the humans to use on those would-be kingdom citizens:

"There is no kingdom! This world is all there is!"

"If there is a kingdom, where is it? Seeing is believing!"

"The kingdom is a fairy tale for weak minds—a crutch, a coping strategy!"

"They will believe me," thought Lucifer. "They always have." He turned and strode toward Galilee to have a word with Herod, the puppet king of the region, about getting rid of the troublemaker John.

Herod didn't like John any more than Lucifer did. Soon, Herod ordered that the activist John be arrested, locked up, and eventually beheaded.[5] Herod didn't care much about the kingdom or those renunciations, but he was *absolutely* fed up with John frequently pointing out Herod's lifestyle to the people, publicly declaring that it was evil and anti-kingdom.

It wouldn't be the last time that Lucifer recruited the support of a local government to deal with those who encourage defection to the kingdom.

*notes for this chapter
start on page 281*

19: Hidden in Plain Sight

The location of an announcement can be almost as important as the announcement itself. Returning to his hometown of Nazareth, Jesus went to the community leaders who greeted him warmly at the local kingdom Justice Center.[1] These men had known Jesus since he was a boy. They had watched him grow up.

"Jesus, we were just gathering for the reading from the books of Israel's founders," one of the elders told him. "Come join us—better yet, read a selection from the book for us." He handed Jesus one of the old books containing the history and wisdom of the nation of Israel.

Jesus knew that heaven's nation on earth had been waiting for hundreds, no thousands of years for what he was about to say. He also knew they weren't expecting it today, especially in dusty little Nazareth. He wondered how they would react.

"I would be honored." Jesus rose, took the book and stood before the leaders and a small gathering crowd. He looked about, smiling as his gaze met eye after familiar eye from his childhood days. He cleared his throat and spoke in a loud voice: "All the power of the kingdom of heaven is upon me."

They all knew Jesus was simply quoting directly from the book of Isaiah, one of Israel's founding fathers, but there was an incredible authority in his voice.² It was almost like it was personal.

Jesus continued reading, "I have been chosen by the King of heaven to give you a message," he paused as the audience strained with anticipation. "He has selected me to set free the prisoners and the oppressed. He has sent me to give sight to people who are too blind to see. I have come to heal those with broken bodies and hearts. I am here to announce to you that the King of heaven is now buying back the earth and his people!"

Jesus closed the book, handed it back, took his seat, and looked down. The silence got more intense.

Jesus then lifted his head and spoke again, "That long-awaited day of freedom for Israel starts right here in Nazareth, and it starts right now, today!" This time he was not quoting from the book but speaking on his own.³

The onlookers were stunned. Some were offended.

It took a few moments before anyone could speak. One person finally whispered, his irritated voice growing in volume as he spoke, "Maybe Jesus has spoken with the Prince himself, or maybe even the King!" With a clear touch of sarcasm, he added, "So what did they say to you, Jesus?"

A family friend of Joseph, Jesus' adoptive father, tried to ease the tension by interjecting a compliment about Jesus' powerful delivery. "Joseph's boy sounds like a founding father himself!"

As much as he had loved his mother's husband Joseph, Jesus knew who his real father was. Turning to the sarcastic elder, he said, "You know from Israel's history that the authority of a founding father of Israel is never appreciated in his own hometown, so the King sent his representatives elsewhere. So be it with Nazareth; the wonders of the kingdom will pass you by."

The leaders looked at each other, "I think he's just insulted us." The crowd's murmuring grew into sharp

19: Hidden in Plain Sight

comments. Regrettable words were thrown. The next thing anyone knew, Jesus was being pushed by a mob toward a nearby cliff on the edge of town.

As they approached the precipice, Jesus made a slight turn into a dimension just beyond their human sight.

"Where did he go?"

"I was holding his arm and he vanished!"

"You idiots!"

Invisible to the agitated crowd, Jesus simply walked away.[4]

So began the public declarations of Jesus. Over the next three years, he repeated the same message day after day: "The border crossing into the kingdom of heaven is about to open!"

The crowds following Jesus grew daily, making it difficult for him to keep up with all the demands on him. The Prime Minister told Jesus, "It's time to establish a team of honorary consuls, a group of men committed to you, who have pre-qualified for citizenship in heaven. We'll train them on getting the kingdom message out in a powerful way, and you will lead them by example."

Jesus knew the plan. He appointed twelve of his followers as honorary consuls for the kingdom.[5] They were not chosen for their social, intellectual or financial status. The Prince was able to just look at someone and know their character.[6] Though some of them were a bit rough around the edges, the Prince knew that these men would eventually embrace the King and the kingdom more tightly than they would embrace life itself.

Interestingly, Jesus didn't choose anyone who worked at the kingdom Justice Center, though the justices there had all heard about Jesus from their colleagues in Nazareth. They were keeping an eye on him.

Jesus gathered his honorary consuls together, "You probably don't even know what an honorary consul is. It is someone who is *not* a citizen of the kingdom but who has been authorized by the kingdom to work on its behalf. As you will soon see, my main objective is to offer kingdom citizenship to citizens of earth, and that offer will start with each of you when the time comes."

"You will hear me say over and over, how people can become citizens of heaven. When my work here on earth is done, the Prime Minister of the kingdom will visit you and give to you, and everyone who is pre-qualified, a kingdom passport, authorizing full access to the kingdom."

Looking at his new honorary consuls, Jesus said, "I expect that most of you in this group, after you become citizens, will be appointed ambassadors, as well. You will then have full authority to call down all the resources of heaven as needed—but I am getting ahead of myself."

"Your main job for now as honorary consuls is to watch me and learn. We want to demonstrate to everyone in Israel, by our words and by our actions, that the kingdom is really real, and the kingdom is right here!" [7] He waved his arms at dimensions that the honorary consuls could not see. "Everything the people have heard from the founding fathers is true. I am about to make it possible for humans to enter the kingdom. Now *that* is good news! All they have to do is turn their back on the warlord Lucifer and take the citizenship deal that is about to be offered."

Not yet sure what the citizenship deal would be, the honorary consuls still had a lot to tell the gathering crowd.

"OK, let's get to it!" said Jesus, stepping into the crowd, to get up close and personal with humans who want to learn what the kingdom is all about.

This was the start of an almost three year "kingdom awareness tour," for Jesus and his entourage. Walking throughout Israel, Jesus met with the people face to face. It was a nonstop series of one-on-one conversations, speeches

19: Hidden in Plain Sight

to the crowds, firm handshakes, and brotherly embraces. Most of all, though, Jesus told stories.

He would speak important truths about the kingdom of heaven in the form of simple stories.[8] The stories were simple, but it wasn't always clear exactly what his point was. At times, even his honorary consuls found themselves baffled by Jesus' stories.

"Why not just give them straight talk on the kingdom?" they asked Jesus, after the crowds had left. "Let them know exactly where it is, and exactly how to get there!"

"I don't want everyone to understand everything I am saying right now," Jesus said. "What I want them to hear from me is that the kingdom is real, and it's right here, right now. I want them to hear what the kingdom is like, as compared to the earth. Then they need to think about where their own allegiances lie and what it might mean for them to give up citizenship on earth and commit to the kingdom. Not everyone is ready to embrace the kingdom."

"You've seen me heal people, and even raise some from the dead, but every one of them is still going to die," Jesus paused to let them think. "But you, my friends, have a greater assignment. You will invite people to live forever in the kingdom. That is why I speak plainly to you. You need to understand the kingdom message more clearly than anyone."[9]

While walking from one town to another, Jesus asked Peter, "What do you hear from the people? Who do they say that I am?"

"They say you're a prophet for sure. Maybe even one of the founding fathers come back to life!"

"I see," he said. "Who do you say I am, Peter?"

Peter stopped walking, looked Jesus in the eye and said, "I know you are the Prince of the Kingdom of Heaven."

Jesus paused, looked Peter in the eye and said, "I never told you that—my father did. But don't tell anyone, Peter."

Peter said, "Okay," but thought to himself, "Why not?"[10]

Those flocking to see and hear Jesus were a cross section of the culture. They were merchants and tax collectors, fishermen and prostitutes, Israelites, Romans, Greeks, Samaritans, the rich and the poor, the holy and the demon-possessed. He met with men, women, and children everywhere he went.

Something, however, was missing. Conspicuous by their absence from the crowds was any of the management or staff of the kingdom Justice Center. If they did show up, it was usually the Justice Center interns, on the fringes of the crowd, listening and taking notes for their superiors. Some of the people wondered, "If the border to the kingdom is opening, why isn't anyone from the Justice Center out here with you, Jesus? *They* are in charge of clearing our kingdom records. Are the kingdom laws changing?"

"Not at all," Jesus replied. "Everything you heard through Israel's founding fathers is exactly the same, then as now.[11] Some people, however," referring to the officials at the Justice Center, "have become more interested in being known as experts in the law, than knowing the one who gave them the law. They like being in charge more than they want to know the kingdom and the Royals." [12]

"That's it!" Lucifer realized. "Turf war!"

*notes for this chapter
start on page 284*

20: Challenging Authority

༄

Calling his minions together, Lucifer mapped out a whisper campaign to get the crowd buzzing, "Jesus is out to undermine the Justice Center by drawing attention to himself."

The officials at the kingdom Justice Center didn't need Lucifer to point out that Jesus was a threat. They watched Jesus closely, looking for an opportunity to discredit him and bring him down.

The crowds were intrigued by the turf war, but they were really excited about the miracles. Jesus knew he needed to address the believability factor. He knew that a man claiming to represent the King of a superpower nation in another dimension needed to back up his words with a little proof.

For person after person, Jesus used his kingdom authority over the dimensions of the universe to do things that are impossible for beings locked in three dimensions.

"I'm doing these miracles, these demonstrations of kingdom power, for two reasons," he explained to his honorary consuls, gathered around their evening campfire.

"Fame and fortune?" asked John, nicknamed by the Jesus as one of the boisterous "thunder brothers." [1] John's brother, James, gave him a corrective slap on the back of his head.

"Thank you, James." Jesus smiled. "No, John, not even close," he continued. "First, it's to show that the kingdom of heaven has a huge desire and ability to meet the needs of its citizens. Receiving a miracle gives a taste of what it's like when one is released from the chains of these three dimensions."

"Secondly, I do them to show the crowds that the reality of the kingdom is far bigger than what they can detect with their senses and understand with their minds—that what they have always believed about the King and the kingdom is *really real*."

Jesus did many miracles in front of many eyewitnesses, feeding crowds of thousands from virtually nothing, turning hundreds of gallons of water into the same amount of fine wine, withering a tree by speaking to it—jaw-dropping miracles for sure—but the most impressive were the healings. Person after person came to Jesus and he cured them of lifelong incurable infirmities including blindness, paralysis, and mental illness. In most cases, however, Jesus told the person being healed not to tell anyone.

The capstone of his miracles was when Jesus' friend Lazarus died. Four days after his friend's death, Jesus stood in front of Lazarus' tomb with dozens watching. He called directly up to the top floor of heaven, "Father! King of heaven! I know that *you* know the plan, but I'm shouting this so everyone watching me here will know that this miracle is *your* doing!"

The King nodded, watching through the Crystal Sea portal. Jesus turned to the tomb and said, "Lazarus, come out!"

An attendant in the kingdom arrivals lounge tapped the new arrival on the shoulder, interrupting his conversation. He whispered, "Mr. Lazarus, please come with me right away."

20: Challenging Authority

Moments later, Lazarus found himself back in his body, staggering toward the open door of his tomb. Everyone was astounded, including Lazarus.

Word of the miracles, this one in particular, spread fast all over the country, and Jesus drew huge crowds, hundreds and even thousands at a time. Often, they showed up to see the miracles and totally missed the message. So when the people saw the miracles, Jesus would challenge them, "Even if you don't understand or believe what I'm saying, at *least* believe me because of the miracles you have seen with your own eyes!" [2]

As he traveled throughout Israel on his kingdom awareness tour, Jesus was constantly dogged by Justice Center staff members who had been sent by their superiors to pepper Jesus with trick questions, trying to trip him up in front of the people. They usually found that they were the ones to be embarrassed by Jesus' common sense, yet deeply profound answers.

After disposing of a trick question, Jesus would turn his back on the antagonists and remind the crowd of the dangers of being blindly committed to anyone or anything other than the kingdom and the Royals themselves.

The thing which really infuriated the men from the kingdom Justice Center was when, right in front of them, Jesus would look a person in the eye and say, "We both know that you have broken the prime directive of heaven, but I hereby grant you a full pardon from your death sentence under kingdom law."

The Justice Center staffers nearly had a stroke! "Now he's handing out pardons for kingdom violations! Who does this guy think he is, the Prince of heaven or something?"

Jesus had no patience for the Justice Center bureaucrats. "You wouldn't know a Royal if you were standing in front of one! You think handing out kingdom pardons is hard for me? You don't even know who I am! How hard do you think *this* is?" Jesus turned to a crippled person sitting on the floor in front of him and said, "Get up and walk!" Jesus then turned and glared at the bureaucrats, as the man jumped up off the floor, whooping and hopping.[3]

On the way out of town, Jesus and his entourage walked along a dusty highway. Peter and John had been talking about Jesus and those amazing healings. When they came alongside Jesus, Peter blurted, "Jesus, we're not trying to tell you what to do, but when you heal people like that, it's big news. If you just tell them who you really are—the Prince of the kingdom of heaven—word would get around. They're all guessing that you are the Prince, but you don't ever tell them! You even tell them not to say anything about the miracles.[4] I don't get it."

They walked in silence for another twenty paces and Jesus asked, "You're not trying to tell me what to do?"

"Oh, no, of course not," Peter responded immediately. John shook his head in agreement.

It was another twenty paces before Peter blurted, "But if I was telling you what to do, I'd say, 'Just tell them!'"

Jesus laughed as they kept walking.

Lucifer was not laughing. "This Prince is walking through my planet, inciting people to openly defy and reject me, their lawful ruler!"

If he could, Lucifer would have orchestrated an unfortunate accident to have Jesus killed. The trouble for Lucifer was that Jesus was no mere human, but a citizen of the kingdom. But there was more—back at the Jordan, the Prime Minister had given Jesus not only a kingdom passport, but full diplomatic credentials as well. Jesus' diplomatic credentials were that of a senior kingdom ambassador, giving access to resources, not just in the lower frontier, but in the Kingdom of Heaven above.

Lucifer, however, was locked into the lower frontier, just the dimensions of the earth and the heavenlies. "I can't even

20: Challenging Authority

see those other dimensions anymore," he said, knowing how much power could be wielded through them. Lucifer knew full well he was no match for Jesus. "Damn that Prince! I can't lay a hand on him directly," he thought in anger. "But I have to get him off my planet somehow. The boys over at the Justice Center are really mad at Jesus and they want him out of the picture as well. There's no telling what they might do if I just give them a little help."

The chief justice was livid. "This Jesus is telling the people to get right with the kingdom, but he isn't even pointing them to the kingdom Justice Center! Who does he think he is? It's like he's rewriting the books of Israel's founding fathers! He announced that he can personally issue kingdom pardons! Only the Prince of heaven can do that! Jesus is a liar and a deceiver! This is treason!"

Other Justice Center officials saw which way the wind was blowing and piled on, "He publicly mocks the Justice Center and all of us, calling us walking dead men. He says we will be excluded from the kingdom's plan for Israel!" [5]

"Enough!" shouted the chief justice. "This man Jesus is an enemy of Israel and of heaven's prime directive. He has to die for the good of the nation!"

The PM turned to the Father and said, "The chief justice doesn't know how right he is!"

"If he did," the Father replied, "he might not go through with it." [6]

Jesus' kingdom citizenship awareness tour had been going on for almost three years. Before Jesus and his followers turned toward Jerusalem, Jesus had them set up camp at the base of a mountain. The next morning, Jesus called, "Peter! James! John! Come with me. I want to show you something. The rest of you stay here. We'll be back in a few hours."

Without a word, the four of them climbed the rocky slope, finally making it to the small, flat peak. They were dusting themselves off when a dimensional doorway opened and Jesus lit up as if he were glowing from within. The light became intense, and two other bright figures appeared through the door and stood beside Jesus. Peter, James and John jumped back. They watched and listened as the three bright figures greeted each other and spoke of a mass exodus, which was just about to start—a migration of humans across the border from earth into the kingdom.[7]

Peter recognized the others, and whispered to John, "It's Moses and Elijah—founding fathers of Israel! They've crossed the border to meet us." He called out, "Jesus!"

The three glowing figures suddenly stopped their conversation and turned their heads in Peter's direction. "We need to make some monuments here—to you!" Peter shouted. "Everyone, everywhere will know who you really are and what you are going to do! We have to tell them!"

Moses whispered, "Is he trying to blow your cover?" Jesus shook his head slightly. "No," Jesus whispered back, "he just doesn't understand the plan." [8] All three quietly looked at Peter, who was beginning to think the monument thing wasn't such a good idea. Behind the bright figures, a dark cloud boiled up, quickly engulfing them. Moses immediately recognized what was happening. It was the Prince's father. Moses recognized the King from their meeting in the clouds on Mount Sinai. A voice boomed from within the cloud, directed at Peter, James and John, "This is my son! Listen to him!" [9]

As quickly as it arrived, the cloud receded. Moses and Elijah also left, closing the door behind them. "C'mon, lets go," Jesus said to his friends. "Now listen this time—do not tell anyone who I really am!" Jesus headed down the steep slope, then paused and turned, "At least not until I return from the dead." The three men were baffled by the part about returning from the dead. They kept their mouths shut regardless.[10]

20: Challenging Authority

They rejoined their friends at the base of the mountain. Over the following weeks, Jesus and his group traveled throughout the region and had many life-changing encounters with people. One morning, Jesus announced, "Time to head for Jerusalem."

Lucifer could hardly contain himself. "Into the hornet's nest," he cackled. "All according to plan..."

*notes for this chapter
start on page 287*

21: The Set-Up

☙❧

The Prime Minister turned to the Royal Father. "All according to plan," he said somberly. The King nodded.

Jesus made a triumphant entry into Jerusalem amidst thousands of cheering admirers. Later that week, knowing he was about to die, Jesus organized a private dinner with just his twelve honorary consuls. His best friend John sat on one side, Judas their trusted treasurer on the other, and the others around the table. He had a lot to share, and he didn't have much time.

Jesus wasted no time. "I hate to tell you this, but one of you is going to turn me in to the authorities."

The men were shocked, but Jesus said it, so they knew it had to be true. Each asked quietly, "Is it me?" and they looked around at each other, wondering. Judas looked Jesus in the eye and whispered the same question.

Judas already knew the answer. Earlier, he had secretly gone to the Justice Center and had offered to help them forcibly arrest Jesus. He had hoped this would compel Jesus to, once and for all, use his kingdom authority to put the justices and the Romans in their place; however, at this moment, his plan didn't seem so smart. He felt about as stupid as Adam wearing a fig leaf in front of the Prince.

Jesus looked long at Judas but didn't answer him directly. Breaking off a piece of flatbread,[1] Jesus held it up.

Looking around the table he said, "This is my body." He dipped it in the dish of herbs and handed it to Judas. "Eat it."[2]

Jesus pushed the basket of flatbread down the table. "all of you, eat it." The others each broke off a piece bread and ate in silence, wondering what Jesus meant by that.

Then Jesus reached for a cup of wine, wrapped his hand around it and mused, "For centuries, the blood of innocent animals has been poured out at the Justice Center to pay for the crimes against the kingdom, committed by the people." Looking around the table and making eye contact with each of his honorary consuls, he said, "Tomorrow, it will be my blood that is poured out, to satisfy kingdom justice for anyone in my family who claims me as their substitute."

He lifted the cup. "This is my blood that frees you from the death penalty. Drink it... and every time you do, remember what family does for family." He took a sip and passed the cup around the table. Each man took a drink. None of them really understood what Jesus had just told them, but he said to do it, so they did it.[3]

Lucifer had been watching from a corner of the room. He was perplexed that Jesus spoke of his blood as being something special. Lucifer thought, "He knows I own the human bloodline, and that by living in his mother's womb for nine months he is part of my bloodline, my family."[4]

He shook his head and focused on the task at hand. "OK Judas," he said to himself, "no turning back now." Lucifer walked across the room and entered into Judas' human body.

No one in the room could see what just happened except Jesus, who looked sternly into the eyes of Judas, addressing Lucifer, and whispered, "Just do it."[5]

To the surprise of the others, Judas got up quickly and rushed out the door, taking Lucifer with him.

Immediately, kingdom guards descended into the room like a SWAT team to secure the perimeter. All of Lucifer's henchmen were hustled away, well out of earshot. It was

21: The Set Up

clear that the Royals wanted to keep the rest of the dinner conversation in the family, at least for now.[6]

Jesus looked around the table at his honorary consuls. "There's not much time. I need to tell you a few things..."

"For over a thousand years, the blood of innocent animals has been offered up at the Justice Center, to pay for people's crimes against the kingdom, but you know there is this nagging dilemma...

Your kingdom record gets cleared, but five minutes after you leave the Justice Center, it happens... It's always something, isn't it? Something you said, or thought, that you know is just wrong. Maybe you did something - or you didn't do something that you should have. You're guilty again, usually before you get home!

Here's the rub: the blood of those animals can only clear past violations. You know you can't pay for a crime before you commit it – justice doesn't work that way."

The consuls had thought about that very question but thinking about it too much gave them a headache.

Jesus explained, "You are all prisoners of time. You move forward through time and you can never go back. An animal can pay for your crime with their life, but once they're dead – they're dead! Their death yesterday can't pay for the crime you'll commit tomorrow." Unless you are sacrificing animals all day every day, you can't ever get ahead of the law.

They all knew he was right, but what could anyone do about it?

"Here's what you need: an innocent, willing, substitute from your family, who is not a prisoner of time. One whose death can pay for your kingdom crimes after you confess and ask for mercy."

Blank expressions all around the table.

"We are family," Jesus continued, "so I can be your substitute, but get your head around this: Our family home is above the dimensions of earth, above length, width, height and time; where past, present and future are all equally accessible.[7] When you ask my father for forgiveness - for anything – even 30 years from today, he can look at what I am about to do tomorrow - as it is happening - and say, 'paid in full.'"

"What are you going to do, to make all this happen?" Peter asked.

"Yes, well," Jesus took a sip of water, and took on a somber tone. "By this time tomorrow, I will be put to death by those who run the kingdom Justice Center. They will have the help and support of the Romans who run the rest of the world."

"No!" Peter shouted. We will never let those...!"

"Peter, stop!" Jesus interrupted. "It's not about them. It is my choice! Don't let anyone tell you that 'this person or that group of people murdered Jesus.' [8] This has been my father's plan to free our family, for more than four thousand years. There will be violent opposition from the enemy, but if you trust me in the battles, even if you die, you live!" [9]

The room was silent. Peter was a little embarrassed at Jesus' pushback. John broke the ice. "So no more long lines of animals at the Justice Center?"

"No longer needed," Jesus responded. "I am the innocent, willing, once-and-for-all substitute from your family in heaven that can cover your kingdom violations forever. The old kingdom Justice Center is going out of business and *I* am replacing it.[10]

"Once your record is clear, the Prime Minister will issue you a kingdom passport, and with one of those, you can never be turned away at the kingdom gates.[11] Best of all, Jesus added with a smile, "In the kingdom, time never runs out and we all live forever."

That part the honorary consuls could grasp, and the atmosphere in the room lightened.

21: The Set Up

"When you know for certain that you are a citizen of the kingdom and that you really will live forever, it's very freeing," Jesus said. "You don't have to worry about the minutia of kingdom law, or even the ups and downs of life. You are free to focus on the big picture of building the kingdom here on earth, with me." [12]

Jesus reached for some hummus, giving them a moment to let it all sink in. The men began to chatter with each other on what lay ahead.

"In a few days I will come with the Prime Minister and bring your kingdom passports. After I have left the earth and returned to the kingdom, the Prime Minister will again visit each of you to deliver diplomatic credentials establishing your status as ambassadors of the kingdom. That often involves the handling of classified information that will be revealed only on a need-to-know basis." [13]

"Do not hesitate to call in the kingdom military as needed. The Prime Minister can provide weapons effective in all dimensions, not just the three dimensions of earth.[14] You will need them since the enemies of the kingdom live in dimensions outside of plain sight.[15] Don't worry," the Prince told them. "I personally have overcome everything he's got in his arsenal, and I have got you covered." [16]

Jesus looked around the room at his team of honorary consuls, who had fallen silent again. They were just now realizing that, while they may become ambassadors, it was apparent that they were about to be posted in a war zone.

"Oh, one last thing," Jesus said. "If anyone asks you to help them become a kingdom citizen, you are authorized to accept their renunciation of the warlord and their pledge of allegiance to me and my Kingdom. Lead them through the water right away, and the Prime Minister will issue them a kingdom passport, on the spot, guaranteeing that new citizen's entry into the kingdom."

"If anyone who is already a kingdom citizen tells you they want to be a kingdom ambassador, bring them to the Prime Minister. He will make the call on exactly what they need and how they should be used in the Diplomatic Corps."

The men felt like they had been hit with a fire hose of last-minute information, too much to take in all at once.

"Don't worry," he told them. "The Prime Minister will help you remember everything I told you." [17] He took a last look around the table. "OK," Jesus said. "Time to go."

Together they all went out past the kingdom security team standing guard and through the east gate of Jerusalem and waited in a garden, in the dark of night.

Lucifer had been waiting for this moment. He took a deep breath and said, "It's show-time!"

*notes for this chapter
start on page 293*

22: Blood Matters

T he next twelve hours were a cacophony of confrontation, arrest, and accusations, with all the noise coming from the accusers. "I want to hear you say it! Are you the Prince of the Kingdom, the One promised in the Garden four thousand years ago?" Jesus hardly spoke, and when he did, it only infuriated the accusers.[1] Jesus endured verbal abuse as well as brutal and bloody physical assaults. The Roman governor, Pilate, asked Jesus directly if he, Jesus, was actually a king. "Yes," Jesus answered, "but right now, my kingdom is not of this world." [2]

"Enough with the nonsensical answers! Don't you know that I have the power to put you to death right now?" demanded Pilate.

Jesus, dripping blood on the marble floor of Pilate's foyer, said softly, "You wouldn't have any power at all if my Father hadn't given it to you." [3]

Not knowing what to do with an answer like that from a man who should have been very intimidated, and, facing an unruly mob of locals calling for Jesus' death, Pilate made a quick calculation. He then did the politically expedient thing; Jesus was flogged, taken outside the city, and was nailed to a cross, the preferred method of execution in the Roman Empire.[4]

Along with two other condemned men, the Prince of heaven hung in public view to die a slow-motion death. It was a surreal view from the perspective of the men on the cross. People gawked at them from just a few feet away, some in stunned silence, some chatting and milling about. Some were just doing their jobs, making sure the execution went off without any trouble.[5]

The condemned man on his left side turned his head and insulted Jesus with his final breaths, "You phony. If you really are the Prince, how could you let this happen?"

"Shut up," gasped the dying man on Jesus' right. "We deserve to die. He doesn't. Prince," he gasped, "remember me—when you get home to your kingdom."

Jesus gathered what was left of his strength and replied, "You will be with me at the kingdom gates today." [6]

As the Prince breathed his final breaths as a human, he felt the entire, fearsome weight of the kingdom's legal system crushing down on him. He was personally absorbing the rightful punishment due all who flaunt the kingdom's prime directive: Total allegiance to the King.

The Prince cried out to his father, but kingdom communications were cut off and the border was shut tight. Jesus was under condemnation, and heaven was sealed off. He hung there in agony and finally died, alone.[7]

The normally bustling great kingdom hall was totally silent. The Royal Father was on his throne, eyes closed, and his head tilted back. The Prime Minister sat nearby, leaning forward, his head buried in his hands.

On earth, just out of human sight, Lucifer was high-fiving every one of the rebels surrounding him. This was a time to celebrate! The invader had been turned back! The human Prince was dead — put to death by the humans he came to save!

"And when those Royals try to claim that Jesus was the acceptable substitute—here to save the humans from kingdom law—*Wham!*" Lucifer slapped his hand on his thigh, "Got him! Jesus, Crusher, the One, what-*ever* your name is! You are from my bloodline, my household, my earth! You can pick up your marbles and go home, Prince. Get off my earth, now!"

When Jesus breathed his last, there was first a ripple, followed by tremors on the earth, then a violent shaking.

Lucifer and his followers stood in stunned silence and watched. At the Royal Father's command, over one thousand members of the kingdom Corps of Engineers grabbed the fabric of the universe, the curtains dividing the dimensions, and began to twist them. First they warped, then they stretched, and finally, a hole was torn.[8] They had torn a permanent wormhole in the universe from the dimensions of heaven to the dimensions of earth.

While there had been temporary wormholes before, this new one was the first permanent road between the three dimensions of earth and the highest dimensions of the heavens. Kingdom engineers were already busy setting up a border crossing checkpoint to allow access exclusively for kingdom citizens. The road was not very wide, however. It was actually quite narrow, and its entrance on the earth's end was in the heavenlies, just out of sight for the humans. By design, a human on earth couldn't find it at all unless the Prime Minister or one of the ambassadors would lead them to it.[9]

Lucifer, however, could see the new border crossing. "What does he think he is doing? Nobody is going up that road! Jesus is not qualified as a kingdom-substitute because he is part of my household, my bloodline and I forbid it! He is not an acceptable substitute under kingdom law!"

He shook his fist upwards, shouting "If you let these people up that road into the kingdom, I am coming up too and so are all my troops! If you don't let us in, our whole deal is off!"

Outwardly defiant, but trembling inside, the warlord of the earth waited silently for a reply. He didn't have to wait long.

Lucifer's lieutenant ran breathless to his leader, "They have tricked us! It's pure Royal blood!"

"What is this nonsense?" he demanded. "Make sense!"

"I overheard some kingdom soldiers. They were laughing at us![10] They were saying that the bloodline in this Jesus is 100% pure Royal blood."

"Impossible! All of you were encouraging the women and men of Israel, and the rest of the world for that matter, to sleep with whomever they wanted—and I know they were doing it. After all these centuries, that so-called Royal bloodline is now mine, and I can prove it!" he screamed.

"I'm telling you, Jesus is totally of the Royal bloodline," Lucifer's lieutenant continued. "The girl, his mother, was a virgin. No man had ever touched her. They said the Prime Minister of heaven is the baby's father."

"I knew she was a virgin!" Lucifer protested. "I read what those founding fathers had written about that. So what? Virgin or not, she is part of my bloodline. After Rahab and all the others, I own the stinking human bloodline!"

"You are completely right about that, sir. You have done a masterful job in capturing Israel's bloodline. However," he continued, "it seems that when the Prince created humans, he constructed them so that no blood from the mother ever comes in contact with the baby—not ever.[11] Blood doesn't even exist in a baby until the father's contribution starts the process. His bloodline is 100% pure Royal, because the Prime Minister of heaven is the father.   The Royals have taken an end run around our claim to his bloodline. It'll be hard to convince any judge that Jesus isn't an acceptable substitute—not on the basis of his bloodline anyway."

Lucifer stood in stunned silence, staring at nothing.[12]

22: Blood Matters

Fearing the traditional shooting of the messenger, Lucifer's lieutenant made a silent and hasty exit as Lucifer processed the devastating news.

Now, after thirty-three years on earth, Jesus was helped out of his dead body by a kingdom military honor guard. He was brought to the kingdom citizens' arrival lounge.

At the lounge entrance, Jesus literally bumped into the man he had just spoken with, back on the hilltop, on the cross next to him. The man did a double-take and, with tears in his eyes, he gave Jesus a bear hug. Jesus received the hug with a big grin.[13]

*notes for this chapter
start on page 297*

23: *Legal Matters*

༄༅

"And here we are!" Jesus said as the entered the KAL with his new friend from the crucifixion. All the man could say was, "Thank you, Jesus! Thank you!"

The Prince walked over to greet friends[1] in the lounge. After a few minutes, he announced, "This has been a big day and it's not over yet." With that, he glanced up at the clock...

Friday, 12:21 AM KST ⌛ 29 AD FST

...and walked out of the lounge and headed down the concourse, through the security gate, down a long corridor, past the entrance to the lower waiting room. The lighting was quite dim. The heat was stifling. At the end of the hallway was a heavy metal door. Etched in stone above the door was a single word:

TARTARUS

The door was guarded by a kingdom trooper. He dropped to one knee as the Prince approached. The Prince nodded and the guard rose to open the door. As he pulled, the hinges creaked and, like breaking the seal on a jar, air rushed through the crack as it opened.

Inside, hundreds, maybe thousands, of Lucifer's troops squatted in the darkness, murmuring.[2] They immediately fell silent and all locked eyes on the Prince. Most of them had been locked in the darkness since shortly after leaving the heavenlies behind, to pursue the human women of earth, thousands of years earlier. Realizing this was not a rescue by their general, they all fell to their knees.[3]

"If you haven't heard," the Prince said in a loud steady voice, "the war is over. Hostilities may continue for a while, but your General Lucifer has lost." The murmuring grew and quickly faded as they leaned forward for more news. "All humans, regardless of their ancestry, can once again become part of the Royal bloodline of heaven and regain their kingdom citizenship."

He paused to let the news sink in. "You gave up everything to become like men, and so you will be judged like men. As I promised when you were deported from the kingdom, each of you will face trial, but I will not judge you. The humans whom you violated will be your judges." [4]

The Prince looked deeply into the eyes of the warriors who, before the General's rebellion, had served bravely in his kingdom army. He sighed, and silently exited the dungeon. The door slammed shut behind him as he strode purposefully up the corridor towards earth.

Jesus died on Friday. At daybreak on Sunday, the Prince returned to the earth in a strong, new human body. It looked much like the old one, even bearing the same scars.

At the Prince's command, one of the kingdom soldiers rolled the stone away from the entrance to the tomb. The Roman soldiers who had been posted to prevent grave tampering sat on the ground, unable to stand, and watched. They were as motionless as they were speechless. A few moments later, they both got up and bolted in the direction of the Jerusalem city gate.

The Prince walked out of the tomb. He was almost out of the garden when he heard a voice calling from behind him, but not calling him by name.

23: Legal Matters

"Where is he?" she called. He knew that voice well. It was Mary, one of his most loyal friends.

Mary was unaware that the man she was speaking to was Jesus until he turned and said, "Mary!" She was stunned. He was supposed to be dead!

She ran toward him, arms ready for a hug, saying, "Jesus!"

The Prince had a huge smile and held up his hands to discourage the hug. "Whoa, Mary. Stop!" Mary stopped short, wondering why Jesus would keep her at arms-length.

"I need to go to the throne room and see my father before anyone can touch me, but I'll be right back.[5] Go tell our friends that you've seen me this morning."

Jesus vanished from Mary's sight when he turned onto the kingdom highway, through the newly opened wormhole. The gates swung open and he was greeted with the thunderous cheering of thousands who lined both sides of the road. He strode purposefully toward the throne room to seek a judgment for the humans, from the King.[6]

The King couldn't wait. He ran out of the throne room to greet his son, with tears in his eyes. He wrapped his arms around the Prince. The Prime Minister joined-in for a three-way hug. Within minutes, they sat to hear the Prince's testimony and to discuss what had just happened on earth.

Pointing to his own blood dripping on the throne room floor, the Prince made the case that his death was sufficient to pay for all crimes against the kingdom, for any human who asked the king for clemency, and showed true remorse.

The King agreed. "Your innocent, voluntary death is sufficient to satisfy kingdom justice once for all time, for any human who confesses, shows remorse, and asks for a pardon. Their records will be cleared."

The Prince then shifted gears, asserting that their former General Lucifer had breached the written agreement that was made in the Garden of Eden.

"He authorized and encouraged his rebel forces to commit repeated physical, sexual assaults on human women – direct descendants of our children, Adam & Eve," the Prince testified. "Had it not been for the actions of the Prime Minister, there would not have been a single person left on earth in the Royal bloodline."

The King agreed again and handed down his ruling. "All authority over the earth, which had been transferred to Lucifer in the Garden of Eden, is hereby revoked. All authority on earth – and in Heaven – is now given to you, the Prince of Heaven." [7] The King reached out and shook hands with his son. The Prime Minister did the same.

"And I look forward to bestowing all that power," said the Prince, "and all that authority, onto my human followers, those who commit themselves to our family." [8]

The King was beaming, "This is a great day, son. Go tell them the good news!"

The Prince took his leave, stopping to shake hands and exchange a quick word with Michael and Gabriel on the way out, and he headed back to earth.

His first task was to take care of some unfinished business with his friend Mary...

*notes for this chapter
start on page 300*

24: Transfer of Authority

~~~

Before Mary made it all the way back from the garden tomb to the room where the honorary consuls were hiding out, Jesus met her on the path, arms spread wide. "Mary!" he said, surprising her. This time he didn't flinch, letting her give him a big hug.[1]

In his new body, the Prince traveled through Israel for forty days, but not always in the conventional way. He used a number of higher-dimensional shortcuts to get where he was going.[2] Time after time, Jesus would suddenly, apparently out of nowhere, step into the presence of people in locked rooms or in private conversations. After engaging them for a while, the Prince would leave, not by walking out the door, but by simply vanishing from their sight.[3] While astonishing to them, from Jesus' perspective, he was simply stepping out of the room.

When Jesus did step in or out of the earthly dimensions like that, it usually gave people a jolt, even those who knew him well. He would suddenly appear, and they would act like he was a ghost. "Don't be afraid," Jesus would say. "Look at me, touch me. I've got skin and bones just like you. I'm not a ghost!"[4] It was not an easy thing for them to get used to.

In his first such meeting, the Prime Minister joined the Prince. Jesus told the men, "Congratulations! Because I have cleared your kingdom record once and for always, and because you have publicly committed yourselves to me and to my kingdom, you are now full citizens of the kingdom of heaven. Receive your kingdom passports!" [5]

Standing directly in front of the group in an unseen upper dimension, the Prime Minister went from man to man, reaching his hand into each chest and sliding a new kingdom passport into each heart, as if into a pocket.[6] He looked at them proudly, then stepped up and out of the room, returning to the kingdom proper.

The Prince continued, "All the rights, privileges, and responsibilities of citizenship in the kingdom of heaven are now yours. And by the way, you are no longer honorary consuls. As citizens of heaven, you are now consuls of the kingdom, no longer just honorary."

"And that means ... ?" asked Peter.

Jesus replied, "It means you are still official representatives of the kingdom, commissioned by the Prime Minister, but now you do it as citizens, kingdom *insiders*. Your job is the same—bring as many humans as possible through the citizenship process. Help everyone who wants to immigrate to heaven."

"But for you," Jesus added, "there will be more. You will be the first ambassadors to the earth from the kingdom of heaven.

As ambassadors, you will have an open line to the Prime Minister, and he will provide you with access to the kingdom arsenal. Trust me, you will need these weapons when the enemy comes out of the heavenlies against you.[7] Whenever you call on me, know that the Prime Minister will support you with the full power and authority of the kingdom."

Peter asked, "But all that authority—how will we even know how to use it? You know we have failed miserably at even the simple things you have taught us."

Jesus smiled and put his hand on his friend's shoulder, "I will head back across the border soon, and I will send the

24: Transfer of Authority

Prime Minister. He will make it clear exactly what your tasks are." Jesus added, "You never saw me do anything that the King didn't tell me to do. The Prime Minister will keep you on track with kingdom policies and initiatives. The only thing is that you've got to listen to him and trust what he tells you. And, be bold enough to act on it! Got it?"

They nodded.

"But don't go anywhere yet," Jesus warned.[8] "As the kingdom Diplomatic Corps, you have all been targeted by the enemy—you are marked men." Jesus looked at the fearsome kingdom military guards one dimension above, surrounding their little group. "Wait here until the Prime Minister brings your diplomatic credentials and a secure communications link is established with the kingdom. Once all the security measures are in place, the Prime Minister will provide your global deployment instructions." [9]

It was time for the Prince to leave earth and return to the kingdom. He met with his consuls and other close friends on a hillside in Galilee to make a stunning geopolitical announcement: "Lucifer's reign on this planet is officially over. I have fulfilled everything required to reclaim the earth for the kingdom. All authority over both the kingdom and the earth has been legally returned to me, and I am giving it to you." [10]

The diplomats glanced at each other, wondering what this world-changing news would mean.

"Lucifer is refusing to relinquish his grip on the earth and its people—he will fight us to the death—but he cannot hold back the forward march of the kingdom. Rest assured that he will be removed.[11] He is only allowed to remain for a time because you have a job to do first. As kingdom diplomats, you need to tell everyone, everywhere, that Lucifer is finished. He and anyone who remains loyal to him will *not* be allowed to stay in the kingdom when its borders are officially moved around the earth." [12]

"Tell the people," Jesus said with a calm urgency, "tell all of them.[13] If they want to even see the kingdom, they must become kingdom citizens. Tell them citizenship is free. They just need to apply for it." [14]

With that, Jesus, the Prince of heaven, said farewell to his friends. "You may not see me—but trust me—I will be with you." He turned slowly up the narrow, newly paved kingdom highway, through the border crossing, and into the throne room of his father.

The Prince was greeted by a crowd of millions. Every being in the kingdom had turned out for the triumphant return of the Prince. He took his seat next to his very proud father while the Prime Minister made preparations for his own imminent departure.

The soon-to-be-ambassadors were very excited. It was a nervous excitement that stayed with them as they settled back into Jerusalem to wait as they had been told. Waiting is hard when you know the entire world, including your own life, is about to be turned upside down.

They stayed close together. Nobody wanted to miss a thing. The kingdom guard continued to keep watch as Lucifer and his men paced nervously.

The Prime Minister, the Prince and the King walked with Michael and Gabriel along the new kingdom highway toward the earth. They paused just short of the border crossing on the kingdom side.

"You know there will be a lot of hate directed at our citizens, because of the Prince," Michael said to the Prime Minister.

"No kidding," replied the PM with mock surprise. "Humans are renouncing their citizenship on earth and are turning their backs on its ruler because of the Prince. No wonder the earth's establishment hates them. It hates us too, you know." [15]

24: Transfer of Authority

"It doesn't matter what our enemies feel about us, Michael," the Prince added. "The Prime Minister will give them everything they need to protect themselves.[16] I told them they would receive direct orders to go out into every place on earth, to tell everyone about immigration to the kingdom. I wouldn't send them out unless they were fully armed, right PM?"

"I will see to it that my ambassadors will be able to exercise the full power and authority of the kingdom," assured the Prime Minister. "They will have a direct line to the Royal family."

The King underscored the point, "These new ambassadors, and those under their protection, will have more firepower available to them than Lucifer ever saw when he was here in the kingdom. These will be the most well-protected diplomats the earth has ever seen. As long as the ambassadors are coordinated with the Prime Minister, Lucifer has no chance against them. The only problem is if they let themselves get distracted with the stuff of life on earth."[17]

"What about the new citizens who don't aspire to become kingdom diplomats?" Gabriel asked.

"They are every bit as much a part of my kingdom as the ambassadors are," the King said with certainty. "But if an unarmed kingdom citizen gets caught in the crossfire with the enemy, well, they may get pushed around a bit."

"Pushed around, but never pushed out of the kingdom," the Prime Minister added.[18] "Better they should aspire to join our Diplomatic Corps, though."

"Absolutely," said the Prince.

All five stood at the border, looking out towards the earth.

"Take care of my family," the Prince said quietly to the Prime Minister.

"Hey, they're my family too!" the PM whispered back with a wink.

The King said, "Let the Prime Minister go, so he can do his job."

The three Royals embraced. The Prime Minister gave a nod to the generals and walked through the border into the heart of Jerusalem.

Lucifer paced back and forth in his mountain hideaway just south and one dimension up from Jerusalem.

"So kingdom justice has been satisfied forever. Anyone who wants, can have their kingdom record wiped clean permanently. It's a pardon from the King that makes them eligible for kingdom citizenship. Hmmm," Lucifer was mulling over the current situation.

It was taking him some time to process this, but Lucifer realized that the one thing he had counted on for thousands of years had slipped away. Lucifer had focused on capturing the bloodline to invalidate Crusher's qualifications to be the One, but the Royals did an end-run. Jesus had paid the ransom making kingdom pardons and kingdom citizenship available to humans!

"But what if I can convince humans to turn their noses up at the pardon...?"

*notes for this chapter
start on page 303*

25: Free Will

∽∾

The King of heaven won't force anyone into taking the pardon, not if these humans really have free will." ¹ The more Lucifer thought about it, the more he liked the idea. He turned to his lieutenants and tested some lines for their next big whisper campaign.

"Kingdom pardon? No thanks. Where is the personal responsibility in someone else taking the blame?"

He tried another, "Accepting that pardon is like admitting you are a failure and you need someone's charity."

One of his officers chimed in, "Who needs a pardon anyway? Look at all the good things you've done. They must count for something!"

Another added, "Forget the pardon, you don't want to be lumped in with a bunch of people who have done despicable things and then beg for a pardon at the last minute. What was that King thinking anyway?"

Still another said, "Taking the pardon is the same as admitting you've done really, really bad things—but you are not that bad. In fact, you're pretty good. This pardon is for losers who haven't accomplished anything in life! It's a crutch for the weak! And you are strong!"

Lucifer offered his favorite, "You think the King wants you in his family, after the way you have let him down? I'm embarrassed that you would even ask him for a pardon!"

He smiled, "We can work with this. Who would even want to ask for a kingdom pardon?"

It was a beautiful morning in Jerusalem. All the kingdom consuls were together in a large room, waiting as the Prince had told them. Also in the room were a number of Jerusalem locals and foreigners from around the world, including Cyprus, Libya, Egypt, and Rome, to name a few. The word was out – something big was about to happen.

The morning stillness was shattered as the Prime Minister entered the room through a wormhole from an unseen upper dimension. Everyone in the room heard the sound of a powerful gust of wind, which shook the house.[2]

The Prime Minister came to all of the consuls at once with the same flickering flame appearance that Moses saw on the bush in the desert more than a thousand years earlier. Everyone in the room saw it dancing on each of the consuls.

The Prime Minister reached into each consul's body and deposited their diplomatic credentials. To each he whispered, "You are now an ambassador of the Kingdom of Heaven!"

The new ambassadors jumped up, eyes wide and mouths open, when they realized what was happening. They started shouting at each other, but they didn't even recognize what they themselves were saying. They were all speaking different languages. "What is going on?" several onlookers wondered aloud.

The foreign bystanders realized before anyone else that these ambassadors were speaking in several foreign languages, their own languages! [3] They were shouting an incredible message: "The borders of the kingdom of heaven are opening for immigration!"

"Comm links all check out sir," reported the senior communications officer in the CSOC. "All human languages plus the kingdom code are available and operational."

25: Free Will

The Prince nodded in approval. He had included the kingdom code as part of the ambassador's equipment, since he was not about to let Lucifer listen-in on critical communications traffic with his ambassadors.[4]

Everyone was amazed. No one had ever heard of anything like this. The room was filled with the sound of voices, those of the ambassadors as well as those of the astonished onlookers.

The Prime Minister tapped ambassador Peter on the shoulder and whispered to him. Peter then stepped up, raised his hands and called for quiet in the room.

"Some of you said you think we've been drinking," Peter said to the crowd. "You're wrong. It's much too early in the day for that!" A few in the crowd chuckled.

"Do you remember Jesus?" Peter asked loudly of the crowd.

Jesus had done countless miracles in Jerusalem over the past few years. Yes, everybody here knew who Jesus was.[5]

"Let me tell you who Jesus really is," Peter said. "Jesus is the Prince of the Royal family of the kingdom of heaven, the same Royal family who established our country Israel and protected it and provided for it since the beginning. Yes, I am saying he has lived forever! That's what people do in the kingdom of heaven—they live forever! Do you know what I am talking about?"

"Yes! Yes! Yes!" the crowd shouted gleefully.

"Yes – Jesus the Prince of Heaven – he is the one you put to death on a cross, less than two months ago!"

A shriek, some gasps and the room fell silent.

*notes for this chapter
start on page 306*

26: Competing Offers

∽∾

The people were stunned. They realized the unspeakable act that they had allowed, and for some, even encouraged to happen.

Finally, a voice cried out, "what should we do?"

"Admit your guilt to the King and show you are sorry! Turn your back on the ruler of the earth. Renounce him and all he stands for. Ask the King of Heaven to count his son's death against your crimes against the kingdom. Then cross through the water into the kingdom!"[1]

Peter shouted with a boldness no one had ever seen in him before, "Anybody want to be a citizen of the kingdom, and live forever?"

The crowd roared, "Yes!"

"Then stand up and do what I just told you. The Prime Minister will issue you a kingdom passport and *that* will give you guaranteed passage through the border into heaven. Even when you die, you will live forever!" [2]

That day, three thousand people in Jerusalem renounced their citizenship of earth. With the help of the ambassadors, they applied for and received kingdom passports.[3]

The word spread quickly. The staff at the kingdom Department of Immigration was busier than ever—and they were loving it.

The ambassadors were on a roll. The more people who accepted this offer to become kingdom citizens, the more people they told.

The ambassadors knew that the best place to spread the Prince's good news had to be at the kingdom Justice Center. After all, Jesus had told them, "I am the new kingdom Justice Center."

"Our citizenship is in heaven!" these ambassadors would shout on the way to the Justice Center.[4] "Turn your back on the ruler of earth and join us!"

The Roman soldiers who heard the ambassadors' message were not sure what to make of it. The ambassadors had said nothing about Rome or Caesar, or even Israel. It was as strange to the soldiers as it was amusing.

It was neither strange nor amusing to Lucifer. He knew exactly what was happening. The Prince had punched a hole in the border and if Lucifer didn't take some action, now, his entire human race would be rushing out of his lower frontier—out of his sphere of influence.

"I will not let this situation spin out of control," he said to himself. Lucifer strode toward the Justice Center. "The chief justice should be looking for some viable options just about now."

The judiciary at the kingdom Justice Center was indeed looking for options. They were getting close to full-scale panic. They looked out the window of their executive conference room to see those motley followers of Jesus, as they called them, at the front of a huge crowd right below their window. These unsophisticated men, these self-proclaimed kingdom ambassadors, were telling the crowds that people could be pardoned for violations of the kingdom's prime directive, without submitting to the authority of the Justice Center.

Caiaphas, the chief justice, understood at least some of what was happening. "The institution of the Justice Center is

26: Competing Offers

under attack. For over a thousand years, this has been the one and only place where people could come to escape the consequences of violating the kingdom's prime directive!"

"The Prince of heaven would be appalled," Lucifer whispered in the chief justice's ear. "He personally organized the first Justice Center. These traitors are feeding lies to the people."

Caiaphas turned to his associates and said calmly, "Our people have forgotten what it means to be a kingdom people. The Prince of heaven showed Moses and Aaron long ago the way to escape the death penalty at the Justice Center. These 'Jesus people' are offering a shortcut to justice where there is none. Our people are believing lies. It is our job to expose the liars."

"Look!" interrupted Nicodemus, pointing out the conference room window. The other justices gathered close around him. "It's that lame fellow who panhandles outside the main gate of the Justice Center. I know he can't walk, but there he is, prancing around like a fool." They saw Peter and John standing near the center of the crowd, just as much the center of attention as the former cripple.[5]

"Now they are doing it too!" Nicodemus exclaimed.

His associates knew Nicodemus was referring to the many healings, and even the raising of people from the dead, for which Jesus had become known. The chief justice knew that Nicodemus had spent quite a bit of time with Jesus before his execution, so he wasn't sure about Nicodemus' political loyalties.

"Nicodemus," said the chief justice, "there is a huge difference between following the ancient teachings of the Prince of heaven as Israel has done for thousands of years, and following a man who claimed to be the Prince himself, but was then killed at the hands of mortal men. Can't you see how ridiculous and impossible that is? The eternal Prince of the kingdom being killed by mere men?" [6]

They could all hear the crowd below shouting, "Prince Jesus!"

"This is not the work of the Prince," whispered Lucifer smoothly. "These men are simply calling attention to themselves, distracting the people from true kingdom justice and the Justice Center."

"It's a trick." Caiaphas said quietly. "As I said, we simply need to expose the liars. Bring those followers of Jesus in, so we can talk with them."

A security team from the Justice Center elbowed its way through the crowd. They grabbed John and Peter who were in the midst of telling the people how to apply for kingdom citizenship. They were dragged away, but before the crowd dispersed that evening, another two thousand applications had been processed and passports had been issued by the kingdom Department of Immigration.[7]

Peter and John spent the night in jail.[8] The next morning, they, along with a man they had healed, were brought before Chief Justice Caiaphas and members of his judicial staff. He had only one question, "By whose authority are you doing this?"

Peter, once a lowly fisherman from Galilee, now an ambassador of the superpower kingdom of the universe, looked the chief justice in the eye and said, "If you are asking about how we healed this man who could not walk yesterday, then I want to be very clear. We are ambassadors of the kingdom of heaven. It is by the power of the kingdom and the authority of the Prince of heaven that this man stands before you tall and healthy."

"Jesus from Nazareth, the One who you brought to Pilate to be killed, is that Prince of heaven. The King of heaven raised him back to life. Jesus, who you opposed, has become the new Justice Center. No one can have their record permanently cleared, and get kingdom citizenship, unless they accept a kingdom pardon from Jesus."[9]

26: Competing Offers

The justices were speechless. Caiaphas ordered the guards to remove the three men from the room. Once they were alone, they discussed their options.

"What are we going to do with these men? They know nothing about kingdom law, but they claim to have a new Justice Center! What nonsense!"

"But that *was* an outstanding miracle. Everyone saw it and we can't deny it."

"We cannot let them keep stirring up the people like this," said Caiaphas. "Just think about it. The real Prince of Heaven wouldn't keep changing the law. He wouldn't build our Justice Center, and then suddenly abandon it. We may not understand all of this, but we do know that these men are seducing our people away from the Justice Center that the true Prince of heaven established himself—and that is just wrong! Bring the prisoners back in!"

*notes for this chapter
start on page 307*

27: Punch - Counterpunch

∽∂

The chief justice gave the men a tongue lashing, reminded them of two thousand years of national history and tradition, and ordered them to stop their divisive behavior immediately.[1]

Peter and John listened respectfully. When it was their turn to respond, Peter said, "Ask yourself what you would do in my place. Obey a man from earth, or obey the King of the universe? We cannot keep quiet about this."

"That doesn't sound much like Peter the fisherman," the King remarked to his son as they watched events unfold from the throne room.

"Amazing! PM certainly is inspiring our ambassadors," said the Prince. "Just look at that!" They watched as Peter and John arrived at the home of a new kingdom citizen who was hosting an Independence Day party with the ambassadors and a number of new citizens. They celebrated their new citizenship and the opening of the kingdom borders by singing patriotic songs of the kingdom, with speeches and rounds of cheering for the Prince.

"PM has the ball and he is running with it!" smiled the Prince, as his father nodded in agreement.

Passport Please - Epic of the Kingdom III

The Prime Minister had his ambassadors fired up. They could not think about anything other than getting the word out about the kingdom. While the Prince often spoke to the crowds with stories that were admittedly cryptic, the ambassadors were all about straight talk. They met with people every day in Jerusalem, reminding them about what Jesus had said, and answering questions about the kingdom.

The ambassadors' number one priority was always the same, to make sure that as many people as possible would hear that the kingdom was opening its borders to those with kingdom passports.

Anywhere they had the opportunity, the ambassadors promoted the kingdom. They were even brazen enough to hold a major citizenship drive at the Jerusalem Justice Center again.[2]

"This is outrageous!" Chief Justice Caiaphas shouted. "They are continuing to make a mockery of the Justice Center! Bring them up here now!" The security chief ran out with his men to grab the troublemakers.

Caiaphas was furious. Sharp words and accusations were thrown and fired back.

"Don't back down!" the Prime Minister whispered to Peter. "Speak the truth! The Prince and I will be your shield and your sword!"

"Don't back down!" Lucifer whispered into the chief justice's ear. "Speak the truth! Everyone knows you speak for the Prince of heaven. These men are traitors!"

"The battle for hearts and minds enters a new phase," the King said to his son.

"Lucifer is frantic to hold onto as many humans as he possibly can," responded the Prince. "But our ambassadors and the PM are hustling to get as many passports issued as possible."

In Jerusalem, Caiaphas signed an executive order authorizing his political officers to seek out and discipline

27: Punch - Counterpunch

revolutionaries. A revolutionary was anyone who attacked their traditional values with the destructive notion that this dead man Jesus was a replacement for the Justice Center in Jerusalem.

One of the most notorious enforcers of the Justice Center was an ambitious and well-schooled young man named Saul, who had made a name for himself as an up-and-comer in the Justice Center hierarchy. He had even participated in the first stoning execution of one of the leaders of this "Jesus movement." Caiaphas had no question about Saul's loyalty. He authorized Saul to use any means necessary to capture and bring these rebels back to Jerusalem to face the consequences of their treason against Israel.

"Now there's a man of action," the Prince said to his father. "Action and passion. Off-track for sure, but this guy has the potential to be a one-man kingdom Diplomatic Corps."

"He's also a Roman citizen, so he can cross any border on earth to get the word out about your kingdom and enroll citizens," replied the King. "Go introduce yourself to him, son. It's time for Saul to begin a new life—to be born into our kingdom!"

The Prince headed down to earth to intercept Saul, who was on his way to break up a kingdom citizenship rally in Damascus. The Prince stood in the middle of the road, just out of human sight in the heavenlies. Saul rounded the bend with his entourage. As Saul passed just inches away, the Prince reached into the three dimensions of earth and grabbed him, yanking Saul to the ground, and pulling him partially into the heavenlies. Saul was blinded by the brilliant light coming from the Prince's face in this higher dimension. Saul's comrades could see he was frightened. They couldn't see the Prince at all—but they heard everything.

"Saul!" yelled the Prince, inches from his face. "What are you doing?"

"Who are you?" Saul implored, now fully blinded.

The Prince explained. "I am Jesus, the Prince of the kingdom, son of the King of heaven. You, Saul, are terrorizing citizens of my kingdom and that is going to stop right now!"

Having Saul's full attention, Jesus told him where to go and what to do to get his vision back. Saul was more than ready to comply.[3]

As Saul recovered, he was visited by the Prime Minister who taught him everything he needed to know about the kingdom. In time, the former "muscle" of the Justice Center became a kingdom citizen, and even the most prominent ambassador of the kingdom. The PM issued his passport and diplomatic credentials. Like Abram two thousand years earlier, the Prince "made a name for him." From now on, Saul would be known throughout the earth as Paul.

Ultimately, Paul become as headstrong an ambassador of the kingdom as he had been as a Justice Center enforcer, but this time he had the full power and authority of the kingdom and its armed forces to back him up.

"The environment is just too hostile to publicly announce the opening of a kingdom consulate here," Paul told the new citizens as they gathered in the locked home of one of his friends in Jerusalem. "For now, we will continue to meet together in secret, but you need to continue to invite those who want to defect to the kingdom."

"We'll never get the word out if we stay underground," said one of the enthusiastic new citizens.

"Everything in its time," responded Paul. "The Prime Minister has directed that I start establishing kingdom consulates in homes throughout the Mediterranean region. I'm heading out shortly to do just that."

27: Punch - Counterpunch

Paul established kingdom consulates throughout the region. The consulates provided instruction on kingdom culture and, of course, kingdom immigration requirements. He appointed local consuls to assist new and prospective citizens. Every new citizen was strongly encouraged to consider a career in the kingdom Diplomatic Corps and to become an ambassador themselves.

Kingdom citizens who wanted to become ambassadors would meet with Paul or another ambassador who could set up a three-way meeting with the Prime Minister. The PM had the final authority in the matter. Often, the diplomatic credentials were slipped to the new ambassador by the PM before the meeting was over.

"Whether it is a large consulate or a small underground cell," Paul explained to his local consuls, "the mission is always the same: first heal anyone who needs it. That will to get their attention.[4] Then tell people about the kingdom, induct new citizens, train them in the ways of the kingdom, and get the word out to everyone on earth that the borders to the kingdom are opening—for kingdom citizens only."

Most people who responded to that message wanted to know the same basic things about the kingdom. The consuls, citizens, and ambassadors got a lot of practice distributing a consistent, understandable message.

They assured the people, "This is not a new program. Israel's founding fathers looked forward to the arrival of the One to clear the way, so you can become kingdom citizens. For thousands of years, the Royals have been preparing a way for humans to cross over into the kingdom and to live forever! So give up your citizenship on earth, become a kingdom citizen and live, even after you die!"[5]

The consuls and ambassadors were peppered with questions from their audience, most of which were the same from day-to-day. They were ready with the answers.

"What do I have to do to get into the kingdom?"
"Come clean! Admit you have violated kingdom law. Publicly renounce Lucifer, the ruler of the earth and swear full allegiance to the kingdom of heaven and its Prince, Jesus. Do that and become a kingdom citizen.[6] That's it! All new citizens are given kingdom passports, and you will need that to get through passport control."

"Is it true that kingdom citizens live forever?"
"It is absolutely true, in the most real way possible, not some hopeful, wispy nonsense. We are talking about real life. The kingdom overlaps the dimensions of this earth and has dimensions you cannot see with human eyes, including time. Even when your earthly body drops away, you will live forever in the kingdom with a new body." [7]

"Aren't there other ways into the kingdom?"
"No! There is no other way! Anyone who wants to get in needs a kingdom passport!" [8]

"Can't we just focus on living our lives on earth, and worry about immigration when we get there?"
"If you don't bother to get a passport when the passport office is open, what will you say to the immigration control officer? Know this, if you have been advised of the entry requirements and you ignore them, he will not let you in! Failing to apply for your kingdom passport is exactly the same as saying, 'I don't really care about entering the kingdom.'" [9]

27: Punch - Counterpunch

"If we want a kingdom passport, do we have to give up everything we've worked for?"
"The building is on fire and you are more worried about your belongings than your life! Grab your passport first and run to safety, then think about your stuff!"[10]

"How can I even be sure my passport is valid?"
"If you find yourself knowing and following what Jesus told us, including telling others about the kingdom and encouraging them to apply for citizenship, that is a very good sign that your passport is valid." [11]

"But the men at the Justice Center tell me I can't qualify for citizenship!"
They are absolutely right, *you* cannot! But your substitute can qualify you! The lifeblood of Jesus that cleared your kingdom record is your pardon. All you need to do is accept the pardon and apply!"

"So I don't have to do anything?"
"You must publicly accept the pardon while you are on earth and apply to become a citizen of the kingdom. A pardon doesn't apply unless it is accepted by the one to whom it is offered.[12] No one can make you do it and no one is going to force you into heaven if you don't. But remember, the penalty for doing nothing is that you will be turned away at the border."

The ambassadors would always encourage the crowd to take action, *now*. "Decide one way or the other! No fence sitters! Dual citizenship is not acceptable! The Royals have no interest in only half of your loyalty.[13]

The kingdom's citizenship enrollment drive continued for many centuries. Citizenship rolls were growing, but response varied by region. In some places being a kingdom citizen became respectable and even fashionable; in others the local government made it punishable by death.

Either way, Lucifer knew that the Prince's immigration push was not going away anytime soon. "New times demand new approaches," he thought. "Let's see where I can stir the pot a little..."

*notes for this chapter
start on page 311*

28: Media Blitz

~~~

Alternative citizenship drives were held by citizens of earth. They pointed humans not to the Prince of the kingdom, but to "princes" by other names. While most of their followers say they know and respect Jesus, many of them were proponents of dual citizenship. Kingdom Department of Immigration policy does not allow issuing passports to anyone until they renounced all such rulers, other than the Prince of heaven and his kingdom.

Lucifer called out to whoever would listen, "Such intolerance! The kingdom of heaven isn't a monopoly and the Prince doesn't run the only game in town! There are a lot of choices and each one is as good as another! Take the best of each, but don't rush your decision. You've got plenty of time to decide."

Saturday, 11:48 AM KST ⧖ 1454 AD FST

In the middle of the main plaza of the great kingdom hall, the Prince spoke with General Michael. "Before we engage direct military action to take back the earth, I want a worldwide airdrop of leaflets directed at the civilians on the earth. Everyone on the planet must know the whole story of what I am offering, from beginning to end." [1]

"I want anyone, anywhere, to be able to pick up a leaflet in their own language and know what is about to happen and why. I want them to know how to protect themselves and their families," the Prince showed Michael a sketch of what he had planned. "Something like this ..."

WARNING!
Here is the record of the Kingdom's dealings with earth...
Here is what is about to happen on the earth...
Here is how you can protect yourself and your family...
Here is what happens to those who ignore this warning...

FOR SHELTER AND PROTECTION:
Find any Kingdom representative and tell them,
"I want in!"

The prototype for the Prince's leaflets had been around for a while in the form of letters written by the first ambassadors. Those letters, combined with the books of the founders of Israel, covered all the points that the Prince wanted to make. Due to the limitations of printing technology, these leaflets had always been in short supply. That was about to change.

"Everywhere! I want them everywhere," the Prince said as he stood in Johann Gutenberg's print shop, in fifteenth century Germany. He gently flipped through the pages of the first mechanically printed Bible, his pre-production "warning leaflet." [2]

By the end of that millennium, printing presses were everywhere. On these presses, literally billions of copies of the Prince's warning leaflets had been printed.

"I don't want anyone on the planet to say they never heard," the Prince said to the PM.

28: Media Blitz

"This is by far the most widely distributed publication in human history," the PM responded. "In thousands of languages, and more on the way! They will *all* hear about our citizenship offer, as long as they don't close their eyes and ears."

Lucifer felt like he was making progress as well, as the race for the allegiance of humans intensified. While mass murder had long been a fact of life on earth, the millennium closed with the twentieth century going down as the bloodiest hundred-year period in history.[3]

"The trick isn't simply wiping them off the planet," Lucifer explained to his soldiers. "It's getting them off the planet as clueless as possible about the kingdom and kingdom citizenship. As long as they are citizens of earth when they leave their bodies, the Prince can't have them, ever."

Lucifer, sounding like a coach at halftime, encouraged his troops. "Keep up the pace! We can't do much against the kingdom ambassadors who have the backing of the Prime Minister, but we can keep people away from them. Let's keep these humans occupied with themselves, with money, sex, power, real estate, good deeds, religion, politics, their kids, with—well, with anything! I don't care, as long as they don't find time to apply for kingdom citizenship.

One of the rebels asked, "How about we tell them they are not smart enough to understand the leaflets for themselves."

"Yes! That's what I am talking about!" Lucifer exclaimed. "No backing down! We have no reason to back down ... to hell with the Prince and his kingdom!"

Both the lower waiting room and the kingdom citizens' arrival lounge were processing an exponential increase in the number of deceased human souls.

*notes for this chapter
start on page 312*

29: Out of Harm's Way

&

"We held up our end of the transaction," the Prime Minister said to the Prince. "You fulfilled every term and condition and paid the full price in accordance with the mortgage, and yet Lucifer acts as if there was no judgment against him."

"That's why the mortgage has penalty clauses," the Prince responded. "If that snake had even a single drop of honor, we'd never have to break the seals and refer to those sections."

"We all know this is not about the contract," the King interrupted. "For him it never has been. Lucifer knows he has never had a legal leg to stand on since you paid off the mortgage. This is personal. He is only out to hurt our family." The King looked at the clock...

Sunday ~~~~ KOH WAR DEPT - CLASSIFIED INFORMATION [1] ~~~~

...and nodded to the Prince.

"Gabriel!" said the Prince. "It's time. Initiate the airlift. Recall all the ambassadors and evacuate our citizens from the earth. Get them out of harm's way, immediately!"

It was not a surprise, but it was certainly a shock when the siren went off in the kingdom citizens' arrival lounge. It surprised some that General Gabriel was in the lounge, personally encouraging all kingdom citizens to, "Walk, not run, but walk to the lounge exit facing the border crossing." For now, honorary citizens of the kingdom from the old days would continue to wait in the lounge until the judgment.²

Everyone knew this day was coming, though it never seemed like it would be today. The citizens gathered outside the kingdom gate and waited, as the sirens wailed all along the secure border of heaven.

Citizens of the earth could not hear them at all, but the sirens from the kingdom were heard clearly all over the earth, by every single naturalized kingdom citizen on the planet.

It was the middle of the night for some, morning for others, mid-afternoon for still others. Each knew instantly what this meant. They jumped from their beds, dropped their work, stopped their conversations, screeched their vehicles to a halt, stood up at their desks, and looked up in the direction of the siren.

Many kingdom citizens on earth who heard the sirens were in the presence of citizens of earth. These friends, family and co-workers watched in awe as the kingdom citizens begin to shimmer. Expressions on their glowing faces looked as if they were seeing something absolutely amazing, because they were. They took a few steps up into the heavenlies, as if a whole new dimension or direction of travel had been opened to them—because it had! They approached the crowd gathering outside heaven's newest border crossing.³

Their citizen-of-earth friends watched as they simply vanished in an instant, without a trace and without a clue to where they had gone.

"Officials now believe that this is the largest case of alien abduction ever," was the unbelievable, yet seriously delivered network news report. Almost everyone thought

29: Out of Harm's Way

that was preposterous, yet the "experts" on TV seemed to be convinced.

Outside the gates of heaven, there was an instant reunion among kingdom citizens arriving from earth and those who had been waiting patiently in the citizens' arrival lounge.

The mother brought down by cancer, the nephew killed on the freeway, the childhood friend shot in the war ... They were all there, in perfect health and elated to see the new arrivals from earth! It was an unbridled atmosphere of celebration as families and friends were joyfully reunited.[4]

The gates of the kingdom proper swung open and the Prince came through into the happy throng. "It's time!" he shouted. "It's opening day! Come on in!"[5]

One by one, the crowd flowed through the hundreds of passport control lanes, as the kingdom immigration officers scanned each one for their kingdom passports. The officers were aware that everyone in this crowd was with the Prince, but they had a job to do and the Prince appreciated that. No one would get into heaven without a kingdom passport; it was their job to see to it.

The crowd poured into the great kingdom hall where a party and banquet had been prepared.[6] Prince stepped up to the speaker's platform and addressed the multitude. "Ambassadors, consuls, citizens of the kingdom! On behalf of my father the King, and the Prime Minister who you already know, I officially welcome you to heaven!"

The crowd erupted in a cheer that shook the roof and sustained itself for a very long time.

The Prince was beaming. He stood on the platform, taking it all in, his eyes darting through the crowd, exchanging smile after smile. He knew every single one of these new citizens, and from the way they were hugging and shaking hands, it looked like a massive family reunion. Finally, the Prince raised his hands and the crowd quieted down.

"If anyone told you that the adventure is over, and now you are simply going to sit on a cloud with a harp, they—were—wrong!"

The crowd erupted in cheers again, ready to follow the Prince anywhere. The Prince gave a wink to the head harpist in the kingdom band, "Unless that's your job!" [7] The crowd cheered loudly for the band, as the harpists strummed a few chords in salute.

The Prince held up his arms and the roar of the crowd diminished a bit. "In accordance with kingdom law and with an agreement which was made over six thousand years ago in the garden colony, I have purchased back the earth for the kingdom." The cheers from the crowd surged. "But," he held his hands up again. "But, the warlord Lucifer has reneged on his agreement and has refused to step down as ruler of the earth."

The mood of the crowd suddenly began to turn. "We will now push him out," the Prince announced. In the span of a few seconds the crowd went from a noisy, cheering throng to an almost silent assembly.

"As I speak, forces of the kingdom of heaven are massing just inside the kingdom border, ready to unleash the awesome power of the kingdom's war machine onto the earth." [8]

The crowd was completely muted. Many of them had just left the earth that day. Most of them had family and friends who were still on the earth.

The Prince continued, "This difficult time on earth will be a last call for humans to renounce their earthly citizenship and apply for kingdom citizenship. During the next seven years, the earth will be under siege by the armed forces of the kingdom. *No one* will be oblivious to what I am doing. During that time, the Prime Minister will continue to send emissaries to enroll as many new kingdom citizens as they can, but the stakes have gotten extremely high. Humans who

29: Out of Harm's Way

become citizens of heaven during this time will very likely be killed as traitors to the earth by their government and Lucifer's loyalist forces. We will receive these new citizens into the kingdom with honor." [9]

The Prince's announcement had a sobering effect on the crowd as they became aware that the tensions and bloodshed which had been escalating on the earth for centuries were now being overshadowed by an even greater terror.

"It will be very bad for people on the earth, but my nation Israel will be protected through the storm as they always have been. Remember Noah, Joseph, Moses and the others? I was with Israel through their disasters then, and I'll stay with them through this one. You'll see. A Royal never takes back a promise!"

"This war will be over soon. When it is, we will return to the earth and for a thousand years. You will rule the planet with me, without the poisonous influence of Lucifer.[10]

"In the meantime, you all have much to see and learn in the kingdom. You may want to visit the Crystal Sea observation platform. From there you can see as events unfold on the earth. But for now, my friends, let's enjoy the kingdom together."

The Prince stepped down from the platform and made his way through the crowd to meet with his father before donning his battle gear.

Generals Michael and Gabriel were ready for the assault on earth. Their troops were positioned just above the border crossing. They were reviewing last-minute instructions with their battalion commanders.

All they needed was a word from the Prince...

*notes for this chapter
start on page 316*

30: Commence Firing

ಌ

The Prince strode into the great kingdom hall. His father, seated on his throne and surrounded by many attendants, was holding a sealed envelope which had just been brought up from the kingdom archives. It was labeled:

MORTGAGE
Terms for Buy-Back of the Earth

The King looked his son in the eye. "Lucifer still refuses to vacate in accordance with the agreement." [1]

"As we knew he would," replied the Prince. "I've done my part, so now we will hit him with the penalties for non-performance as spelled out in the mortgage. The envelope, please, Father."

The King handed him the thick envelope with the official seal of the kingdom office of land records on the outside.

"Michael! Gabriel!" the Prince called to his generals, "Bring in the enforcers!"

The huge doors to the hall swung open and Generals Michael and Gabriel let four armed troopers, each riding a massive horse, step into the hall toward the Prince.

Passport Please - Epic of the Kingdom III

The mortgage envelope contained seven envelopes. Inside each were written specific penalties for breaching the mortgage agreement that was made in the garden long ago.

The Prince handed an envelope to each of the four riders. They read their orders, saluted the Prince and headed for the Crystal Sea, to wait for the trumpet signal to assault earth.[2]

As the Prince opened the fifth envelope to read its contents, an attendant from the Kingdom Arrivals Lounge burst into the room. "Pardon me, your highness, but the new arrivals in the KAL are crying out, wanting to know how much longer the terrorists will rule the earth!"

He glanced again at the note, "A few more from earth need to join them first. Tell them it's almost time."[3]

The Prince ripped open the sixth envelope. The earth and the sky went black, and panic gripped the earth.[4] Outside the hall, a cheering crowd had gathered around the kingdom army which was assembling at the edge of the Crystal Sea.

The Prince tore open the final envelope. Suddenly, everything and everyone in the Kingdom fell silent.[5] For the next 30 minutes the only sound to be heard was breathing, and horses snorting, as members of the Army Signal Corps positioned themselves, getting ready to blow their trumpets.

The Prince handed General Michael a box, spewing smoke. The General carried it to the edge of the Sea, held it up for all to see, and threw it in. As it descended, lightning, thunder and earthquakes shook the earth.[6] The trumpeters let out blasts, and the entire kingdom army rushed through the Crystal Sea to capture Lucifer and liberate the earth.

Spectators jumped back from the edge of the portal, as blinding flashes again rocked the earth below. Mountains slid into the ocean creating massive tsunamis, wrecking thousands of ships. Nuclear plants melted down, poisoning drinking water for millions.[7] Every hallmark of civilization was being destroyed. The institutions of government, industry, commerce, agriculture, medicine, and law were

30: Commence Firing

decimated. Millions of humans died. The vast majority of them were hustled into the lower waiting room, which was straining to accommodate the inflow. It was shocking that any humans were surviving on earth, but incredibly, many were somehow able to dodge the destruction.

In spite of the chaos and carnage on earth, the Prime Minister was still on the ground, issuing passports as fast as humans would publicly renounce Lucifer and apply for kingdom citizenship.

The Prince stepped down to the earth and told the PM, "Lets get Israel into the fight." The PM introduced the Prince to 144,000 humans from Israel—as the One promised to them some six thousand years earlier in the Garden of Eden. They immediately pledged themselves to the Prince and became kingdom citizens.[8] They were all sworn-in by the Prime Minister as special emissaries to encourage wartime immigration to the kingdom. It was a hard message for some to hear, given the political climate, but easy for others, given the bleak outlook for the earth. More people were applying for and getting kingdom citizenship, in spite of the carnage going on around them.

These Israeli emissaries were working under the direct protection of the Prime Minister. Not even Lucifer himself could touch them. Their message was very clear: "Last call for kingdom citizenship!"

Everyone on earth knew that the kingdom was behind these devastating attacks, and world leaders were scared to death. The governments enacted a zero-tolerance policy against anyone who renounced Lucifer and professed loyalty to the kingdom. Violators were to be executed immediately, publicly beheaded as traitors.[9]

"You can't hide the truth!" yelled a woman who had received her kingdom passport from the Prime Minister just minutes earlier. The authorities had been tipped off to her public renunciation. One officer taped her hands behind her back and forced her to her knees while the other captured the gruesome scene on cellphone video.

"I watched my sister shimmer and disappear across the border into the kingdom," the woman screamed at the armed men. "Just before she vanished, the last thing she said was, 'I see Mom!'" It's true! Everyone is talking about it! You *know* it's true!"

Grabbing a fistful of hair, the officer shook her head violently. "You are a traitor! That kingdom of yours is killing our people! May your kingdom die with you!"

She looked up, "Is that the worst you can do?" [10]

With that, he swung down a large machete and her body dropped to the floor, releasing her from the earth.

Even before her assailants had left the room, a kingdom soldier picked the woman up out of her lifeless body and carried her to the Kingdom Arrivals Lounge, which was once again filling up with new citizens. As she sank into a chair, she heard, "Welcome to the kingdom, ma'am. You've been through a lot today, but it will get much better from here on out. May I get you a drink?" [11]

In heaven, the embankment of the Crystal Sea was packed. Recent immigrants from earth were shocked to see the end of their former civilization. They were in awe of the courage displayed by those who accepted the offer of kingdom citizenship, despite the dire consequences.

Most of all, the new kingdom citizens looking down were amazed and saddened at the stubborn refusal of so many humans to accept the still-free offer of kingdom citizenship, even when it was clear to everyone that time was just about up for Lucifer and his earth.[12]

"We need a leader who can rally the world against the Prince," Lucifer said. He encouraged Toman Darta, a brutal former dictator who had been in hiding, to come out and be that leader. Lucifer sent his troops to rally the support of

30: Commence Firing

regional leaders as Darta and his chief of staff, Blick Runson, prepared for a global telecast.[13]

CNN, SkyNews, Al Jazeera, BBC, RT, France24, China Central TV, and other networks that were still operating, carried Darta's address, solidifying the image that Toman Darta spoke for all citizens of the earth.

"Fellow citizens, I want to be very clear with you. The terror that has rained down upon this planet is not the work of any citizen of earth. Rather, this unspeakable evil has come directly from the kingdom of heaven and its chief terrorists, the Royals. We must not allow anyone to live, not for a moment, who holds sympathy or loyalty to that despicable kingdom or its murderous rulers."

"In keeping up our global war on terror, the governments of the earth have expanded the cash bounty program for any citizen bringing proof of the execution of a kingdom citizen. You will be required to show some video or other evidence that they indeed renounced our benefactor Lucifer. By doing this you will be doing a great service to your fellow man."[14]

"Additionally, in order to restore order to the global financial markets, and to halt widespread corruption, I have ordered an immediate transition to global cashless commerce. Dr. Runson will explain."

"Thank you President Darta. In order to halt runaway inflation, tax evasion, money laundering and currency speculation, we are instituting blockchain-based [15] global system of commerce. All it requires is the insertion of a simple chip," he held up his wrist to the camera, "There—you can barely see it—just a small mark to show it is properly installed." The mark looked like a tiny tattoo resembling three superimposed sixes. He continued, "All financial institutions worldwide are already linked with all merchant accounts, and regional currencies are all being converted to a single electronic currency called the LUCI. The LUCI will replace the confusing mix of dollars, pounds, euros, bitcoin, yuan, pesos, and a hundred other currencies. This conversion will give criminals no place to hide."

"Thirty days from today, cash transactions, and the corruption that comes with them, will be a thing of the past. Details of how to enroll are online." A web address flashed on the screen. "All police and fire stations worldwide have been equipped with the chips and everything needed for you to get yours installed. This program is not optional. Without the chip installed, you will not be able to access financial accounts or sell or purchase anything." [16]

"Hey, I thought Darta was dead," said one of the onlookers at the Crystal Sea observation platform. He was hanged for crimes against humanity. It was all over the Internet.[17]

"I thought so too," replied his friend. "But it looks like you and I are deader than he is."

"More dead and more alive!" he responded, as they gave each other a high-five.

Tensions on earth continued to rise as the kingdom army kept up the pressure, month after month. Darta was doing everything he could to keep the population under control, focusing them on the evils being thrust upon them by the kingdom and it's hate-filled ruling family.

After three years, the LUCI was faltering.[18] Darta was faced with an imminent collapse of his global financial system.

"What the hell are we going to do?" he demanded of Runson.

Four television news networks playing on video screens in Darta's office were all reporting on the same disaster. What had started as a double spike in the global prices of gold and oil, had triggered hyper-inflation, killing the LUCI.

"What kept the LUCI up was confidence you and in our government," Runson explained. He knew that Darta already knew what he was going to say, but Runson said it anyway...

30: Commence Firing

"This war on the earth by the kingdom has unified the people behind you, but they have all watched as our entire civilization has collapsed, right before their eyes."

"People have been whispering that we fraudulently bypassed the blockchain – which we did - conjuring up piles of counterfeit LUCIs to pay for the war. In the process we destroyed the value of everyone's personal assets. The word is out - LUCIs are worthless - nobody wants them!"

"I don't give a damn about their assets!" Darta bellowed. "They can't just abandon the LUCI! Make them use it!"

Looking out the window at the boiling clouds, Runson sensed that he was not going to have time to address that problem.

*notes for this chapter
start on page 321*

31: The Take-Down

∽∾

The Prince thundered up to the great kingdom hall on his white horse and called, "Kingdom citizens from earth! Saddle up and follow me! You and I are going to put away the squatters!"

Members of the kingdom regular army brought white horses for all the new citizens. Each swung up into the saddle as if they had been doing it all their lives.[1] "This is awesome," said one new cavalryman to another. They had been waiting a long time for this day. The liberation of earth!

The viewing platform over the Crystal Sea was packed, everyone straining to see the end of Lucifer's reign on the earth.

The Prince's horse reared up. He looked up to the Kingdom Hall balcony with a salute and shouted, "For the King!"

"For the King!" roared the response, as millions of former residents of the earth, along with kingdom regular army galloped behind the Prince down the kingdom road, past a huge crown of kingdom citizens, waving to the troops and cheering wildly.

The armies of the earth had been expecting the Prince's assault, but they were no match for a multi-dimensional army falling down on them. It was like attacking a troop of blind men. They couldn't even see the Prince's army coming.

Passport Please - Epic of the Kingdom III

The cavalry spread out across the earth chasing down Lucifer's rebels. General Michael and a squad of cavalry burst into Darta's office. They grabbed Darta and Runson by their collars and ran them straight through the plate glass window of his high-rise headquarters. Michael led them to a lake, much smaller than the Crystal Sea of heaven, but it was neither smooth nor crystal. It looked like a liquid inferno. General Michael gave the order and his troops threw Darta and his chief-of-staff headfirst into the molten, sulfurous boil.[2]

The Prince spotted Lucifer and made a direct line for him. He grabbed his former General by the neck while kingdom troopers bound him in chains. Lucifer was carried to the Pit as his rebels scattered. Just mention of the Pit threw them into a panic.

The kingdom security team lifted the cover of the pit. Smoke poured out. The sound of vibrating wings from millions of killer locusts filled their ears.

"See you in a thousand years!" the Prince shouted as Lucifer was hastily thrown in. "Lock it up!" he shouted to his soldiers, who dropped the lid into place, sealing the pit in all dimensions.[3]

The Prince smiled as he heard victory cheers from the crowd above.[4] He called out, "Michael! Gabriel! Cease fire! It's over! Tell the new arrivals in the KAL to join us. We want to greet them!"

Once again, Gabriel made an announcement in the citizens' arrival lounge: "All citizens of the kingdom who arrived in the past seven years, please join us now as we meet the Prince in the new garden colony on earth."

"All others, honorary citizens of the kingdom, please continue to relax here in the lounge. You will be seen by the judge in about a thousand earth years. Trust me, up here, it'll only be a day here, so relax and enjoy." The honorary

31: The Take-Down

citizens didn't mind the extra wait, since it most of them had just arrived just a few KST minutes ago.

Back on the earth, the citizen-soldiers of the kingdom gathered on horseback around the Prince. The kingdom regular army, on horseback and on foot filled the large field behind them. It was over!

The excitement of victory was in the air. From a distance, they heard music. It was a parade of new kingdom citizens who had been killed on the earth in the war. As they came closer, the crowd heard the marchers singing patriotic kingdom songs.

"Make way for the newest citizens of the kingdom!" the Prince shouted, as Michael and Gabriel led the parade of martyrs down from the citizens' arrival lounge and back to the earth which they had so recently, and violently, left. At the same time, from another direction, the Prime Minister's 144,000 emissaries, kingdom citizens from Israel, joined the festivities.

The entire company of kingdom citizens broke into spontaneous cheering and joined in with the patriotic kingdom songs. The cheering went on and on as they celebrated their return to earth.

The Prince finally held up his hands for quiet, and the crowd went silent.

"This is our new home, for now," announced the Prince. "Every human who rode with me into battle today, down the kingdom highway, will rule with me here on the earth. Addressing the new arrivals, he declared, "You who were killed for becoming kingdom citizens in the last seven years, you will rule with us! [5] Now let's return the earth to the splendor that we enjoyed in the garden so long ago!"

"But this time we're staying in the garden—" came a shout from the crowd, "with you!"

The Prince smiled and waved to the enthusiastic citizen as the crowd erupted in cheers yet again.

Now that the Prince and his co-regents were installed as rulers on earth, the kingdom Office of Foreign Affairs got busy, knowing they would soon annex the entire frontier as part of the kingdom proper.

Many families started and grew large. People lived much longer; the population exploded, and the earth repopulated quickly. In many ways it was much like the old garden. Under the Prince's reign and with his knowledge of agriculture, the ground of the earth returned to the fertile state of the garden, yielding many times more crops per acre than any of the humans had ever seen when they lived on the earth. Fish returned in abundance to the streams, rivers, and oceans, and ranchers watched over huge herds. There was plenty of food for everyone.[6]

The Prince was always in sight. He walked among the people and just visited, talked and laughed. "We're all family," he would always say, and he meant it.

Over time they were joined by citizens of earth who had survived the carnage of the war but had still not become kingdom citizens. These somewhat shell-shocked refugees were also enjoying the peace and prosperity under the leadership of the benevolent rulers. Citizens of earth were granted refugee status by the Prince on the condition that keeping the prime directive would be their first priority.

There is no kingdom policy that provides automatic granting of citizenship to the refugees, or to anyone in a kingdom territory; however, it was very easy to become a citizen, since there were ambassadors everywhere and the Prime Minister was always pleased to preside over induction ceremonies. When they came of age, all persons born on the earth since the Prince's return still needed to personally renounce their citizenship on earth and apply for full kingdom citizenship, if they wanted to keep it as adults. They would then receive their own kingdom passport.

31: The Take-Down

For whatever reason, many of them never found time to apply for kingdom citizenship. If one chose not to become a kingdom citizen, they were not compelled to do so. This was in accordance with long-standing kingdom policy for territories outside the kingdom proper.

The next thousand years was a time of restoration, growth, peace, and prosperity on the earth.

In the conference room of the great kingdom hall, the Royals and their generals were holding a special session.

"You had a question Michael?" the Prince asked.

"Sir, when you announced to the crowd that the earth was once again like the garden, that citizen shouted, 'This time we're staying!'"

"He did," replied the Prince with a smile, "and he meant it."

"Well, are they staying?" Michael inquired. "It's been a almost a thousand years since Lucifer was put away. We understand from the Prime Minister that under the terms of the agreement with Lucifer, it won't be much longer until he is released from the pit, back onto the earth." He motioned toward the clock...

Sunday, 11:58 PM KST ⧖ 2994 AD FST

"...and we know what happened last time Lucifer had contact with the humans."

.

*notes for this chapter
start on page 323*

32: Last Gasp

～∞～

The King understood Michael's concern. "I am sure our kingdom citizens know Lucifer and his schemes well enough, especially since the PM is with them always. But for those who are still citizens of earth, the descendants of those who survived the great war, it will be the same as with Adam and Eve. They could live in this peaceful garden of earth for a million more years; but they would still choose to embrace evil when Lucifer shows up, just like in our first garden colony."

"What we are doing here is exposing Lucifer's great lie," the Prime Minister explained. "He has always whispered into human ears that it's the social environment or corrupt governments which are to blame for all the world's troubles. He has always encouraged the humans to, 'Pour all your efforts into fixing those, then there will be lasting peace and security...' and that's nonsense!"

"That's right, PM," said the King. "The Prince gave the earth a perfect government and social environment for a thousand years. Michael, you just watch how many citizens of earth *run* to Lucifer and embrace him when he shows up."

"So, will you make any changes in your plan to deal with that?" the general asked.

"No, we will not take away the right of humans to choose between good and evil. The plan stays the same—each human must choose of their own free will," the Prince responded firmly. "We will continue to offer pardons and kingdom citizenship to the humans. The process has been made abundantly clear.[1] Those who take our offer will be protected by the kingdom. Those who refuse—well, they are on their own."

The era of peace and prosperity on the earth had been continuous for a thousand years since the victory celebration.

The Prince turned to Michael and quietly gave the order, "It's time. Let him out."

Silently, the kingdom border gates swung open. A kingdom Special Forces team headed toward the Pit. As the massive lid was lifted, acrid smoke poured around its edges and billowed into the sky. The officer yelled into the blackness, "Lucifer! Come out!"

"Damn!" Lucifer shot out from the depths of the pit, through the earth's three dimensions and into the heavenlies, as far as he could go. He breathed deep gulps of clean air and shook off the last of the clinging locusts.

For a very long time Lucifer had been planning what he would do upon his release.

"The real prize," Lucifer thought, "will be to seduce those born on earth in the past thousand years, after the return of the Prince. They had never been with the Prince in the kingdom proper, so just like Eve in the garden, they will be easy targets."

Anyone who had not yet made the commitment to become a kingdom citizen was a target for Lucifer. He needed to find a willing accomplice to deal with this opportunity.

Lucifer headed directly to the far-off home of Gog, an ancient enemy of the Prince who had survived the global destruction and chaos.[2] Although Gog knew how to get along in this postwar world, Lucifer was sure that Gog never liked playing the "prime directive game" with the conquerors from

32: Last Gasp

the kingdom. "Gog will be ready to listen," Lucifer thought confidently.

Gog was absolutely ready to listen. He was sick of playing the role of "humble vanquished human" before the Prince, but he was good at knowing which way the political winds were blowing. If there really was a chance to crush the Prince, or at least send him packing, Gog was in; but he told Lucifer that he doubted it could be done.[3]

"His co-rulers are weak," Lucifer explained to Gog. "They took part in only that one battle, and mostly, they just watched the Prince fight."

"What about all the other people and their descendants? There are millions and most of them are kingdom citizens, aren't they?" Gog asked, knowing that he and the citizens of earth were greatly outnumbered.

"That, my friend, is the beauty of this plan," Lucifer smiled. "There are a lot of people who have still not committed to the kingdom. They aren't 'in' with the Prince as his co-rulers are. Every one of those people wants to make a name for themselves; and you Gog, will give them that opportunity to become leaders on earth." Gog nodded slowly as he thought. "What about the Prince?" he asked.

"He will never be in a weaker position," Lucifer lied convincingly. "He is fully occupied with his little family in the three dimensions of Jerusalem. Gog, I've looked at the numbers. Dimension for dimension, this will be a fair fight, except you will have the overwhelming advantage of surprise."

Lucifer knew the Prince was active and powerful in all dimensions, making him absolutely invincible against Gog and his army, but this was Lucifer's chance to create havoc and doubt amongst the human population, and to smear the Prince as an occupying warlord on their earth.

Just like in the garden, where he won over Adam's wife, he planned to trump the Prince by winning over the entire alien resident population of the earth; and maybe—just maybe—the rest would follow like Adam did, leaving the Royals without a human family.

Looking his newest friend in the eye, he asked, "So, Gog, are you in?"

"I'm in." [4]

Gog and his army marched toward Jerusalem, recruiting more citizens of earth every mile, encouraging them to make a name for themselves, and step up to the challenge of real leadership. His offer appealed to the young men of earth. "The privileged few have been ruling the planet with the Prince, but what about you? Come join us as we take our leadership positions in the new government of our planet."

Not all the young citizens of earth were suckered in by the deceit, but many were. The army swelled in size, almost uncountable as they approached Jerusalem.

The Prince drove his horse-powered gold-plated war-chariot through the midst of the kingdom cavalry, assembled and waiting for him. He stopped at the edge of the Crystal Sea, stepped down and joined his generals, standing by their steeds. The Prince asked, "Is everything ready?"

"Yes, sir!" shouted the generals.

The Prince nodded and took on the determined expression of a warrior about to step into battle. "No flood this time, gentlemen. Today, Lucifer's treachery ends in a firestorm." [5] The generals nodded solemnly as they strapped on their helmets. After a final word, they mounted up.

Amongst the cavalry, all the eyes were on the Prince. He jumped into his chariot, raised his hand and pointed toward the King and Prime Minister on the Kingdom Hall balcony. His voice thundered out, "Who do we follow?" A million voices shouted in unison, "The King! The King! The King!" The Prince saluted his family, and they saluted back.

The Prince turned and pointed to the sea. He shook the reigns and shouted, "For the King!" The ground shook as all

32: Last Gasp

of the kingdom cavalry raced down through the Crystal Sea. From the earth, the cavalry looked like a fiery cluster of comets falling out of the heavens.[6]

Before the firestorm hit Lucifer's army, Kingdom Special Forces, pre-deployed across the border, had scooped Lucifer up and carried him to the molten lake. Without ceremony, they threw him in to join Darta and Runson.[7]

"Damn you, Prince!" were Lucifer's final words as he hit the burning surface of the lake.

Just as he had never been allowed to reenter the kingdom proper, Lucifer realized that there was now no hope of ever reentering the earth or anywhere in the lower frontier. He descended many dimensions below the gates of heaven, into a most miserable place.

The kingdom cavalry encircled Jerusalem in front of Gog and Lucifer's army, and also surrounded them from behind. A tsunami of fire washed over millions of rebels. Jerusalem was spared, but the flames and acrid smoke of Lucifer's burning army rose high into the sky.

The Prince shouted over the roaring inferno, "Gabriel, evacuate the planet! Get all the humans across the border. Kingdom citizens into the KAL, and all the rest to immigration detention!" Gabriel galloped off with a battalion.

The entire region surrounding Jerusalem was in flames and filled with burned bodies and a river of blood. It was an awful sight.[8]

Soon, Gabriel returned to report, "all humans have been cleared from the planet."

The Prince asked, "Jerusalem as well?"

"Of course," responded Gabriel.

"Then let's get back across the border," the Prince ordered. "It's about to get very uncomfortable around here!"

Michael and Gabriel signaled for the cavalry to retreat back through the Crystal Sea. The earth began to shake

Passport Please - Epic of the Kingdom III

violently. With a load roar, darkness rolled across the sky. All lights in the heavens were extinguished, much like when Lucifer's rebellion had been crushed, some 10,000 years earlier, but this time it was destruction by fire, not water.[9] The view of the lower frontier from the Crystal Sea observation deck and the CSOC was one of total blackness.

The returning army was greeted outside the great kingdom hall by the Prime Minister and the King. The Prince hopped down from his chariot to receive a hug from his Dad, "Well done, son! Well done." The PM gave him a hug as well.

The King and Prime Minister also congratulated Michael and Gabriel on a job well done. The Prince wiped off some soot from his face and said, "Let's head to the conference room for a debrief before we head to court."

The Prime Minister agreed, "No time to waste. There are several billion people waiting to stand before the judge." [10]

*notes for this chapter
start on page 327*

33: Immigration Hearing

Michael was almost reluctant to bring it up but blurted it out anyway. "Most of the new kingdom citizens from earth have loved-ones waiting to stand before the judge," Michael said.[1] "Many will have a reason why someone or other down there should be let into the kingdom, even though throughout their life, that person may have consciously ignored or rejected all kingdom offers of citizenship."

The Prime Minister jumped in, "Look, Michael, a thousand years of peace and prosperity were just put at risk by a single hater of the King. Millions of alien residents in the lower frontier jumped up to follow Lucifer the minute he returned. There are *millions* in the lower waiting room who would bring poison into the kingdom by following their own desires instead of following the King. This last thousand years could not have made it any clearer." [2]

"Kingdom justice is perfect justice," said the King with finality. "Everybody gets what they want. Those who wanted to immigrate to the kingdom are in. Those who wanted to be free from the kingdom will get their wish. We respect every human's earthly choice to come into the kingdom, or to go their own way. I understand that some of our citizens could think it is a good idea to pull former friends into the kingdom—but I will not allow anyone to be dragged into the kingdom against their will, not by me, not by our citizens, not by *anybody*."

In the lower waiting room below the charred earth, conditions were worse than ever. After Gog and Lucifer's final attack, millions more citizens of earth had recently been jammed into those dark, crowded conditions. Even the video screens had finally gone blank.

In the kingdom citizens' arrival lounge, it was as pleasant as ever for the honorary citizens who were still patiently waiting.

Guests in both rooms would not have to wait much longer.

"Escort the humans from immigration detention [3] into the alien-resident section of the judicial center," the bailiff instructed the kingdom deputy. "Immigration detention" was the kingdom's official name for Lucifer's old lower waiting room, where all the citizens of earth waited after leaving their mortal bodies.

The deputy called the detention center security station and passed the message.

A voice boomed through the detention center, "All citizens of the old earth are to report immediately to the high court of the kingdom!" Automatic gates swung open and the court alien-resident section. There were literally billions of humans moving from the dimly-lit lower waiting room into the massive courtroom in the Valley of Jehoshaphat.[4] Each person had a story and they were ready to tell it to the judge.

As they moved up into the courtroom, all the lights in the lower concourse flickered and went dark behind them.

In his melodious announcer voice, Gabriel advised the honorary kingdom citizens in the citizens' arrival lounge that the court was ready to receive them.

"There will be a lot of unsavory characters in the courtroom," Gabriel explained, "but we have a special, honorary citizens' section to which you will be escorted." [5]

33: Immigration Hearing

Recent arrivals from earth who did not join Gog, who had never applied for kingdom citizenship, were reminded by the deputies that as aliens they had no right to remain in the kingdom unless the judge granted them kingdom citizenship. They had been brought up to join the throng in the alien-resident section.

All the kingdom citizens evacuated from earth before it's destruction were escorted into the spectators' chambers of the courtroom.

The Prince stood in his chambers at the door leading into the courtroom, waiting.[6]

"All rise for the judge!" called the bailiff. Billions of spectators and alien residents rose to their feet.[7]

A division of kingdom regulars under General Michael was already posted around the courtroom. The Prince strode through the doorway behind the judge's bench. Huge 4-D video screens above and behind the bench, and throughout the courtroom, made it possible for everyone in the room to see the judge, the speaker, and all the evidence.[8] This proceeding was to be a very public event.

The Prince, wearing a flowing judge's robe, paused before he sat and scanned the room. It was an awesome sight. Every human who had ever lived, who was not a kingdom citizen, stood in the defendants' arena. Each was as ready as they would ever be for their day in court before the Prince. Jesus swung himself down into the judge's great white throne.[9]

"The immigration and deportation tribunal for citizens of the old earth who are now alien residents in the kingdom of heaven, is now in session," boomed the bailiff. "The honorable Ambassador Extraordinary and Plenipotentiary to the Lower Frontier, former citizen of the old earth, Prince of heaven, and high Judge of the kingdom, Jesus, is presiding. These proceedings are now in session." The bailiff hammered his staff on the floor of the main courtroom. It echoed off the high arched ceiling.

"Good morning all," said the Prince. Addressing those in the alien resident's section he said, "Citizens of the old earth! You are here today because you are stateless persons. Your homeland has been decimated by war. Judgment has already been carried out on Lucifer, your former leader. The government of the old earth is no more. As you are no doubt aware, kingdom immigration policy allows entry and residency only to citizens holding kingdom passports. Without a kingdom-issued passport, entry is denied, and those without a passport are deported to exile alongside the leader of the old earth. Do you understand?"

The courtroom was dead quiet.

The Prince continued, "But this proceeding is a judgment, not a condemnation. Each one of you will be heard individually. As needed, this court is prepared to review all the evidence in your life, since every detail is a matter of public record." He rested his hand on a stack of books on his bench. The micro-data contained in those books detailed the events of the life of every individual who had ever lived on earth.

"In these proceedings, there is one subject of primary interest to the court: *While living on earth, did you willfully and consciously reject or ignore the opportunity to gain citizenship in the kingdom?*"

"If you did in fact ignore or reject that opportunity, then the other matters of your life will have no bearing on your judgment, so please spare the court explanations and lists of justifications, which do not have direct bearing on the subject of interest.[10] Also, this is not a hearing on the merits of the kingdom's long-held and widely published immigration policy—the need for kingdom citizenship in order to gain entry."[11]

33: Immigration Hearing

"The Royal family, and I personally, went to great lengths to make pardons freely available, so you could be eligible to apply for kingdom citizenship. This information was widely advertised for thousands of years on the earth, through our kingdom consulates, embassies, and a leaflet-dropping campaign lasting more than five hundred years."

"This court will respect the wishes of those who have consciously rejected the kingdom's offer of citizenship, in favor of remaining a citizen of earth.[12] By the end of this proceeding, all citizens of the former earth will be escorted out of the kingdom to follow their ruler, Lucifer, to share his fate. They will never be allowed reentry into the kingdom."[13]

"The court is well aware of the possibility of mitigating circumstances. The court reserves its sovereign right to pass judgment, based on the merits of each case, consistent with kingdom law.[14] As an example, there are millions standing in the defendants' arena today who were killed before they were born, prior to taking a single breath on the earth. The wrath of this court is *not* reserved for you."

"There may be others upon whom the court will extend leniency within the law, but remember this—when you make your case before me," the Prince leaned forward over the bench, "I have very little patience for foolish excuses and lies.[15] All statements made in court will be reviewed against the evidence of the defendant's life on earth, as recorded in the books. Those sentenced to deportation will have been convicted by their own testimony." [16]

The judge turned his eye to the honorary citizens arena, smiling as he saw friend after old friend from as far back as before Noah's flood, and before. "Finally," he said, "many here today received honorary citizenship in the kingdom before the arrival of the promised One. Your long-standing and often long-suffering commitment to this kingdom is appreciated by the Royal family. I especially look forward to seeing you before my bench, and having the Prime Minister confer full kingdom citizenship upon you." He caught the eye of his oldest friend Adam and gave him a personal nod and smile.

The Prince scanned the defendants' arena.

"There are a lot of people here today. When coming before the bench, the name of each defendant will be looked up in the register of issued and accepted pardons." The Prince placed his hand on the other book on his bench. "This ensures that no one is wrongly convicted and sentenced." [17]

Scanning the huge courtroom, the Prince was silent for a moment, preparing himself for a long session.

"Open the books of human deeds," he instructed, "and bring forward the first defendant."

"Your honor, I bring before you ..."

And so began the great judgment of the citizens of earth, which did not end until the last human had been heard and received justice.

The Prince rose from his bench, turned to Michael and said, "It's time. Tear down that disgusting lower waiting room. Toss it all into the molten lake. Then resurrect the earth and the entire lower frontier again, and make it ready for a new age in the new kingdom." [18]

*notes for this chapter
start on page 331*

34: Moving Day

∽∾

In the great kingdom hall, there was a bustling of a different sort. Boxes were being stacked high outside the entranceways and piles of furniture were being hauled on carts across the shiny floor of the hall.

The King, the Prince and the Prime Minister sat around the conference table, along with Michael and Gabriel, in the only room that still had all of its furniture.

"Moving day!" announced the Prince, ready to assume the throne in his new, expanded kingdom in the lower frontier. The borders had officially been moved and the frontier had been formally annexed by the kingdom. The Royal city, New Jerusalem, was about to be established on the earth as the new capital of the kingdom.

"It was a long time coming," said Michael.

"And costly," added the King softly. He looked at his son with intense pride. "Very costly."

"But like I said, totally worth it!" responded the Prince. "By the way, have you met my new family?" he said as he waved his hand toward the window overlooking the crowds of new citizens walking through the kingdom proper.

They all chuckled.

"I would say," the Prime Minister steered them back to the original purpose of the meeting, "the Immigration Project was a complete success."

The Prince added, "Michael, Gabriel, you and your troops were magnificent. Your service to the kingdom is appreciated beyond measure."

The generals nodded modestly and quietly thanked the Prince. "We are who we are, because of you—all of you," Gabriel responded.

"Michael," the Prince asked with a wink, "do you think my people still see me as an ogre?"

Blushing at the reference to his comment from some seven thousand earth years earlier, the general responded, "You demonstrated the purest love for them by what you did.[1] You proved that there was absolutely *nothing* you wouldn't do for them. They saw it. They know you're not— not an— um—ogre—sir."

The Prince smiled at the response from his uncharacteristically flustered general. Turning to the King, he said, "You reached out to them first, Father, and you sent me to bring them into the family—and they love you for it."[2]

"I didn't send just you, son. I sent you both," the King responded, with a nod to the Prime Minister.[3] "You two are quite a team."

They sat quietly around the table, enjoying the moment.

The Prime Minister was anxious to springboard the discussion on to the next topic. "Generals, I want to tell you about our next initiative, which will stand on the shoulders of the Immigration Project!" He glanced at the clock...

Monday, 12:01 AM KST ⧖ 0000 NJST

"As soon as we move to New Jerusalem, a new week begins in the Kingdom," the PM announced. "No one in our human family could have expected how good this will be!" [4]

Michael and Gabriel exchanged glances; both having expected at least a short break in the action. Gabriel took a

34: Moving Day

deep breath, and said, "Never a dull moment in the kingdom, sir. Please, tell us about it."

There was a soft knock on the conference room door, and a mover stuck his head in. "When would be a good time to pack this room?" he asked.

The Prime Minister knew the Prince was anxious to move to New Jerusalem, so he deferred with a nod to the Prince. The Prince responded, "Right now would be great, thanks."

Standing up, the Prince looked at his generals and said, "Let's move to the conference room in New Jerusalem. The Prime Minister will tell you more about our next project when we get there."

The Prince smiled and asked, "Who wants to join me in heaven on earth?" [5]

*notes for this chapter
start on page 331*

35: Another Age Begins

~~~

Moses was impressed. With drawings spread out before them, the King explained to his old friend, "We're almost done setting up a whole new cosmos, from the lights in the heavens to the smallest details of earth - everything."[1]

"And," interrupted the Prince, pointing to the sky, "our pre-fabricated city. New Jerusalem will cover almost two million square miles and reach into the limitless power supply of the earth's core over 1,200 miles down. It's 1,400 miles top to bottom, with walls that are two hundred feet thick."

The King grinned and said to Moses, "I think it will remind you of what you saw every morning, looking out from Pharaoh's palace in Egypt." [2]

Moses couldn't wait. The entire crowd was now looking straight up.

"Here it comes!" the King announced. "Earth is now officially part of the kingdom proper," "The Crystal Sea is no more, and our New Jerusalem is the last thing to pass through that portal." [3]

They all stopped, looked up, and watched as the pyramid-shaped New Jerusalem settled into place on the refurbished earth,[4] sliding into a precisely engineered hole in the new earth. The city descended, as water from the old Crystal Sea gushed down the sides of the city, lubricating it as it lowered into place. It slid far below the earth and when it finally came to rest it would still extend far into the sky, providing an incredible view from the top.

The citizens were shouting and cheering and crying all at the same time. The noise was incredible.[5]

"Look at those materials," added the prime minister as mile after mile of the city slid into its foundation. "Crystal, pearls, precious stone inlays everywhere. Even the streets are paved with gold."[6]

"So *that's* what you've been doing," Peter said to the Prince. "You said you were going to prepare a place for us, but this is outstanding![7] All it needs is a good place for fishing," grinned the big fisherman from Galilee.

"Check it out," said the Prince. "Not only do we have hundreds of miles of oceanfront, but also a river flowing down, right out of the throne room, through the city, out across the earth—and it is teeming with fish! If you get hungry while you're fishing, it has the Tree of Life on both sides of the river, giving delicious fruit all year long!"

The Prince's first friend Adam exclaimed, "One tree standing on two sides of the river! Like you said back in the garden, these extra dimensions are beyond what I could ever have imagined!" [8]

"Told you," said the Prince, grinning at his friends and fellow rulers of the new earth.

One of the citizens asked the Prince, "What do you have planned once we are all settled into our new city?"

The Prince smiled at him, put his hand on the man's shoulder and said, "Excellent. A man of action! Come, follow me and you will see …" [9]

Appendix 1: Time Zones and Time Lines

Appendix 1:

Time Zones and Time Lines

Time Zones and Time Lines in the Kingdom

Humans have traditionally counted time in years before and after the Prince of Heaven was born on earth as a human.

The Bible is clear that Adam and Eve lived about 4,000 years before the Prince arrived,[a] and today we live about 2,000 years after his arrival. That is, 4000 BCE [b] and 2000 AD.

In the Kingdom, however, we are told:

> "With the Lord a day is like a thousand years, and a thousand years are like a day." 2 Peter 3:8

Passport Please takes that position that there are two time zones in our world... **Kingdom Standard Time**, measured in days and **Frontier Standard Time**, (including the earth) which is measured in years. The table to the right shows major events in *Epic of the Kingdom*, in both time zones.

In the first two verses of the Bible, time is not mentioned.

> "In the beginning God created the heavens and the earth. Now the earth was formless and empty, darkness was over the surface of the deep, and the Spirit of God was hovering over the waters." Genesis 1:1-2

Passport Please takes the position that many weeks, possibly millions of them, passed (in KST) before *Volume 3* began...

> 1 million KST weeks = 7 billion FST (earth) years

---

[a] Genesis tells the age of Adam and his descendants, all the way to Abraham, and tells how old each one was when they had their son. Simple arithmetic shows that Abraham was born 1948 years after Adam was created. Virtually all historians agree that Abraham lived approximately 2000 BCE. That dates Adam and Eve to around 4000 BCE.

[b] BCE is *Before the Common Era*. Many prefer to use the traditional nomenclature "BC," for *Before Christ*. *Passport Please* uses "BCE," not to make a statement, but simply to follow a present-day naming convention.

Appendix 1: Time Zones and Time Lines

TIME ZONES AND TIME LINES

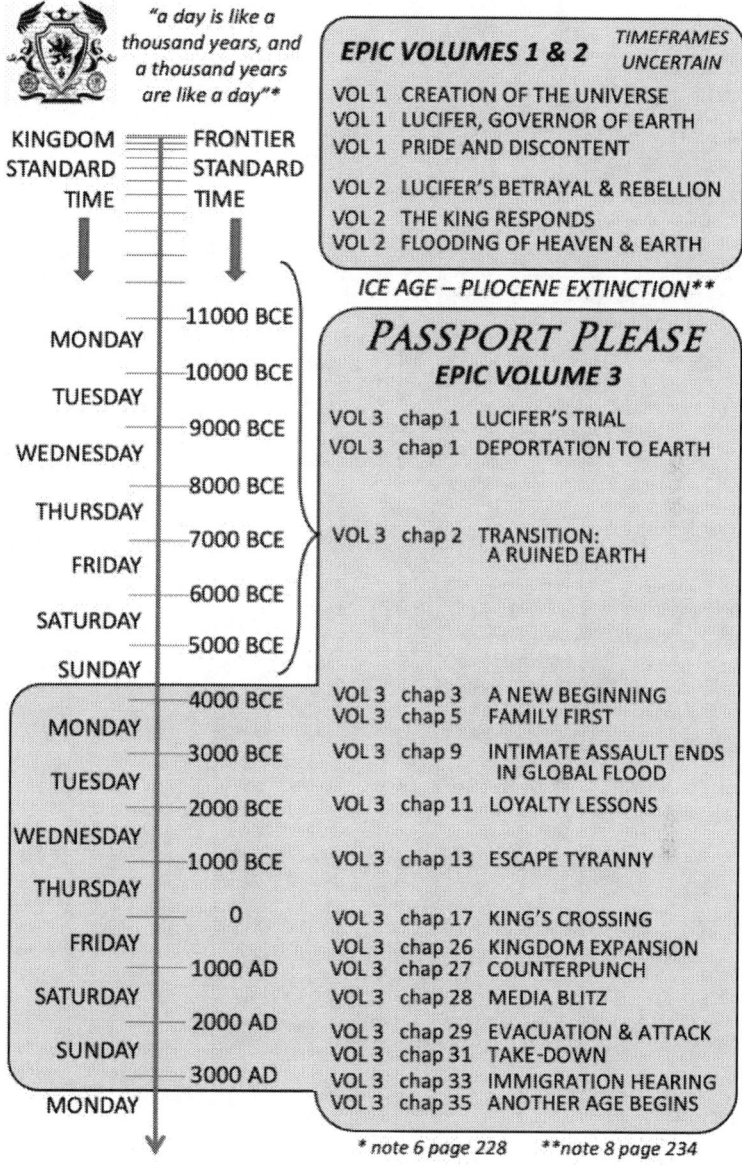

"a day is like a thousand years, and a thousand years are like a day"*

KINGDOM STANDARD TIME — FRONTIER STANDARD TIME

EPIC VOLUMES 1 & 2	**TIMEFRAMES UNCERTAIN**
VOL 1	CREATION OF THE UNIVERSE
VOL 1	LUCIFER, GOVERNOR OF EARTH
VOL 1	PRIDE AND DISCONTENT
VOL 2	LUCIFER'S BETRAYAL & REBELLION
VOL 2	THE KING RESPONDS
VOL 2	FLOODING OF HEAVEN & EARTH

ICE AGE – PLIOCENE EXTINCTION**

PASSPORT PLEASE
EPIC VOLUME 3

- MONDAY — 11000 BCE
- TUESDAY — 10000 BCE
- WEDNESDAY — 9000 BCE — VOL 3 chap 1 LUCIFER'S TRIAL / DEPORTATION TO EARTH
- THURSDAY — 8000 BCE
- FRIDAY — 7000 BCE — VOL 3 chap 2 TRANSITION: A RUINED EARTH
- SATURDAY — 6000 BCE
- SUNDAY — 5000 BCE
- MONDAY — 4000 BCE — VOL 3 chap 3 A NEW BEGINNING / chap 5 FAMILY FIRST
- TUESDAY — 3000 BCE — VOL 3 chap 9 INTIMATE ASSAULT ENDS IN GLOBAL FLOOD
- WEDNESDAY — 2000 BCE — VOL 3 chap 11 LOYALTY LESSONS
- THURSDAY — 1000 BCE — VOL 3 chap 13 ESCAPE TYRANNY
- FRIDAY — 0 — VOL 3 chap 17 KING'S CROSSING
- SATURDAY — 1000 AD — VOL 3 chap 26 KINGDOM EXPANSION / chap 27 COUNTERPUNCH / chap 28 MEDIA BLITZ
- SUNDAY — 2000 AD — VOL 3 chap 29 EVACUATION & ATTACK / chap 31 TAKE-DOWN
- MONDAY — 3000 AD — VOL 3 chap 33 IMMIGRATION HEARING / chap 35 ANOTHER AGE BEGINS

*note 6 page 228   **note 8 page 234

Appendix 2: Endnotes

Passport Please is a novel based completely on the Bible.

Novels rarely have endnotes, but without them, a reader might incorrectly assume that one or another part of the *Passport Please* story is not based on the Bible.

The references and notes that follow, are presented to show where the characters and plot elements in *Passport Please* came from, to help you come to your own conclusions.

The endnotes that follow are not exhaustive. Since *the Epic of the Kingdom* tells the big picture of the Bible from the before the earth was formed to the end of the world, the endnotes could easily have been longer than the story.

With a few noted exceptions, Bible quotes are taken, with permission, from the New International Version (NIV) and they are in quotation marks. If a contextual clarification is added inside the quotation marks by the author, it is in brackets, for example:

Luke 8:31 "And they [the demons] begged Jesus ..."

The author's goal is not to prove that the Bible is true, but rather to show that this story is true to the Bible.

It is hoped that these endnotes will demonstrate that it is.

―――――――――――――――――

Pages 1 to 4 — *Introduction*

1. John 3:3 Jesus tells Nicodemus, "no one can see the kingdom of God unless he is born again."

2. String theory bridges the gap between Einstein's theory of relativity and Bohr's theory quantum mechanics, and it shows that there are at least 11 dimensions in our universe (length, width, height, time plus 7 others). See *The Elegant Universe,* by Dr. Brian Greene (1999)

3. John 18:36 "Jesus said, 'My kingdom is not of this world... But now my kingdom is from another place.'"

   John 8:23 "he [Jesus] continued, "You are from below; I am from above. You are of this world; I am not of this world."

4. *Passport Please* takes the position that the summaries of *Epic of the Kingdom I & II* in this book are a reasonable reconstruction of information scattered throughout the Bible. We know there is much more to this story than was ever written down, and seeking out that story is a noble task.

   John 21:25 "Now there are also many other things that Jesus did. Were every one of them to be written, I suppose that the world itself could not contain the books that would be written."

   Proverbs 25:2 It is the glory of God to conceal a matter; to search out a matter is the glory of kings.

Appendix 2: Endnotes

Pages 5 to 8 Epic of the Kingdom I: Beginnings

[1] Even before time began, the King was making plans...

1 Corinthians 2:7 "we declare God's wisdom, a mystery that has been hidden and that God destined for our glory before time began."

Titus 1:2 "the hope of eternal life, which God, who does not lie, promised before the beginning of time."

2 Timothy 1:9 "He has saved us and called us... before the beginning of time."

Paul was unable to describe, and he was forbidden to tell about, what he was shown in the Kingdom of Heaven.

2 Corinthians 12:4 "[I] was caught up to the third heaven... [where I] heard inexpressible things, things that no one is permitted to tell."

[2] John 14:2 "My Father's house has many rooms; if that were not so, would I [Jesus] have told you that I am going there to prepare a place for you?"

Revelation 5:11 "...many angels, numbering thousands upon thousands, and ten thousand times ten thousand, They encircled the throne and the living creatures and the elders."

[3] Malachi 2:15 "What does the one God seek? Godly offspring."

[4] There are actually 11 dimensions. See note 2, page 226.

[5] Luke 8:17 "There is nothing hidden that will not be disclosed, and nothing concealed that will not be known or be brought out into the open."

Luke 12:3 "What you have whispered in the ear in the inner rooms will be proclaimed from the roofs."

Revelation 20:12 "I saw the dead, great and small, standing before the throne, and books were opened. Another book was opened, which is the book of life. The dead were judged according to what they had done as recorded in the books."

6   A thousand years on earth is like a day in the Kingdom. See note 5 page 242, note 6 page 256 and Appendix 1.

2 Peter 3:8 "With the Lord a day is like a thousand years and a thousand years are like a day."

Ecclesiastes 3:11 "He has also set eternity in the human heart; yet no one can fathom what God has done from beginning to end."

7   The King's plan was secret, until He revealed it:

1 Corinthians 2:7-9 None of the rulers of this age understood it [God's plan], for if they had, they would not have crucified the Lord of glory. However, as it is written: 'What no eye has seen, what no ear has heard, and what no human mind has conceived'— the things God has prepared for those who love him.'"

1 Peter 1:12 "Even angels long to look into these things."

8   Genesis 1:1 "In the beginning, God created the heavens and the earth."

John 1:3 "Through him [Jesus] all things were made; without him nothing was made that has been made."

The Bible is silent regarding *how* all things were made. As a literary device, the marble-sized sphere is borrowed from the first book ever written in English by a woman, *Revelations of Divine Love*, by Lady Julian of Norwich, published around 1373 AD. It recounts visits by Jesus to Lady Julian...

Appendix 2: Endnotes

"...he [the Lord] showed me a little thing in the palm of my hand, about the size of a hazelnut, and as round as a ball. I looked at it and thought: 'What can this be?' And the answer came: 'This is all that is made.'"

9   The Earth was originally created, ready to be inhabited.

Isaiah 45:18   "For this is what the Lord says—he who created the heavens, he is God; he who fashioned and made the earth, he founded it; he did not create it to be empty, but formed it to be inhabited—he says: "I am the Lord, and there is no other."

10   Many were present at the creation of earth.

Job 38:4,7 "Where were you when I laid the earth's foundation... when the morning stars sang together, and all the angels shouted for joy?

11   Lucifer was the beloved guardian of the Garden of Eden.

Ezekiel 28:12-14 "You were the model of perfection, full of wisdom and perfect in beauty. You were in Eden, the garden of God; every precious stone adorned you: ruby, topaz and emerald, chrysolite, onyx and jasper, sapphire, turquoise and beryl. Your settings and mountings were made of gold; on the day you were created they were prepared. You were anointed as a guardian cherub, for so I ordained you. You were on the holy mount of God; you walked among the fiery stones."

As guardian of Eden, Lucifer sounds "good," but Jesus calls him evil, and his friend John agreed:

John 8:44 [Jesus said] "He [the devil] was a murderer from the beginning, not holding to the truth, for there is no truth in him. When he lies, he speaks his native language, for he is a liar and the father of lies."

1 John 3:8 "...the devil has been sinning from the beginning."

Jesus and John contradict Job and Ezekiel (note 10 & 11, above), unless they are referring to two different beginnings.

Passport Please takes the position that Ezekiel and Job referred to the beginning of planet earth (Genesis 1:1), while Jesus and John referred to the beginning of the resurrected earth, which was "raised from the dead" starting in Genesis 1:3. Only then their statements do not conflict.

Lucifer started loyal, and later rebelled.

Pages 9 to 10   Epic of the Kingdom II: Betrayal

[1] Humans were destined to rule the earth.

Psalm 8:4-6 [King David wrote] "what is mankind that you are mindful of them, human beings that you care for them? You have made them a little lower than the angels* and crowned them with glory and honor. You made them rulers over the works of your hands; you put everything under their feet."

*The Hebrew word "Elohim," translated above as "angels," appears in the Bible 2605 times. 99.4% of the time it is translated as "God" and only this once as "angels." Accordingly, *Passport Please* takes the position that the correct translation is that man was made "lower than God," as opposed to "lower than angels."

The King was about to create humans, a little lower than himself, to rank higher than all other beings.

Appendix 2: Endnotes

This made Lucifer jealous of humans and angry with the King. He had been the King's favorite, but now humans, who could become children of the Royal family, would stand between Lucifer and the throne.

John 1:12 "to all [humans] who did receive him, to those who believed in his name, he gave the right to become children of God..."

2 *Passport Please* takes the position that a civilization lived on the earth before Lucifer's rebellion, and it was destroyed during that war, and Jeremiah saw its ruins...

Jeremiah 4:23-27 "I looked at the earth, and it was formless and empty; and at the heavens, and their light was gone. I looked at the mountains, and they were quaking; all the hills were swaying. I looked, and there were no people; every bird in the sky had flown away. I looked, and the fruitful land was a desert; all its towns lay in ruins before the Lord, before his fierce anger."

The only other reference in the Bible to an earth that is formless and empty, is before the seven-day resurrection of the earth...

Genesis 1:2 "And the earth was formless and empty..."

This destroyed civilization has since been forgotten...

Psalm 9:5-6 "You [God] have rebuked the nations and destroyed the wicked; you have blotted out their name for ever and ever. Endless ruin has overtaken my enemies, you have uprooted their cities; even the memory of them has perished."

Who the inhabitants and builders of those towns and cities were remains a mystery, but archeological evidence indicates they existed thousands, even millions of years ago, *Passport Please* takes the position that these human-like beings were fundamentally different from descendants of Adam and Eve. See note 5 on page 237 and note 8 page 243 regarding those differences.

3   Ezekiel 28:17 "Your heart became proud on account of your beauty, and you corrupted your wisdom because of your splendor."

Isaiah 14:13-14 "You [Lucifer] said in your heart, 'I will ascend to the heavens; I will raise my throne above the stars of God; I will sit enthroned on the mount of assembly, on the utmost heights of Mount Zaphon. I will ascend above the tops of the clouds; I will make myself like the Most High.'"

4   Revelation 12:7-8 "Then war broke out in heaven. Michael and his angels fought against the dragon, and the dragon and his angels fought back. But he was not strong enough and they lost their place in heaven."

Passport Please takes the position that the King of Heaven crushed Lucifer's rebellion by shaking and flooding the earth and the heavens, which left the planet dead and ready for resurrection. See note 2, above, and note 6, page 234. Shaking of heaven and earth will happen again near the end of days...

Hebrews 12:26 "Once more I will shake not only the earth but also the heavens."

Haggai 2:6 "the Lord Almighty says: 'In a little while I will once more shake the heavens and the earth, the sea and the dry land."

Appendix 2: Endnotes

⁵ This flood was so massive, it even extinguished light in the heavens.

Genesis 1:2 "And the earth was* formless and empty, darkness was over the surface of the deep..."

Where could so much water come from, to extinguish the lights in the heavens? A web search for "massive water in space," for example, will show multiple articles like... *"Enormous water reservoir found in space is bigger than 140 trillion earth oceans,"* (zmescience.com) which says this water appears to be spread over hundreds of light years. The discovery came as part of a 2008 quasar study called "APM 08279+5255", made using the California Institute of Technology's Submillimeter Observatory near the summit of Mauna Kea in Hawaii.

With so much water covering earth, it is not surprising that the King's first step in restoring earth, after turning on the light, would be to separate the waters on the earth from the waters above the earth. See note 1 on page 240.

* A little-known but long-running debate among Hebrew grammar experts is whether Genesis 1:2, above, should read "the world *was* formless and empty" or "the world *became* formless and empty." Grammatically, the Hebrew word "hayah," can be correctly translated either way, and both are found many times in the Bible.

Passport Please takes the position that the world *became* formless and empty after Lucifer's rebellion was crushed. *In the Beginnings* by Dr. Steven Dill (2010) has much to say on this topic.

⁶ Lucifer was responsible for the earth's destruction, and everyone in the Kingdom knew it.

Isaiah 14:16-17 "Those who see you [Lucifer] stare at you, they ponder your fate: "Is this the man who shook the earth and made kingdoms tremble, the man who made the world a wilderness, who overthrew its cities and would not let his captives go home?"

⁷ Heavenly beings, as well as earthly beings, will be called to stand before Kingdom justice.

Isaiah 24:21-22 "In that day the Lord will punish the powers in the heavens above and the kings on the earth below. They will be herded together like prisoners bound in a dungeon; they will be shut up in prison and be punished after many days."

⁸ This sudden wave of death on the earth is consistent with what scientists call the "Pliocene extinction," which came upon the earth quickly between 13,000 and 9,000 BCE, around the last ice age. A quick internet search will reveal a trove of information on this global catastrophe.

Pages 11 to 16   *1: End of the Age*

¹ Lucifer was not always the King's enemy. In the very beginning, he was a "team player" in the kingdom. See note 11 on page 229.

² *Passport Please* takes the position that renouncing the Prime Minister and the kingdom citizenship he confers, is final and "unpardonable." A citizen's free-will decision to renounce their citizenship will be honored.

Mark 3:29 "whoever blasphemes against the Holy Spirit will never be forgiven; they are guilty of an eternal sin."

Appendix 2: Endnotes

Luke 12:10 "And everyone who speaks a word against the Son of Man will be forgiven, but anyone who blasphemes against the Holy Spirit will not be forgiven."

3   *Passport Please* takes the position that "in the beginning" the earth was created beautiful and ready for life and that Lucifer's rebellion led to the destruction of the earth, leaving it formless and empty. (see pages 5-10)

4   Lucifer was in the Garden of Eden before leading his rebellion. See note 11 on page 229.

5   The presence of God has a distinct aroma, of life or death.

2 Corinthians 2:15-16 "For we are to God the pleasing aroma of Christ among those who are being saved and those who are perishing. To the one we are an aroma that brings death; to the other, an aroma that brings life."

6   Lucifer's rebels will be judged by humans.

1 Corinthians 6:3 "Do you not know that we will judge angels?"

7   There is a body of water between heaven and earth. Jesus' friend John was shown what the Crystal Sea above the sky looks like from there...

Revelation 4:6 (John saw) "in front of the throne there was what looked like a sea of glass, clear as crystal."

Ezekiel looked up from earth and saw the King's throne. He said it was like looking through a sheet of ice...

Ezekiel 1:22, 25-26 "Spread out above the heads of the living creatures was what looked something like an expanse, sparkling like ice... Above the expanse over their heads was what looked like a throne of sapphire, and high above on the throne was a figure like that of a man."

235

As a reminder that water separates earth from the Kingdom, a model of the Crystal Sea was constructed in the Jerusalem Justice Center. An 11,500 gallon pool of water called "the Sea," rested above (not next to) twelve metal bulls, like the sea that is above the things of earth.

2 Chronicles 4:2-4 "He made the Sea of cast metal, circular in shape, measuring ten cubits from rim to rim and five cubits high ... The Sea stood on twelve bulls, three facing north, three facing west, three facing south and three facing east. The Sea rested on top of them."

8 Revelation 12: 9 "the devil, or Satan, who leads the whole world astray... was hurled to the earth, and his angels with him."

Revelation 12:4a "Its [the dragon's] tail swept a third of the stars [angels] out of the sky and flung them to earth."

Isaiah 14:12, 15 "How you have fallen from Heaven, O morning star ["Lucifer" in KJV], son of the dawn! ... you are brought down to the grave, to the depths of the pit."

Luke 10:18 "I [Jesus] saw Satan fall like lightning from heaven."

Pages 17 to 22   2: Transition

1 The King is a proponent of people groups being identified by their own flags...

Numbers 2:1-2 "The Lord said to Moses and Aaron, "The Israelites are to camp... each man under his standard [flag] with the banners of his family."

2 The King's throne has wheels!

Daniel 7:9b "His [God's] throne was flaming with fire, and its wheels were all ablaze."

Appendix 2: Endnotes

3   Isaiah 66:1 "This is what the Lord says: 'Heaven is my throne, and the earth is my footstool.'"

4   After the capital city of the Kingdom moves to earth, the Royal family will live there. (notes 2/4, pages 331-333)

Revelation 21:3 "God's dwelling place is now among the people, and he will dwell with them. They will be his people, and God himself will be with them and be their God." (this is from the next to last chapter of the Bible)

5   The first human, Adam, was a "new" creation, unlike men and women who lived on earth in a prior age. See note 8 on page 243 and note 2 on page 231. Plants and animals created on Days 3, 5 and 6 (above) were the same kind that inhabited the earth prior to the flood of Genesis 1:2.

plants & trees *according to their kind*	Gen 1:11-12
birds & fish *according to their kind*	Gen 1:21
animals *according to their kind*	Gen 1:24

Adam was not like the old kind of man that existed before the flood of Genesis 1:2.

Starting with Adam, humans would be created to be like their creator, destined to be rulers over the earth, and their bodies would be a home for the Prime Minister.

Genesis 1:26 God said, "Let us make mankind in our image, in our likeness, so that they may rule over the fish in the sea and the birds in the sky, over the livestock and all the wild animals, and over all the creatures that move along the ground."

6   Earth will ultimately be united under the King...

Ephesians 1:9-10 "he [God] made known to us the mystery of his will ... when the times reach their fulfillment—to bring unity to all things in heaven and on earth under Christ."

1 Corinthians 15:24 "Then the end will come, when he [Jesus] hands over the kingdom to God the Father after he has destroyed all dominion, authority and power."

Revelation 11:15 "The seventh angel sounded his trumpet, and there were loud voices in heaven, which said: 'The kingdom of the world has become the kingdom of our Lord and of his Messiah, and he will reign for ever and ever.'"

Isaiah 26:15 "You have enlarged the nation, Lord; you have enlarged the nation. You have gained glory for yourself; you have extended all the borders of the land."

7. Genesis 1:3,5 "And God said, let there be light... evening and morning, the first day."

On the first day, there was light, but not from the sun, which would be re-lit days later. See note 1, page 240. The light came from the Prince himself. This will happen again at the end of the age...

Revelation 21:23 "The city [which came down from heaven] does not need the sun or the moon to shine on it, for the glory of God gives it light, and the Lamb [Jesus] is its lamp."

When anyone from the Kingdom enters the lower frontier, their brightness can rival the sun.

John 1:4-5 "In him [Jesus] was life, and that life was the light of all mankind. The light shines in the darkness, and the darkness has not overcome it."

John 8:12 "I [Jesus] am the light of the world."

Appendix 2: Endnotes

The King shines so brightly, it could kill a human, so he cloaks himself in thick clouds. Once he told Moses to shield his eyes. See note 3, page 268.

Matt 17:1-5 "Jesus took with him Peter, James and John the brother of James, and led them up a high mountain by themselves. There he was transfigured before them. His face shone like the sun, and his clothes became as white as the light. Just then there appeared before them Moses and Elijah, talking with Jesus... a bright cloud covered them, and a voice from the cloud said, 'This is my Son, whom I [the King] love; with him I am well pleased. Listen to him!'"

The Roman Centurion Cornelius described his encounter with a kingdom soldier:

Acts 10:30 "Suddenly a man in shining clothes stood before me."

1 Timothy 6:16 [God] "alone is immortal and who lives in unapproachable light"

1 John 1:5 "God is light; in him there is no darkness at all."

[8] Hebrews 11:3 "By faith we understand that the universe was formed at God's command, so that what is seen was not made out of what was visible."

Isaiah 44:24b "I am the Lord, who has made all things, who alone stretched out the heavens, who spread out the earth by myself"

John 1:3 "Through him [Jesus] all things were made; without him nothing was made that has been made..."

Pages 23 to 26   **3: A New Beginning**

[1] Restoring the earth would take seven days. Details on days 1-7, and the King's reactions, are found in Genesis 1:3 through 2:2.

> Day 1: Light – *It is good!*
> Day 2: Separate oceans above from oceans on earth*
> Day 3: Plants, trees and fruit – *It is good!*
> Day 4: Lights in sky for signs & seasons *It is good!*
> Day 5: Fish and birds – *It is good!*
> Day 6: Land animals – *It is good!* Man – *very good!*
> Day 7: A day to rest
>
> * The King didn't say that separating the oceans above and below was "good." See note 3 page 241.

Each day in the "week of creation" starts with:
"And God said...",
and concludes with:
"Evening and morning, the first (or 2nd or 3rd) day."

Passport Please takes the position that "creation week" took six 24-hour days to restore an extremely old earth, which had died. See notes 5-8, pages 233-234. This week marked the resurrection of the heavens and earth which had been corrupted and perished and was then brought into a new life through immersion in water.

2 Peter 3:5-7 "For they deliberately forgot that long ago the heavens came into being, and the earth was formed out of water and by water [during "creation week"]. By these waters also the world of that time [the old heavens and earth] was deluged and destroyed..."

Passport Please takes the position that when the Prince used water-immersion to restore the once-dead heavens

Appendix 2: Endnotes

and earth, corrupted under Lucifer's rule, he gave a preview of water baptism for humans (note 9, page 278).

Ephesians 2:1-2 "you were dead in your transgressions... you followed the ways of this world and of the ruler of the kingdom of the air [Lucifer]."

Romans 6:4 "We were therefore buried with him [Jesus] through baptism into death in order that... we too may live a new life."

2   Psalm 11:4 "The Lord is in his heavenly temple... on his heavenly throne. He observes the sons of men, his eyes examine them."

Psalm 113:5-6 "Who is like the Lord our God, the One who sits enthroned on high, who stoops down to look on the heavens and the earth?"

3   Genesis 1:6-8 "God said, 'Let there be an expanse between the waters to separate water from water.... evening and morning, the second day.' So God made the expanse and separated the water under the expanse from the water above it. And it was so. God called the expanse 'sky.'"

Passport Please takes the position that the water above the sky is the Crystal Sea of heaven (note 7, page 235). As long as Lucifer remains on earth, it will remain as an important barrier between heaven and the earth, like a moat, keeping Lucifer and his rebels out of the kingdom.

When the waters were separated, leaving the Crystal Sea above earth, the King did not say, "it is good," as he did about all his other creations. (note 1, page 240) The sea above is not "good," it is "necessary." It will continue to be a necessary barrier, until evil is purged from earth at the end of the age, when this sea will be removed.

Revelation 21:1 "Then I saw 'a new heaven and a new earth,' for the first heaven and the first earth had passed away, and there was no longer any [Crystal] sea."

To this day, humans who commit their lives to the Prince and come under his protection, mark their entry into the kingdom by passing through water—it's called baptism. That is a "picture" of passing through the Crystal Sea into the kingdom of Heaven.

4. Genesis 1:14-19 "God said, "Let there be lights in the expanse of the sky to separate the day from the night, and let them serve as signs to mark sacred times, and days and years, and let them be lights in the expanse of the sky to give light on the earth.... evening and morning, the fourth day"

Special events are signaled through the heavens. The "three wise men" were guided nearly 700 miles from Persia, by following a star to Bethlehem when Jesus was born. See note 3 on page 277. For millenia, mariners have used stars as a sign to guide them around the world.

5. Time is relative, not constant or universal.

2 Peter 3:8 "With the Lord a day is like a thousand years and a thousand years are like a day."

Psalm 90:4 "For a thousand years in your sight are like a day that has just gone by, or like a watch in the night." [a "watch" is a maritime term, usually four hours.]

NASA proved experimentally that time moves forward at different rates depending on the relative speed of the timekeeper. In NAVEX, a 1985 experiment, an atomic clock flew on STS-61A/Challenger. Compared to an identical clock on the ground, the clock in motion

Appendix 2: Endnotes

measured a slowdown of time: 0.000,000,000,295 seconds for each second of flight, a time difference between observers of 0.13 seconds over a five-day flight. exactly as predicted by Einstein's formulas.

Time measurement discrepancies between observers become huge as relative speed between observers approaches light-speed. Then "hours" pass for one observer while "years" pass for another, during the same period, and they are both accurate. *The Elegant Universe*, Dr. Brian Greene, chapter 2.

6   Plants and creatures were created using the same designs as creatures that had lived on earth before, before the great flood of Genesis 1:2. See note 5 on page 237 and note 2 on page 231.

7   Ephesians 6:12 "our struggle is not against flesh and blood, but against the rulers, against the authorities, against the powers of this dark world and against the spiritual forces of evil in the heavenly realms."

8   *Passport Please* takes the position Adam and Eve (and descendants) were designed as a residence for the Prime Minister. The Bible goes out of its way to note that all other life forms were created "according to their kind," but not humans. See note 5 on page 237. The Bible is silent as to the "kingdom status" of men and women who lived before Adam and Eve. That remains a mystery. See note 2 on page 231.

1 Corinthians 6:19 "do you not know that your bodies are temples of the Holy Spirit, who is in you, who you have received from God? You are not your own."

9   Psalm 103:14 "he knows how we are formed; he remembers that we are dust."

Genesis 2:7 "God formed a man from the dust of the ground and breathed into his nostrils the breath of life, and the man became a living being."

Leviticus 17:11 "For the life of a creature is in the blood"

Pages 27 to 30   4: *Rebel's Dare*

[1] This conversation between the Prince and Lucifer is patterned after the conversation between God and Satan in the Book of Job. After that conversation, Satan was allowed limited interaction with Job, to test his loyalty.

Job 1:6-12 "One day the angels came to present themselves before the Lord, and Satan also came with them. The Lord said to Satan, 'Where have you come from?' Satan answered the Lord, 'From roaming through the earth and going back and forth in it.' Then the Lord said to Satan, 'Have you considered my servant Job? There is no one on earth like him; he is blameless and upright, a man who fears God and shuns evil.' 'Does Job fear God for nothing?' Satan replied. 'Have you not put a hedge around him and his household and everything he has? You have blessed the work of his hands, so that his flocks and herds are spread throughout the land. But stretch out your hand and strike everything he has, and he will surely curse you to your face.' The Lord said to Satan, 'Very well, then, everything he has is in your hands, but on the man himself do not lay a finger.' Then Satan went out from the presence of the Lord."

The name Job comes from the Hebrew "hated." In the Bible, Lucifer is the only one we know who hated Job. Lucifer hates humans who are made to be a home for the Prime Minister. See note 8 on page 243.

Appendix 2: Endnotes

Passport Please takes the position that what happened to Job is a "picture" of what happened to Adam, and his descendants. Lucifer asks the Prince for permission to persecute Adam and Eve. Once authorized, he relentlessly pursues his targets, putting them through many trials, but persistent trust in the Prince ends well.

Job 42:12 "The Lord blessed the latter part of Job's life more than the former part..."

2   *Passport Please* takes the position that Adam was fundamentally different than any humans who inhabited the earth earlier. See note 5 on page 237.

3   John 8:44b [Jesus said regarding Lucifer] "when he speaks, he speaks his native language, for he is a liar and the father of lies."

4   Romans 6:16 "you are slaves of the one whom you obey"

5   Job 42:1-2 "Job replied to the Lord: 'I know that you can do all things; no purpose of yours can be thwarted.'"

Psalm 33:11 "the plans of the Lord stand firm forever, the purposes of his heart through all generations."

6   John 15:18 [Jesus said] "If the world hates you, keep in mind that it hated me first."

Pages 31 to 38   *5: Rule 1 – Family First*

1   Genesis 2:8 "Now the Lord God had planted a garden in the east, in Eden; and there he put the man he had formed."

Matthew 12:33 [Jesus said] "Make a tree good and its fruit will be good, or make a tree bad and its fruit will be bad, for a tree is recognized by its fruit."

2. As a resident of the Kingdom proper, the Prince can live and move in higher dimensions than humans of earth. Barriers and constraints of earth are inconsequential to Kingdom residents. See note/page: 3/300 and 3/308.

John 8:23 "You are from below; I [Jesus] am from above. You are of this world; I am not of this world."

John 20:19 " On the evening of that first day of the week, when the disciples were together, with the *doors locked* for fear of the Jews, Jesus came and stood among them and said, 'Peace be with you!'"

Luke 4:29-30 "They got up, drove him [Jesus] out of the town...in order to throw him down the cliff. But he walked right through the crowd and went on his way."

John 13:36 "Simon Peter asked him, 'Lord, where are you going?' Jesus replied, 'Where I am going, you cannot follow now, but you will follow later.'"

3. Waters above the sky are like a moat. (note 3, page 241)

4. The King wants a family of human children (see note 6, page 228) and they will have a seat at his table...

Ephesians 2:6 "God raised us up with Christ and seated us with him in the heavenly realms in Christ Jesus."

5. Genesis 2:19 "Now the Lord God had formed out of the ground all the wild animals and all the birds in the sky. He brought them to the man to see what he would name them; and whatever the man called each living creature, that was its name."

6. Physicists have identified at least eleven dimensions in our universe. Humans can only move freely in three of them. See note 2, page 226.

Appendix 2: Endnotes

[7] Genesis 2:9 "The Lord God made all kinds of trees grow out of the ground—trees that were pleasing to the eye and good for food. In the middle of the garden were the tree of life and the tree of the knowledge of good and evil."

[8] Genesis 2:16-17 "And the Lord God commanded the man, 'You are free to eat from any tree in the garden; but you must not eat from the tree of the knowledge of good and evil, for when you eat from it you will certainly die.'"

[9] Genesis 2:24 "a man will leave his father and mother and be united to his wife, and they will become one flesh."

Ephesians 5:25 "Husbands, love your wives, just as Christ loved the church and gave himself up for her"

[10] Psalm 115:16 "The highest heavens belong to the Lord, but the earth he has given to man."

Pages 39 to 44   *6: Betrayal*

[1] When given permission, some heavenly beings have the ability to enter into human beings and even animals.

Mark 5:12-13 "The demons begged Jesus, "Send us among the pigs; allow us to go into them." He gave them permission, and the impure spirits came out and went into the pigs."

Matthew 12:43-44 [Jesus said] When an impure spirit comes out of a person, it goes through arid places seeking rest and does not find it. Then it says, 'I will return to the house I left.'

Passport Please takes the position that Lucifer entered into an innocent snake to accomplish his plan, much as he did later with Judas...

John 13:27 "As soon as Judas took the bread, Satan entered into him."

2. Eve misquoted the instructions the Prince had given Adam, and Satan pounced on her uncertainty.

Genesis 3:2-3 (Eve speaking to Lucifer, who appeared as a serpent) "but God did say, 'You must not eat fruit from the tree that is in the middle of the garden, *and you must not touch it*, or you will die.'"

3. Genesis 3:4-5 "You will not certainly die," the serpent said to the woman. For God knows that when you eat from it your eyes will be opened, and you will be like God, knowing good and evil."

4. Rather than confessing, Eve rationalized her actions.

Proverbs 30:20 "This is the way of an adulteress, she eats and wipes her mouth and says 'I've done nothing wrong.'"

5. Adam was not tricked by Lucifer. He made a conscious choice to disobey the Prince.

1 Timothy 2:14 "And Adam was not the one deceived; it was the woman who was deceived and became a sinner."

6. Proverbs 1:7 "The fear of the Lord is the beginning of knowledge"

7. The Prince said he will send a "crusher" from the descendants of Eve, a human, who will destroy Lucifer.

Genesis 3:15 "And I [God] will put enmity between you [Lucifer] and the woman [Eve], and between your offspring and hers; he will crush your head, and you will strike his heel."

Appendix 2: Endnotes

When God said "your offspring" to Lucifer, he was referring to offspring of the Nephilim from Lucifer's army, and their descendants. See note 2, page 257.

[8] Romans 6:23 "For the wages of sin is death"

Ezekiel 18:20 "The soul who sins is the one who will die."

Pages 45 to 52   7: Consequences

[1] Genesis 3:21 "The Lord God made garments of skin for Adam and his wife and clothed them."

Hebrews 9:22 "without the shedding of blood there is no forgiveness."

Passport Please takes the position that when the Prince killed the animals in the garden, he established the Biblical pattern for how the deadly consequences for crimes against the kingdom can be borne by an innocent, willing substitute from their household. These animals were innocent of any wrongdoing. As beasts of burden, they were willing to carry their master's burdens, and the animals were part of the human's household.

The "kinsman redeemer" pattern was made part of Jewish law in Leviticus 25, where a blood relative (*your kin*) who was qualified (*he had the money, free of debt*), could redeem someone's lost property, if they wanted (*they were willing*).

A kinsman redeemer "redeemed" a relative out of a situation from which they were unable to extract themselves. The animals killed in Genesis were the first kinsman redeemers, extracting Adam and Eve from the death penalty.

Leviticus 25:23-28 "The land must not be sold permanently, because the land is mine and you are but aliens and tenants. Throughout the country that you hold as a possession, you must provide for the redemption of the land. If one of your countrymen becomes poor and sells some of his property, his nearest relative is to come and redeem what his countryman has sold. If, however, a man has no one to redeem it for him but he himself prospers and acquires sufficient means to redeem it, he is to determine the value for the years since he sold it and refund the balance to the man to whom he sold it; he can then go back to his own property. But if he does not acquire the means to repay him, what he sold will remain in the possession of the buyer until the Year of Jubilee. It will be returned in the Jubilee, and he can then go back to his property."

Leviticus 25:49 "any blood relative in his clan may redeem him"

Joseph, son of Jacob, Genesis 37-50 is also a kinsman redeemer, sent ahead by circumstances to save his family and his nation from death. See note 4 on page 264.

Boaz, the rich Jew in the book of Ruth, also fits the pattern, as does Jesus, the ultimate kinsman redeemer.

Ruth 3:20 (Ruth speaking of Boaz) "That man is our close relative, he is one of our kinsman redeemers."

1 John 4:10 "This is love: not that we loved God, but that he loved us and sent his Son as an atoning sacrifice for our sins."

[2] Hebrews 10:1,4 "The law is only a shadow of the good things that are coming—not the realities themselves. For this reason it can never, by the same sacrifices repeated

endlessly year after year, make perfect those who draw near to worship ... It is impossible for the blood of bulls and goats to take away sins."

Hebrews 9:12 "He [Christ] did not enter [God's presence] by means of the blood of goats and calves; but he entered the Most Holy Place once for all by his own blood, thus obtaining eternal redemption."

3. Life after death for animals? The Bible does not give many details. We know that the King cares deeply for animals. He saved Noah's family, and the entire animal kingdom. After they left from the ark, the King declared six times in a row that he was making an everlasting covenant with humans *and* with every living being on the earth. He specifically called out domesticated and wild animals and birds. (Genesis 9:8-17)

Psalm 36:6b "Oh, Lord, you preserve both people and animals."

4. Genesis 3:22-23 "And the Lord God said, "The man has now become like one of us, knowing good and evil. He must not be allowed to reach out his hand and take also from the tree of life and eat, and live forever. So the Lord God banished him from the Garden of Eden to work the ground from which he had been taken."

5. Hebrews 9:27 "Just as man is destined to die once, and after that to face judgment"

6. Luke 4:5-6 "The devil led him up to a high place and showed him in an instant all the kingdoms of the world. And he said to him, 'I will give you all their authority and splendor; for it has been given to me, and I can give it to anyone I want to.'"

Jesus did not challenge Lucifer's statement of ownership of the earth, above; however, God said he is the ultimate owner of the earth and promises as our kinsman redeemer, to redeem the earth. See note 1, page 249.

Leviticus 25:23-24 "The land must not be sold permanently, because the land is mine and you are but aliens and my tenants. Throughout the country that you hold as a possession, you must provide for the redemption of the land."

7   Ephesians 6:12 "For our struggle is not against flesh and blood, but against the rulers, against the authorities, against the powers of this dark world and against the spiritual forces of evil in the heavenly realms."

8   Genesis 3:22 "And the Lord God said, "The man has now become like one of us, knowing good and evil. He must not be allowed to reach out his hand and take also from the tree of life and eat, and live forever."

9   Terms of significant land deals were written and sealed.

Jeremiah 32:9-11 "so I bought the field at Anathoth from my cousin Hanamel and weighed out for him seventeen shekels of silver. I signed and sealed the deed, had it witnessed and weighed out the silver on the scales. I took the deed of purchase - the sealed copy containing the terms and conditions, as well as the unsealed copy."

Passport Please takes the position that the plan to recover Adam's lost inheritance was written down and kept safe in the Kingdom until the time it was needed.

The seven-sealed scroll of Revelation contains the terms on which Adam's lost inheritance may be redeemed.

Appendix 2: Endnotes

This is the "mortgage for the earth." See *35 Simple Studies on the Major Themes in Revelation,* M.R. DeHaan, MD, (1946) page 94

The mortgage for the earth will be opened near the end of time, to provide the legal basis for returning the earth to the Royal family.

Revelation 5:6-7 "I saw a lamb, looking as if it had been slain... He came and took the scroll from the right hand of him who sat on the throne."

[10] Genesis 3:19 "dust you are, and to dust you will return."

Hebrews 9:27 "people are destined to die once, and after that to face judgment"

Pages 53 to 60 *8: Into the Wild*

[1] Genesis 3:24 "After he drove the man out, he placed on the east side of the garden of Eden cherubim [four-winged angel] and a flaming sword flashing back and forth to guard the way to the tree of life."

[2] Isaiah 28:24-29 "When a farmer plows ... [followed by a summary of instructions for plowing and planting cumin, wheat, caraway, barley, spelt, and grain] His God instructs him and teaches him the right way. [more instructions on threshing and grinding grains, for bread] All this also comes from the Lord Almighty, whose plan is wonderful, whose wisdom is magnificent."

[3] Romans 3:23 "for all have sinned and fall short of the glory of God"

Romans 6:23 "For the wages of sin is death"

[4] The place of the dead, known in the Greek as "Hades" has two distinct zones — a comfortable one with cool

drinks and an uncomfortable one with fire and torment.

The early church father, Tertullian (160-220 AD), referred to the comfortable Hades as the "refrigerium interim." "Refrigerium" is the origin of the words "refreshment" and "refrigerator." Jesus referred to the comfortable Hades as "paradise"

Luke 23:43 "Jesus answered him [the thief dying on the cross next to him], "Truly I tell you, today you will be with me in paradise."

Passport Please calls these Kingdom Arrivals Lounge (KAL) and the Lower Waiting Room (LWR). The KAL is for those who have, during their lives, committed themselves to the Kingdom. The LWR is for citizens of earth who declined the opportunity to be part of the Kingdom. We know these places are only temporary accommodations, since all deceased humans in both places will eventually rise out from there.

1 Thessalonians 4:16b "the dead in Christ will rise first."

Revelation 20:13 "death and Hades gave up the dead that were in them"

An un-crossable chasm separates the LWR and the KAL, as Jesus tells us in his narrative about Lazarus and the rich man...

Luke 16:19-31 "There was a rich man who was dressed in purple and fine linen and lived in luxury every day. At his gate was laid a beggar named Lazarus,* covered with sores and longing to eat what fell from the rich man's table. Even the dogs came and licked his sores. The time came when the beggar died and the angels carried him to Abraham's side. The rich man also died and was buried. In Hades, where he was in torment, he looked up and saw

Appendix 2: Endnotes

Abraham far away, with Lazarus by his side. So he called to him, 'Father Abraham, have pity on me and send Lazarus to dip the tip of his finger in water and cool my tongue, because I am in agony in this fire.' But Abraham replied, 'Son, remember that in your lifetime you received your good things, while Lazarus received bad things, but now he is comforted here and you are in agony. And besides all this, between us and you a great chasm has been set in place, so that those who want to go from here to you cannot, nor can anyone cross over from there to us.' He answered, 'Then I beg you, father, send Lazarus to my family, for I have five brothers. Let him warn them, so that they will not also come to this place of torment.' Abraham replied, 'They have Moses and the Prophets; let them listen to them.' 'No, father Abraham,' he said, 'but if someone from the dead goes to them, they will repent.' He said to him, 'If they do not listen to Moses and the Prophets, they will not be convinced even if someone rises from the dead.'"

* Jesus told many stories which may not have been about a specific person, i.e. *"There was a man, who..."* The narrative above is the only story (or parable) that Jesus told in which a main character had a name, in this case, Lazarus. If this story is fictional, then "Lazarus" was very confusing name to use, since Jesus had a real-life friend named Lazarus who died and came back from the dead (John 11:1-44). *Passport Please* takes the position that Jesus told the above, a true story about real people and real places, to describe the KAL and LWR, and tell how people can end-up in one place or the other.

[5] Faithfully offering blood sacrifices, as the Prince had instructed, secured a place in the kingdom for Abel.

Hebrews 11:4 "By faith Abel offered God a better sacrifice than Cain did. By faith he was commended as a righteous man, when God spoke well of his offerings."

6 *Passport Please* takes the position that the 'variance in time zones' is a benefit to humans who have died and are waiting in the KAL or in the lower waiting room. For example, Abel's was the first death recorded in the Bible, approximately 3850 BCE on earth (FST), nearly 6,000 years ago. From the perspective of Kingdom Standard Time, that was six days ago. What we call 2000 AD is around midnight Saturday night in KST, so Abel has been waiting in the KAL longer than any human, but he has only been there since last Monday, in KST. See note 5 on page 242.

7 Genesis 4:10 [God said] "What have you done? Listen! Your brother's blood cries out to me from the ground."

8 An "outlaw" is one who lives outside the responsibilities of the law. They give up the law's protection as well, giving the outlaw the same legal status as a wild animal. *Whatever Happened to Justice?*, Richard Maybury, (2004) Chapter 6.

9 Both the King and Prince used sarcasm on occasion.

Job 38:18, 21 "Have you [Job] comprehended the vast expanses of the earth? Tell me, if you know all this. Surely you know, for you were already born! You have lived so many years!"

Mark 7:9 [Jesus to the religious leaders] "You have a fine way of setting aside the commands of God in order to observe your own traditions!"

Appendix 2: Endnotes

[10] The Royals protect their family, even when it is undeserved.

Genesis 4:15 "if anyone kills Cain, he will suffer vengeance seven times over.' Then the Lord put a mark on Cain so that no one who found him would kill him."

Pages 61 to 66   *9: Intimate Assault*

[1] Genesis 5:4 "Adam lived 800 years and had other sons and daughters."

Genesis 1:29 "[God] said to them, "Be fruitful and increase in number; fill* the earth and subdue it.

* The King James version says "replenish" the earth. Since the King had already restored the plant and animal kingdoms, the only thing Adam and Eve could now "replenish" was the human population of earth, which had been wiped out and forgotten. See note 2 page 231.

[2] Lucifer's rebels intermarried with women on the earth.

Genesis 6:1-2, 4-5a "When men began to increase in number on the earth and daughters were born to them, the sons of God saw that the daughters of men were beautiful, and they married any of them they chose ... The Nephilim were on the earth in those days—and also afterward—when the sons of God [a common reference to angels] went to the daughters of men and had children by them. They were the heroes of old, men of renown. The Lord saw how great man's wickedness on the earth had become"

[3] Genesis 6:5,7 "The Lord saw how great man's wickedness on earth had become ... I will wipe mankind ... from the face of the earth."

4   Genesis 6:9 "Noah was a righteous man, blameless among the people of his time, and he walked with God."

"Blameless among the people," is more clearly translated as "perfect in his generations." That refers to an unblemished family line, a direct descendant of Adam.

5   Those in the lower waiting room can *see* across the chasm into the citizens' arrival lounge, but no one can cross over. See note 4 on page 253.

Luke 16:23 "In hell, [original Greek is "Hades"] where he was in torment, he looked up and *saw Abraham far away*, with Lazarus by his side."

Luke 13:28 "There will be weeping there, and gnashing of teeth, when you *see* Abraham, Isaac and Jacob and all the prophets in the kingdom of God, but you yourselves thrown out."

6   Genesis 9:18-27 tells of Noah's episode of drunkenness, and how when he realized that Ham had gossiped about him to his brothers, Noah cursed his youngest son Ham, who then packed up and left.

7   Hundreds of years after the flood, giant descendants of the Nephilim inhabited the earth—but how? All humans, except those in the ark, had perished in the flood.

Genesis 7:21 "Every living thing that moved on land perished—birds, livestock, wild animals, all the creatures that swarm over the earth, and all mankind."

Numbers 13:17, 32-33 "Moses sent them to explore Canaan… And they spread among the Israelites a bad report about the land they had explored. They said, 'The land we explored devours those living in it. All the people we saw there are of great size. We saw the

Appendix 2: Endnotes

Nephilim there (the descendants of Anak come from the Nephilim). We seemed like grasshoppers in our own eyes, and we looked the same to them.'"

Passport Please takes the position that a human of Nephilim descent was a passenger on Noah's ark. Most, if not all of the evil giants mentioned in the Bible are descendants of Noah's son, Ham.

In Genesis 10:15, "Canaan [Ham's son] was father of ... the Amorites." In Amos 2:9, we learn that these Amorites were "tall as cedars." In Deuteronomy 3:1-11 we learn that one of the Amorite kings, Og, King of Bashan, was so tall, that his bed was 14 feet long and 6 feet wide. In Genesis 10:13-14, "Egypt" (another son of Ham, Genesis 10:6) was father of "the Kasluhites (from whom the Philistines came)," and the most famous Philistine in the Bible was a giant—Goliath.

1 Samuel 17:4 "A champion named Goliath, who was from Gath, came out of the Philistine camp. His height was six cubits and a span" (9 feet, 9 inches tall)

Ham's descendants also established or settled in Ninevah, Babylon, Assyria, Sodom, and Gomorrah (Genesis 10:10, 11, 19). These were all famous in the Bible as hotbeds of evil. One of Ham's sons was named Canaan. Hundreds of years later, when Moses sent spies to search out the land of Canaan (see Numbers 13, in this note), they found the land was populated with giants.

We know Ham's father, Noah, was of pure lineage (note 4, page 257), but we are told virtually nothing about Ham's wife—not even her name.

Based on the Nephilim-like characteristics in so many of Ham's descendants, *Passport Please* takes the position that Ham's wife carried Nephilim DNA onto the ark.

It is possible, though not mentioned in the Bible, that the "Sons of God" (Genesis 6:1-2) came to earth *again* to marry human women after the flood. *Passport Please* allows for that possibility (see novel, page 71).

Pages 67 to 72   *10: Three Prongs*

1. Genesis 11:4 "Come, let us build ourselves a city, with a tower that reaches to the heavens, so that we may make a name for ourselves"

2. The earth was only temporarily turned over to Satan. The King has the right to redeem it, or "buy it back." (see note 1 on page 249)

   Leviticus 25:13 "In this year of Jubilee, everyone is to return to his own property."

3. The King's staff was concerned no one was qualified to fulfill or enforce the provisions of the mortgage.

   Revelation 5:2-4 "And I saw a mighty angel proclaiming in a loud voice, 'Who is worthy to break the seals and open the scroll?' But no one in heaven or on earth or under the earth could open the scroll or even look inside it. I wept and wept because no one was found who was worthy to open the scroll or look inside."

4. The mortgage was held, to be accessed in the future.

   Jeremiah 32:14 "This is what the Lord Almighty, the God of Israel says: Take these documents, both sealed and unsealed copies of the deed of purchase and put them in a clay jar so they will last a long time."

Appendix 2: Endnotes

Revelation 5:1 "Then I saw in the right hand of him who sat on the throne a scroll with writing on both sides and sealed with seven seals."

5   Unrestrained sexual activity is part of Lucifer's strategy. Humans can follow this path, and its consequences, if they choose.

Romans 1:24-26 "Therefore God gave them over in the sinful desires of their hearts to sexual impurity ... God gave them over to shameful lusts."

Pages 73 to 78 *11: National IDs*

1   Abram was Noah's great-great-great-great-great-great-great-great grandson. Noah's male descendants are listed in Genesis 10:21 to 11:26, along with the ages at which they fathered their sons, so it is a matter of simple arithmetic to show that Abram (AKA Abraham) was 58 years old when Noah finally died.

2   Genesis 12:2 "The Lord said to Abram ... I will make you into a great nation"

Genesis 12:3 "all peoples on earth will be blessed through you."

3   Genesis 16:11-12 "The angel of the Lord also said to her [Hagar]: 'You are now pregnant and you will give birth to a son. You shall name him Ishmael, for the Lord has heard of your misery. He will be a wild donkey of a man; his hand will be against everyone and everyone's hand against him, and he will live in hostility toward all his brothers.'"

4   Genesis 17:17b "[Abraham] said to himself, 'Will a son be born to a man a hundred years old? Will Sarah bear a child at the age of ninety?'"

5   Deuteronomy 7:3 "Do not intermarry with them [the non-Israelite nations] Do not give your daughters to their sons or take their daughters for your sons."

6   Genesis 34 tells the riveting story of how Jacob's daughter Dinah was violated by a young man, in a region where the local men were uncircumcised. She called out to her brothers who took care of the offender, along with every man in his city, in an unusual and violent way.

7   Since Abram was 58 when his forefather Noah died (note 1, above), *Passport Please* takes the position that Noah and Abram knew each other well, and that Noah had told Abram about the Nephilim, so that when the Prince gave Abraham circumcision instructions, he understood the importance of protecting the Royal bloodline.

8   While DNA from both parents contributes to establishing the traits of a child, the child's bloodline is established by it's father. In *The Chemistry of the Blood,* (Grand Rapids, MI, Zondervan, 1943) pages 30-32, M.R. DeHaan, MD quotes from *Williams Practice of Obstetrics, Nurses Handbook of Obstetrics, Howell's Textbook of Physiology.*

All essentially say that the mother's blood has no contact with the baby in the womb, thanks to the placenta, also known as "the blood barrier."

All nutrients pass through the blood vessel walls from the mother's circulatory system to the baby's system, but the mother's blood never mixes with the child's. They are completely separate circulatory systems.

Any person with a Jewish *mother* is considered to be Jewish. This view is rooted in Jewish tradition.

Appendix 2: Endnotes

With Mary as His mother, Jesus was undeniably Jewish, even while He is part of his father's royal bloodline.

9   Exodus 34:15-16 "Be careful not to make a treaty with those who live in the land; for when they prostitute themselves to their gods and sacrifice to them, they will invite you and you will eat their sacrifices. And when you choose some of their daughters as wives for your sons and those daughters prostitute themselves to their gods, they will lead your sons to do the same."

10 The King knew Israel would not obey his command to marry only within the nation. He even predicts it and writes a song about Israel's upcoming rejection of Him.

Deuteronomy 31:16 "these people will soon prostitute themselves to the foreign gods of the land they are entering. They will forsake me and break the covenant I made with them.'"

Deuteronomy 31:19 "Now write down for yourselves this song and teach it to the Israelites and have them sing it, so that it may be a witness for me against them."

The lengthy musical indictment of Israel's unfaithfulness (Deuteronomy 32:1-43) ends with the assurance that the King will, in the end, save his people. The King is not surprised by human unfaithfulness, and he provides a way to escape punishment.

11 If a father is of pure royal blood, then the child is royal, regardless of the mother's bloodline. See note 8, above.

Isaiah 7:14 "Therefore the Lord himself will give you a sign: The virgin will be with child and will give birth to a son, and will call him Immanuel." [Immanuel means "God with us"]

Pages 79 to 86   12: Loyalty Lessons

1. Genesis 22:1-18 is the story of Abraham almost sacrificing his son Isaac.

2. Jacob wrestled with the Prince, as did the nation of Israel.

   Genesis 32:26 "The man [the Prince] said 'Let me go ...' but Jacob replied, 'I will not let you go unless you bless me.'"

   Genesis 35:10 "God said to him, your name is Jacob, but you will no longer be called Jacob; your name will be Israel." [Israel means "he struggles with God"]

3. 1 Peter 5:8 "Your enemy the devil prowls around like a roaring lion looking for someone to devour."

4. The story of Joseph is in Genesis chapters 37-50.

   M.R. DeHaan describes Joseph as a "picture" of Jesus. Rejected by his own people, he suffers undeserved punishment and ultimately welcomes everyone who will confess their guilt and accept his provision. See M.R. DeHaan, MD, *Portraits of Christ in Genesis* (Grand Rapids, MI, Zondervan, 1966) Chapter 22

   Genesis 50:20 "You [Joseph's brothers] intended to harm me [Joseph], but God intended it for good to accomplish what is now being done, the saving of many lives."

5. Exodus 1:6, 11-13 "Now Joseph and all his brothers and all that generation died, but the Israelites were fruitful and multiplied greatly and became exceedingly numerous, so that the land was filled with them .... So they [the Egyptians] put slave masters over them to oppress them with forced labor, and they built Pithom and Rameses as store cities for Pharaoh.

Appendix 2: Endnotes

But the more they were oppressed, the more they multiplied and spread; so the Egyptians came to dread the Israelites and worked them ruthlessly."

6 Genesis 4:12 "When you [Cain] work the ground, it will no longer yield its crops for you."

7 Genesis 15:13 "Know for certain that your descendants will be strangers in a country not their own, and they will be enslaved and mistreated for 400 years." [prediction, looking forward]

Exodus 12:40 "Now the length of time the Israelite people lived in Egypt was 430 years." [fulfillment, looking backwards]

8 Exodus 1:22 "Then Pharaoh gave this order to all his people: 'Every boy that is born you must throw into the Nile, but let every girl live.'"

Exodus 2:3 "But when she [Moses' mother] could hide him no longer, she got a papyrus basket for him and coated it with tar and pitch. Then she placed the child in it and put it among the reeds along the bank of the Nile"

Exodus 2:10 "When the child grew older, she took him to Pharaoh's daughter and he became her son. She named him Moses, saying, 'I drew him out of the water.'"

Pages 87 to 92   13: Escape from Tyranny

1 Communications between the King and Moses through the burning bush is described in Exodus 3.

A "wormhole" is a dimensional "shortcut" from one region of the universe to another. See Brian Greene, *The Elegant Universe*, (New York, Random House, 1999) 265, 268

2   Exodus 11:5 "Every firstborn son in Egypt will die"

The story of the Passover is found in Exodus 11 & 12.

3   Exodus 13:21 "a pillar of cloud to guide them ... a pillar of fire to give them light so that they could travel by day or night."

Exodus 12:37 "The Israelites journeyed from Rameses to Sukkoth. There were about six hundred thousand men on foot, besides women and children."

The nation of Israel is estimated at 600,000 men, plus 600,000 women, plus 800,000 children, about 2,000,000 persons.

4   Exodus 14:5 "Pharaoh and his officials changed their minds ... 'What have we done? We've let the Israelites go and have lost their services!'"

5   Israel's escape through the Red Sea is described in Exodus 14:19-31. The exact location of the Red Sea crossing has been a topic of much speculation. In 1978, American Ron Wyatt discovered Egyptian chariot wheels and other artifacts on the bottom of the Gulf of Aqaba (part of the Red Sea). www.wyattmuseum.com

The Egyptians trapped Israel on the west side of the Gulf, on the wide beach at modern-day Nuweiba. Mountains to the north and south, and only one entrance through the mountains from the west, left the Israelites trapped against the sea. (see map) The miles-wide beach on the Gulf and the narrow gap through the imposing mountains can clearly be seen on Google Earth.

Appendix 2: Endnotes

Ten miles across the Red Sea is the land of Midian, in modern day Saudi Arabia. Moses had raised a family in Midian (Exodus 2:15, 21-22). Crossing the Red Sea at this location was a homecoming for him. Before he had gone to Egypt to lead Israel, Moses sent his wife Zipporah to her father's house in Midian (Exodus 18:2). After Israel crossed the Red Sea and camped at Mt Sinai (note 2 on page 268), Moses was reunited with his wife.

Exodus 18:5 "Jethro, Moses' father-in-law, together with Moses' sons and wife, came to him in the wilderness, where he was camped near the mountain of God."

Pages 93 to 98   14: Law School

[1]   "Manna" in Hebrew is translated as, "what is it."

Psalm 78:24-25 "he rained down manna for the people to eat, he gave them the grain of heaven. Men ate the bread of angels; he sent them all the food they could eat."

Centuries later, Jesus compared himself to manna.

John 6:33-35a "'For the bread of God is the bread that comes down from heaven and gives life to the world.' 'Sir,' they said, 'always give us this bread.' Then Jesus declared, "I am the bread of life.""

[2]   Most Bible maps show Mt Sinai in the south-central part of the Sinai Peninsula, in Egypt; however, the Apostle Paul tells us that Mount Sinai is actually across the Red Sea in modern-day Saudi Arabia, which correlates to the Red Sea crossing at the Gulf of Aqaba. (note 5, page 266)

Galatians 4:25 "Now Hagar stands for Mount Sinai in Arabia and corresponds to the present city of Jerusalem, because she is in slavery with her children."

[3]   Psalm 104:2 "He [God] wraps himself in light as with a garment"

Revelation 21:23 "The city does not need the sun or the moon to shine upon it, for the glory of God gives light"

1 Timothy 6:15-16 "God, the blessed and only Ruler, the King of kings and Lord of lords, who alone is immortal and who lives in unapproachable light, whom no one has seen or can see."

James 1:17 "Every good and perfect gift is from above, coming down from the Father of the heavenly lights, who does not change..."

Appendix 2: Endnotes

> Exodus 33:20-23 "he [God] said, 'you [Moses] cannot see my face, for no one may see me and live ... There is a place near me where you may stand on a rock. When my glory passes by, I will put you in a cleft in the rock and cover you with my hand until I have passed by. Then I will remove my hand and you will see my back; but my face must not be seen.'"

See note 7 on page 238.

4   Exodus 33:11 "The Lord would speak to Moses face to face, as one speaks to a friend."

5   Deuteronomy 7:6 "For you [Israel] are a people holy to the Lord your God. The Lord your God has chosen you out of all the peoples on the face of the earth to be his people, his treasured possession."

Passport Please takes the position that the ten commandments were not just laws to be followed, but (at least the first four) were like vows between lovers... 1) be faithful to me, 2) love no one more than me, 3) when you take our family name, carry it with honor, 4) set aside a weekly 'date' with me. The King loved the Israelites so much, he considered their relationship to be a marriage.

Isaiah 54:5 "...your Maker is your husband – the Lord Almighty is his name."

Jeremiah 31:32 "I [God] was a husband to them [Israel]"

Isaiah 62:5 "As a young man marries a young woman, so will your Builder [God] marry you [Israel]; as a bridegroom rejoices over his bride, so will your God rejoice over you."

6   Exodus 31:18 "When the Lord finished speaking to Moses on Mount Sinai, he gave him the two tablets of

the covenant law, the tablets of stone inscribed by the finger of God."

7. Exodus 32:1-7 "When the people saw that Moses was so long in coming down from the mountain, they gathered around Aaron and said, 'Come, make us gods who will go before us. As for this fellow Moses who brought us up out of Egypt, we don't know what has happened to him.' Aaron answered them, 'Take off the gold earrings that your wives, your sons and your daughters are wearing, and bring them to me.' So all the people took off their earrings and brought them to Aaron. He took what they handed him and made it into an idol cast in the shape of a calf, fashioning it with a tool. Then they said, 'These are your gods, Israel, who brought you up out of Egypt.' When Aaron saw this, he built an altar in front of the calf and announced, 'Tomorrow there will be a festival to the Lord.' So the next day the people rose early and sacrificed burnt offerings and presented fellowship offerings. Afterward they sat down to eat and drink and got up to indulge in revelry. Then the Lord said to Moses, 'Go down, because your people, whom you brought up out of Egypt, have become corrupt.'"

8. Romans 3:20 "Therefore no one will be declared righteous in his sight by observing the law; rather, through the law we become conscious of sin."

9. Starting in Numbers 3, there is a detailed description of the construction and operations of the tabernacle, the "portable Justice Center." The tabernacle centralized the sacrifices, so they would be done correctly, and in order.

Leviticus 17:5 "This is so the Israelites will bring to the Lord the sacrifices they are now making in the open fields. They must bring them to the priest, that is, to the

Appendix 2: Endnotes

Lord, at the entrance to the tent of meeting and sacrifice them as fellowship offerings."

[10] By saving the firstborn from all twelve tribes of Israel in the Passover, the King effectively "bought" their lives for himself.

Exodus 13:2 "Consecrate to me every firstborn male. The first offspring of every womb among the Israelites belongs to me, whether man or animal."

Numbers 3:39-48 details how God "traded" the firstborns he had saved, for the entire tribe of Levi. The Levites were then tasked with performing service in the Tabernacle, and later, the Temple.

[11] Matthew 22:29 "Jesus replied, 'You are in error because you do not know the Scriptures or the power of God.'"

Pages 99 to 104   *15: Freedom Ahead*

[1] Deuteronomy 8:15 "He led you through the vast and dreadful desert, that thirsty and waterless land, with its venomous snakes and scorpions."

Numbers 11:14-15 "I [Moses] cannot carry all these people by myself; the burden is too heavy for me. If this is how you [God] are going to treat me, put me to death right now."

[2] Numbers 13:17, 32-33 (quoted in note 7 on page 258) tells the story of the report of the spies sent into Canaan, including confirmation of Nephilim-descended giants in the land.

[3] Numbers 14:2-3 "All the Israelites grumbled …'Why is the Lord bringing us to this land only to let us fall by the sword?'"

4. Numbers 14:11-12 "How long will these people treat me [God] with contempt? How long will they refuse to believe in me, in spite of all the miraculous signs I have performed among them? I will strike them down with a plague ... but I will make you into a nation greater and stronger than they."

5. Numbers 14:15-16 (Moses to God) "If you put these people to death all at one time, the nations who have heard this report about you will say, 'The Lord was not able to bring these people into the land he promised them on oath; so he slaughtered them in the desert.'"

    Numbers 14:17-18 "The Lord is slow to anger, abounding in love and forgiving sin and rebellion. Yet he does not leave the guilty unpunished."

    Isaiah 1:18 "'Come now, let us reason together,' says the Lord."

6. Minors are not tried as adults in kingdom justice.

    Numbers 14:29 "In this desert your bodies will fall—every one of you twenty years old or more who was counted in the census and who has grumbled against me"

    Numbers 14:33 "Your children will be shepherds here for forty years, suffering for your unfaithfulness, until the last of your bodies lies in the desert."

7. Numbers 20:2-12 tells the story of Moses deciding to ignore God's directive to command the rock to yield water.

8. The King always let Moses plead his case, but sometimes, even for God, enough is enough!

    Deuteronomy 3:26 "'That is enough,' the Lord said. 'Do not speak to me anymore about this matter.'"

Appendix 2: Endnotes

[9] Deuteronomy 3:28 "But commission Joshua, and encourage and strengthen him, for he will lead this people across and will cause them to inherit the land that you will see."

[10] Jude 9 "But even the archangel Michael, when he was disputing with the devil about the body of Moses, did not dare to bring a slanderous accusation against him, but said, 'The Lord rebuke you!'"

[11] Moses couldn't lead the nation of Israel into the land promised by the Prince, but hundreds of years later he played a role in opening the way to an even greater promised land, for an even greater number of people. (see novel, page 136) The King decided that getting Israel into the Kingdom by themselves was good, but it was "too small" a plan. The King wanted to reach out to every human on the planet.

Isaiah 49:6 [The Lord says] "It is too small a thing for you to... restore the tribes of Jacob and bring back those of Israel... I will also make you a light for the Gentiles, that my salvation may reach to the ends of the earth."

Pages 105 to 112   *16: School of Government*

[1] Joshua 1:4 "Your territory will extend from the desert to Lebanon, and from the great river, the Euphrates—all the Hittite country—to the Great Sea on the west."

Genesis 15:18 "On that day the Lord made a covenant with Abram and said, 'To your descendants I give this land, from the Wadi of Egypt to the great river, the Euphrates.'"

Exodus 23:31 and Numbers 34:1-12 also describe these boundaries.

2. Joshua 5:2-3, 7b-8 "At that time the Lord said to Joshua, 'Make flint knives and circumcise the Israelites again.' So Joshua made flint knives and circumcised the Israelites at Gibeath Haaraloth [Hebrew for "hill of foreskins"] …They were still uncircumcised because they had not been circumcised on the way. And after the whole nation had been circumcised, they remained where they were in camp until they were healed."

3. Joshua 2 tells the story of Rahab the prostitute who helped Joshua take the city of Jericho and who later joined the family of Israel.

4. Joshua 10 & 11 describe battles in which Israel was victorious, and some of which the King miraculously tipped the scales in Israel's favor, including crushing the enemy with hailstones and stopping the sun in the sky to extend the fighting time.

5. 1 Samuel 8:7 "they have rejected me [God] as their king."

6. 1 Samuel 8:10-18 "Samuel told all the words of the Lord to the people who were asking him for a king. He said, 'This is what the king who will reign over you will claim as his rights: He will [*draft your sons into the army, put your daughters to work for himself and he will take what you grow and give it to his friends. He will take your servants and your livestock for his own use*] and you yourselves will become his slaves. When that day comes, you will cry out for relief from the king you have chosen, but the Lord will not answer you in that day.'"

Appendix 2: Endnotes

[7] In all of recorded history up to 1900 AD, an estimated 133,147,000 people were murdered by governments that were mostly, but not exclusively, totalitarian. This does not count war combatants. Then, in the 20th century, 169,198,000 were added to the number of those murdered by governments. *Death by Government,* by R.J. Rummel (1994), chapters 1 and 2.

[8] The kingdom plan had always been that the Prince would establish and head his government on earth.

Isaiah 9:6-7 "For to us a child is born, to us a son is given, and the government will be on his shoulders. And he will be called Wonderful Counselor, Mighty God, Everlasting Father, Prince of Peace. Of the greatness of his government and peace there will be no end. He will reign on David's throne and over his kingdom, stablishing and upholding it with justice and righteousness from that time on and forever. The zeal of the Lord Almighty will accomplish this."

[9] 1 Kings 11:1-3 says Israel's King Solomon, regarded as the wisest man who ever lived, had over 700 wives, a great number of them from foreign countries of which God had specifically said "do not intermarry with them!"

Ezra 9:1-2 "'The people of Israel, including the priests and the Levites, have not kept themselves separate from the neighboring peoples ... They have mingled the holy race with the peoples around them.'"

Ezekiel 16:26,28,29,32,60,63 "You [Israel] engaged in prostitution with the Egyptians ... the Assyrians ... Babylonia ... You adulterous wife! You prefer strangers to your own husband! ... Yet I will remember the covenant I made with you ... I make atonement for you for all you have done"

Malachi 2:11, 15b "Judah has been unfaithful. A detestable thing has been committed in Israel and in Jerusalem: Judah has desecrated the sanctuary the Lord loves, by marrying women who worship a foreign god ... he [the Lord] was seeking godly offspring."

Passport Please takes the position that circumcision could have protected the Royal bloodline, if only Israel had obeyed the King's command not to intermarry.

10. Rahab the prostitute was an ancestor of Jesus, on both his mother and father's side. Matthew 1:5-16 details Joseph's genealogy. Luke 3:23-38 details Mary's genealogy.

11. In his attempt to "crush the Crusher," Lucifer was actually playing into God's hand. The Prophet Isaiah foretold that an innocent substitute would be punished, to pay the penalty earned by humans for their misdeeds, allowing justice to be fulfilled, and allowing humans to accept the pardon and go free.

Isaiah 53:5, 6b, 8b, 12b
"he was crushed for our iniquities"
"the Lord has laid on him the iniquity of us all."
"for the transgression of my people he was punished."
"he bore the sin of many"

Pages 113 to 120   *17: King's Crossing*

1. The Bible is not specific as to the year of Jesus' birth. The wise men from Persia told Herod the Great of Jesus' birth almost two years after Jesus' birth. (hence Herod's order to kill all Jewish males under 2 years old) Most historians date the death of Herod the Great around 4 BCE. For this reason, *Passport Please* takes the position that Jesus was born around 6 BCE.

Appendix 2: Endnotes

2 Luke 1:26b-31 "God sent the angel Gabriel to Nazareth, a town in Galilee, to a virgin pledged to be married to a man named Joseph, a descendant of David. The virgin's name was Mary. The angel went to her and said, 'Greetings, you who are highly favored! The Lord is with you.' Mary was greatly troubled at his words and wondered what kind of greeting this might be. But the angel said to her, 'Do not be afraid, Mary; you have found favor with God. You will conceive and give birth to a son, and you are to call him Jesus.'"

3 Matthew 2:1-2 "Magi from the east* came to Jerusalem and asked, 'Where is the one who has been born king of the Jews? We saw his star when it rose and have come to worship him.'"

   * The "wise men" were from Babylon (present-day Iraq) where centuries earlier, a Jewish government official named Daniel wrote the Bible's Book of Daniel.

4 Luke 2:13-15 "Suddenly a great company of the heavenly host appeared with the angel, praising God and saying, 'Glory to God in the highest heaven, and on earth peace to men on whom his favor rests.' When the angels had left them and gone into heaven, the shepherds said to one another, 'Let's go to Bethlehem'"

5 Isaiah 7:14 "the Lord himself will give you a sign: The virgin will conceive and give birth to a son, and will call him Immanuel" [Immanuel means "God with us"].

6 Matthew 2:13 "an angel of the Lord appeared to Joseph in a dream ... 'take the child and his mother and escape to Egypt ... for Herod is going to search for the child to kill him.'"

7 Joseph was Jesus' adoptive father. The Prime Minister of the Kingdom of Heaven was his biological father. Not surprisingly, this was hard for many to understand.

John 8:18-19 [Jesus, speaking to the Jewish leaders] "'...my other witness is the Father, who sent me.' Then they asked him, 'Where is your father?' 'You do not know me or my Father,' Jesus replied. 'If you knew me, you would know my Father also.'"

8 Mark 1:5 "The whole Judean countryside and all the people of Jerusalem went out to [John]. Confessing their sins, they were baptized by him in the Jordan River."

9 Renunciation of citizenship to one's old country and pledging allegiance to the new one, has historically been a requirement for naturalized citizenship.

Passport Please takes the position that baptism is the renunciation of one's old way of life, and of Lucifer himself, and it is oath of allegiance to heaven and a commitment to its ruler. See the similarities below.

<u>US Oath of Allegiance:</u> "I hereby declare, on oath, that I absolutely and entirely renounce and abjure all allegiance and fidelity to any foreign prince, potentate, state, or sovereignty of whom or which I have heretofore been a subject or citizen; that I will support and defend the Constitution and laws of the United States of America against all enemies, foreign and domestic; that I will bear true faith and allegiance to the same... and that I take this obligation freely without any mental reservation or purpose of evasion; so help me God."

www.uscis.gov, US Citizenship & Immigration Svcs

Appendix 2: Endnotes

Church of England baptism liturgy:

Questions from clergy to the person being baptized:

Do you reject the devil and all rebellion against God?
Do you renounce the deceit and corruption of evil?
Do you repent of the sins that separate us from God and neighbor?
Do you turn to Christ as Saviour?
Do you submit to Christ as Lord?
Do you come to Christ, the way, the truth and the life?

www.cofe.anglican.org, Church of England

Passport Please takes the position that baptism is also a "picture" of passing though the Crystal Sea, away from Lucifer and into the safety of the Kingdom, much like when the Israelites passed through the Red Sea into a land of safety, away from the tyrannical Pharaoh. It is also like the restoration of earth (note 1, page 240).

Prior to the death of Jesus, *Passport Please* refers to passing through the water as a "pre-qualification" for Kingdom citizenship. The qualified substitute, Jesus, must be put to death before a human's record of crimes against the Kingdom can actually be cleared.

10 Luke 15:7 "there will be more rejoicing in heaven over one sinner who repents than over ninety-nine righteous persons who do not need to repent."

11 James 4:4b "Anyone who chooses to be a friend of the world becomes an enemy of God."

Matthew 6:24a "No one can serve two masters."

12 Matthew 3:15 "Jesus replied, 'Let it be so now; it is proper for us to do this to fulfill all righteousness.' Then John consented."

13 The fabric of Heaven was *torn* at Jesus' baptism.

Mark 1:10 "As Jesus was coming up out of the water, he saw heaven being torn open and the Spirit descending on him like a dove."

A *tear* in the fabric of space is the basis for a "wormhole," or bridge, connecting to new spatial territories. Brian Greene, *The Elegant Universe*, (New York, Random House, 1999) 265, 268

14 John 1:32 "Then John gave this testimony: 'I saw the Spirit come down from heaven as a dove and remain on him.'"

15 Jeremiah 8:6 "No one repents of his wickedness, saying, 'What have I done?' Each pursues his own course like a horse charging into battle."

16 The Prime Minister speaks softly...

1 Kings 19:12 "After the earthquake came a fire, but the Lord was not in the fire. And after the fire came a gentle whisper."

Pages 121 to 124   *18: Summit Meeting*

1 Luke 4:1-2a "Jesus, full of the Holy Spirit, left the Jordan and was led by the Spirit into the wilderness, where for forty days he was tempted by the devil."

Isaiah 53:2 Jesus had "nothing in his appearance that we should desire him"

2 Lucifer offered Jesus all the kingdoms of the world, if Jesus would simply submit to Lucifer. Jesus did not deny that the world was Lucifer's to give as he chose. Neither did he submit.

Appendix 2: Endnotes

Luke 4:5-6 "The devil led him to a high place and showed him in an instant all the kingdoms of the world And he said to him, 'I will give you all their authority and splendor; it has been given to me, and I can give it to anyone I want to. If you worship me, it will all be yours."

Passport Please takes the position that Lucifer did not care so much about owning the world, but he knew that if the King's own son submitted to Lucifer as his superior, there would be no grounds to keep Lucifer and his rebels out of the Kingdom and it's leadership circle.

3   Luke 4:9 "The devil led him to Jerusalem and had him stand on the highest point of the temple. 'If you are the Son of God,' he said, 'throw yourself down from here.'"

4   Matthew 4:11 "Then the devil left him, and angels came and attended him."

5   Matthew 14:3 "Herod had arrested John and bound him and put him in prison because of Herodias, his brother Philip's wife"

Matthew 14:10 "and had John beheaded in the prison."

Pages 125 to 130   19: Hidden in Plain Sight

1   Luke 4:16 "He went to Nazareth where he had been brought up, and on the Sabbath day he went into the synagogue, as was his custom."

2   Mark 1:22 "The people were amazed at his teaching, because he taught them as one who had authority, not as the teachers of the law."

3   Luke 4:17-21 "The scroll of the prophet Isaiah was handed to him. Unrolling it, he found the place where it is written: 'The Spirit of the Lord is on me, because he

has anointed me to preach good news to the poor. He has sent me to proclaim freedom for the prisoners and recovery of sight for the blind, to release the oppressed, to proclaim the year of the Lord's favor.' Then he rolled up the scroll, gave it back to the attendant and sat down. The eyes of everyone in the synagogue were fastened on him. He began by saying to them, "Today this scripture is fulfilled in your hearing."

4   Luke 4:29 "They got up, drove him out of the town …in order to throw him down the cliff … But he walked right through the crowd and went on his way."

5   As noted on page 3, an Honorary Consul is a citizen of the country they live in, who represents a foreign country. (in this case, a citizen of earth representing the Kingdom of Heaven) After they become kingdom citizens, they will become consuls, no longer "honorary."

6   Jesus can see what is in people's hearts...

John 1:47-48 "When Jesus saw Nathanael approaching, he said of him, "Here truly is an Israelite in whom there is no deceit.' 'How do you know me?' Nathanael asked. Jesus answered, 'I saw you while you were still under the fig tree before Philip called you.'"

1 Samuel 16:7 "the Lord said to Samuel... The Lord does not look at the things people look at. People look at the outward appearance, but the Lord looks at the heart."

"FLATLAND, a Romance of Many Dimensions" written in 1884 by Edwin Abbot, is about a character from a 3-dimensional world who enters a world of only two dimensions: forward & back, left & right, *but no up & down*. The 3-dimensional character is unseen by Flatlanders until he intentionally intersects their world.

Appendix 2: Endnotes

When he is "above," he can look down and see inside each Flatlander's heart & thoughts, much like Jesus could see into Nathanial's heart.

7 Luke 17:20b-21 "The kingdom of God does not come with your careful observation, nor will people say, 'Here it is,' or 'There it is,' because the kingdom of God is in your midst."

8 Matthew 13:34 "Jesus spoke all these things to the crowd in parables; he did not say anything to them without using a parable."

9 Matthew 13:10 "The disciples came to him and asked, 'Why do you speak to the people in parables?' He replied, 'The knowledge of the secrets of the kingdom of heaven has been given to you, but not to them.'"

John 14:12 "whoever believes in me will do the works I have been doing, and they will do even greater things than these, because I am going to the Father."

10 Mark 8:29-30, "'But what about you?' he asked. 'Who do you say I am?' Peter answered, 'You are the Messiah.' Jesus warned them not to tell anyone about him."

11 Matthew 5:18 "I tell you the truth, until heaven and earth disappear, not the smallest letter, not the least stroke of a pen, will by any means disappear from the Law until everything is accomplished."

12 Mark 12:38-40 "As he taught, Jesus said, 'Watch out for the teachers of the law. They like to walk around in flowing robes and be greeted in the marketplaces, and have the most important seats in the synagogues and the places of honor at banquets. They devour widows' houses and for a show make lengthy prayers. Such men will be punished most severely.'"

Pages 131 to 138   20: Challenging Authority

1. Mark 3:17 "James son of Zebedee and his brother John (to them he [Jesus] gave the name Boanerges, which means "sons of thunder")"

2. The Bible books of Matthew, Mark, Luke and John are packed with miracle after miracle performed by Jesus, too many to list in this endnote.

    John 10:38 "...even though you do not believe me, believe the miracles, that you may know and understand that the Father is in me, and I in the Father."

3. Luke 5:18-26 "Some men came carrying a paralytic on a mat... When Jesus saw their faith, he said, 'Friend, your sins are forgiven.' The Pharisees and the teachers of the law began thinking... 'Who can forgive sins but God?' Jesus knew what they were thinking and asked, 'Why are you thinking these things in your hearts? Which is easier: to say, 'Your sins are forgiven,' or to say, 'Get up and walk'? But that you may know that the Son of Man has authority on earth to forgive sins …' He said to the paralyzed man, 'I tell you, get up...'" Immediately he stood up in front of them, took what he had been lying on and went home praising God. Everyone was amazed and gave praise to God. They were filled with awe..."

4. Again and again, Jesus told people to keep news of the miracles to themselves—after Jesus heals a deaf man (Mark 7:36), after Peter tells Jesus that he (Peter) knows Jesus is the son of God (Mark 8:30), after Jesus heals a man of leprosy (Luke 5:14), after raising a girl from the dead (Luke 8:56), after explaining to his disciples about his upcoming death and resurrection (Luke 9:21) and after healing everyone in a crowd (Matthew 12:16).

Appendix 2: Endnotes

5   Jesus taught that the institutional religious leaders can be dangerous. It was the religious leaders insisted that Jesus should be killed. See note 6, below.

Matthew 23:27 Jesus said, "Woe to you, teachers of the law and Pharisees, you hypocrites! You are like whitewashed tombs, which look beautiful on the outside but on the inside are full of dead men's bones and everything unclean."

Matthew 16:6,12 "'Be careful,' Jesus said to them. 'Be on your guard against the yeast of the Pharisees and Sadducees...' Then they understood that he was not telling them to guard against the yeast used in bread, but against the teaching of the Pharisees and Sadducees."

Matthew 23:15 [Jesus said] "Woe to you, teachers of the law and Pharisees, you hypocrites! You travel over land and sea to win a single convert, and when you have succeeded, you make them twice as much a child of hell as you are."

Matthew 12:14 "But the Pharisees went out and plotted how they might kill Jesus."

6   John 18:14 "Caiaphas was the one who had advised the Jews that it would be good if one man died for the people."

Caiaphas wanted to be rid of one troublemaker. He didn't realize that Jesus was "the One," whose death would save all people who want to be saved.

7   Luke 9:30-31 "Two men, Moses and Elijah, appeared in glorious splendor, talking with Jesus. They spoke about his departure,* which he was about to bring to fulfillment at Jerusalem."

* "Departure" is from the Greek word "exodos." A thousand years earlier, Moses led the exodus of Israelites out of Egypt into the Promised Land. Moses and Elijah came to discuss details of a larger exodus, where Jesus will lead the way for humans from the tyranny of Lucifer into the Promised Land of the kingdom. This mountaintop meeting is also known as "the transfiguration, where the "glorious splendor" of beings from the kingdom was clearly evident. See note 7, page 238.

8   Romans 11:25-26 "I do not want you to be ignorant of this mystery, brothers and sisters, so that you may not be conceited: Israel has experienced a hardening in part until the full number of the Gentiles has come in, and in this way all Israel will be saved."

Passport Please takes the position that the kingdom plan, of which Peter had been unaware, was that many in Israel were "blinded" or "hardened" to the truth of Jesus' identity, as the promised One who would crush Lucifer's head and rescue the people of Israel. Jesus had been careful not to spread the word too obviously that he was "the One."

If the Jewish leaders realized that Jesus was the One promised in the Garden of Eden, it is unlikely they would have pushed for his death. Without the death of Jesus, humans would not be able to have their crimes against the kingdom paid for under kingdom law, and they would be barred from access to heaven.

Appendix 2: Endnotes

John 4:22 [Jesus said] "salvation is from the Jews."

9 Luke 9:34-35 "While he was speaking, a cloud appeared and covered them, and they were afraid as they entered the cloud. A voice came from the cloud, saying, 'This is my Son, whom I have chosen; listen to him.'"

10 Mark 9:9-10 "As they were coming down the mountain, Jesus gave them orders not to tell anyone what they had seen until the Son of Man had risen from the dead. They kept the matter to themselves, discussing what 'rising from the dead' meant."

Pages 139 to 144   *21: The Set Up*

1 "The last supper" was a traditional Jewish Passover meal, commanded by the King. Bread containing yeast was not allowed, so the bread was flat.

Exodus 12:15 [God said] "For seven days you are to eat bread made without yeast... remove the yeast from your houses."

Luke 22:15 "he [Jesus] said to them, "I have eagerly desired to eat this Passover with you before I suffer."

The King said this meal was only for his family, not for outsiders...

Exodus 12:43 "The Lord said to Moses and Aaron, 'These are the regulations for the Passover meal: 'No foreigner may eat it...'"

2 The four gospels each provide different details of "the last supper." Jesus' friend John tells us about Judas and the bread...

John 13:21-26 "Jesus was troubled, 'One of you is going to betray me.' His disciples stared at one another, at a loss...

Simon Peter motioned [to John] and said, 'Ask him which one he means...' Jesus answered, 'It is the one to whom I will give this piece of bread when I have dipped it in the dish.' Then, dipping the piece of bread, he gave it to Judas."

Also see note 5, page 289.

3   Matthew 26:26-28 "While they were eating, Jesus took bread, and when he had given thanks, he broke it and gave it to his disciples, saying, 'Take and eat; this is my body.' Then he took a cup, and when he had given thanks, he gave it to them, saying, 'Drink from it, all of you. This is my blood of the covenant, which is poured out for many for the forgiveness of sins.'"

When Jesus had spoken on this subject earlier, no one seemed to "get it."

John 6:52-53, 59-60 "Then the Jews began to argue sharply among themselves, 'How can this man give us his flesh to eat?' Jesus said to them, 'Very truly I tell you, unless you eat the flesh of the Son of Man and drink his blood, you have no life in you ... He said this while teaching in the synagogue in Capernaum. On hearing it, many of his disciples said, 'This is a hard teaching. Who can accept it?'"

Jesus gave a clear command for his followers to eat and drink his body and blood, but Jesus did not chastise anyone for not fully understanding. It seems that full grasp of how Communion "works," is not commanded, but participation by Kingdom citizens is.

Appendix 2: Endnotes

[4] *Passport Please* takes the position that by the time of Jesus, not a single human left on earth still had pure Royal blood, a direct descendant of Adam. That is because Israel neglected to "protect their bloodline." See note 10 page 263, and note 7 on page 258.

Jesus seems to confirm this position when he responded to devout Jews by calling them "sons of their father the devil." He also called religious leaders as "a brood of vipers," a clear dig at Lucifer, the snake in the garden.

John 8:44 "You belong to your father, the devil..."

Matthew 3:7 "he [Jesus] said to them [the Pharisees and Sadducees]: 'You brood of vipers!'"

[5] John 13:27 "As soon as Judas took the bread, Satan entered into him. 'What you are about to do, do quickly,' Jesus told him."

[6] The Royal family has secrets, which they often reveal on a need-to-know basis. Sometimes they reveal secrets to a select few, who will share it widely later. Sometimes they reveal a secret, intending that it not be understood until later. Some of the Royal family secrets are hidden even from his angels.

1 Peter 1:12b "Even angels long to look into these things."

Matthew 24:36 "No one knows about that day or hour, not even the angels in heaven, nor the Son, but only the Father."

Ephesians 3:8b-10 [Paul says he will] "preach to the Gentiles the unsearchable riches of Christ, and to make plain to everyone the administration of this mystery, which for ages past was kept hidden in God, who created all things. His intent was that now, through the church, the manifold wisdom of God should be made known to the rulers and authorities in the heavenly realms"

Luke 18:34 "The disciples did not understand any of this. Its meaning was hidden from them, and they did not know what he was talking about."

Luke 24:15-16, 31 "As they talked and discussed these things with each other, Jesus himself came up and walked along with them; but they were kept from recognizing him." [hours pass] "Then their eyes were opened and they recognized him, and he disappeared from their sight."

7 John 8:23 "You are from below; I am from above. You are of this world; I am not of this world."

Ephesians 2:6 "God raised us [humans who join his family] up with Christ and seated us with him in the heavenly realms in Christ Jesus"

8 Jesus did not want anyone to be blamed for his death.

John 10:17-18 "I lay down my life—only to take it up again. No one takes it from me, but I lay it down of my own accord. I have authority to lay it down and authority to take it up again."

Passport Please takes the position that the King sent his own son across the border to be the willing sacrifice, to clear the criminal records of humans in His family. He chose to execute that plan in Jerusalem, at the temple, under the direction of the High Priest, just as kingdom-ordered sacrifices had been done for a thousand years. Jesus' death was not a senseless murder of a good man. He made it clear by his words that his death, and resurrection, were voluntary.

Appendix 2: Endnotes

9   Ever since John the Baptist began announcing the arrival of the Prince of Heaven onto the planet, the battle for the people of earth has turned increasingly violent.

Matthew 11:12 "And from the days of John the Baptist until now the kingdom of heaven has been subjected to violence, and the violent take it by force."

Mark 6:23-25 [King Herod promised the Queen's daughter] "Whatever you ask I will give you, up to half my kingdom....' [She replied] 'I want you to give me right now the head of John the Baptist on a platter.' So he immediately sent an executioner with orders to bring John's head. The man went, beheaded John in the prison, and brought back his head on a platter."

But the Prince said his people would be overcomers.

John 16:33 [Jesus said to his followers] "In this world you will have trouble. But take heart! I have overcome the world."

John 11:25 [Jesus said] "The one who believes in me will live, even though they die"

10   Mark 14:58 "We heard him [Jesus] say, 'I will destroy this man-made temple and in three days will build another, not made by man.'"

Acts 13:38-39 "Therefore, my brothers, I want you to know that through Jesus the forgiveness of sins is proclaimed to you. Through him everyone who believes is justified from everything you could not be justified from by the law of Moses."

11. John 10:27-29 "My sheep listen to my voice; I know them, and they follow me. I give them eternal life, and they shall never perish; no one will snatch them out of my hand. My Father, who has given them to me, is greater than all; no one can snatch them out of my Father's hand."

12. Romans 8:2 "because through Christ Jesus the law of the Spirit of life set me free from the law of sin and death."

    Galatians 5:13 "You, my brothers and sisters, were called to be free. But do not use your freedom to indulge the flesh; rather, serve one another humbly in love."

13. John 16:12-13 "But when he, the Spirit of truth, comes, he will guide you into all truth. He will not speak on his own; he will speak only what he hears, and he will tell you what is yet to come."

    Messages from the Prime Minister are often given to specific individuals, for specific times and purposes...

    1 Corinthians 12:8 "To one there is given through the Spirit a message of wisdom, to another a message of knowledge by means of the same Spirit..."

14. 2 Corinthians 10:4 "The weapons we fight with are not the weapons of the world. On the contrary, they have divine power to demolish strongholds."

15. Ephesians 6:12 "For our struggle is not against flesh and blood, but against the rulers, against the authorities, against the powers of this dark world and against the spiritual forces of evil in the heavenly realms."

16. John 16:33 "In this world you will have trouble. But take heart, I have overcome the world."

[17] John 14:26 "But the Counselor, the Holy Spirit, whom the Father will send in my name, will teach you all things and will remind you of everything I have said to you."

Pages 145 to 150   *22: Blood Matters*

[1] The high priest demanded Jesus state clearly whether or not he was The One promised in the Garden, and Governor Pilate demanded to know if Jesus was the King of the Jews. The gospels record that the answers Jesus gave were anything but clear.

To Pilate's question, Jesus responded:

> Matthew 27:11, Mark 15:2, Luke 23:3 "You have said so"
>
> John 18:34 "'Is that your own idea,' Jesus asked, 'or did others talk to you about me?'"

To Caiaphas, he responded:

> Matthew 26:64 "You have said so"
>
> Luke 22:70b "You say that I am."
>
> Mark 14:62 "I am"

"I am," above, appears to be an affirmative statement, but it had a provocative double meaning. "I am" was the name by which the King of Heaven wanted to be known.

Exodus 3:14 "God said to Moses, 'I am who I am. This is what you are to say to the Israelites: "I am has sent me to you."'"

With this answer, Jesus is not only saying that he is The One sent by the King, he is also saying he is the human embodiment of the King himself. To Caiaphas, "I am" was an incomprehensible, absurd and arrogant answer.

At this time, Jesus was not trying to help Pilate or Caiaphas know his true identity. He was on a mission, and he knew he needed to put Jesus to death.

Isaiah 53:7 "He was oppressed and afflicted, yet he did not open his mouth; he was led like a lamb to the slaughter, and as a sheep before its shearers is silent, so he did not open his mouth."

If Jesus' true identity and mission were clear, no one would have dared to put him to death.

1 Corinthians 2:8 "None of the rulers of this age understood it, for if they had, they would not have crucified the Lord of glory.

2. John 18:36 "Jesus said, [to Pilate] 'My kingdom is not of this world. If it were, my servants would fight to prevent my arrest by the Jews. But now* my kingdom is from another place.'"

*Jesus stated that *now* his kingdom is from another place, but in the future, his kingdom will be on earth.

3. John 19:11 "Jesus answered [Pilate], 'You would have no power over me if it were not given to you from above.'"

4. The crucifixion of Jesus is detailed in all four gospels:

Matthew 27, Mark 15, Luke 23, John 19

5. Psalm 22:14-18 "I am poured out like water, and all my bones are out of joint. My heart has turned to wax; it has melted away within me. My strength is dried up like a potsherd, and my tongue sticks to the roof of my mouth; you lay me in the dust of death. Dogs have surrounded me; a band of evil men has encircled me, they have pierced my hands and my feet."

Appendix 2: Endnotes

Isaiah 53:8b-10a "For he was cut off from the land of the living; for the transgression of my people he was stricken. He was assigned a grave with the wicked, and with the rich in his death, though he had done no violence, nor was any deceit in his mouth. Yet it was the Lord's will to crush him and cause him to suffer"

[6] Luke 23:39-43 "One of the criminals who hung there hurled insults at him: 'Aren't you the Christ? Save yourself and us!' But the other criminal rebuked him. 'Don't you fear God,' he said, 'since you are under the same sentence? We are punished justly, for we are getting what our deeds deserve. But this man has done nothing wrong.' Then he said, 'Jesus, remember me when you come into your kingdom.' Jesus answered him, 'I tell you the truth, today you will be with me in paradise.'"

Passport Please takes the position that the thief's only claim to kingdom citizenship was on a last-minute citizenship application to the Prince. "Paradise" which Jesus promised, refers to the comfortable Hades where followers of the Prince wait after death. It is not the eternal heaven (the 'kingdom proper' on page 33 of the novel). Also see note 4, page 253.

It seems unlikely that the thief would have entered the kingdom proper (the eternal heaven) ahead of all the rest of the dead in Christ who are waiting for the trumpet.

1 Thessalonians 4:16 "For the Lord himself will come down from heaven, with a loud command, with the voice of the archangel and with the trumpet call of God, and the dead in Christ will rise first."

7   Jesus dies alone on the cross, forsaken even by his father.

Matthew 27:46 "About the ninth hour Jesus cried out in a loud voice, 'Eloi, Eloi, lama sabachthani?'—which means, 'My God, my God, why have you forsaken me?'"

On the cross, Jesus had just quoted the Hebrew Bible.

Psalm 22:1 "My God, my God, why have you forsaken me? Why are you so far from saving me, so far from the words of my groaning?"

8   By January 1993, string theory had determined that space can indeed tear. When space tears, it can create a wormhole, or tunnel, to a distant part of the universe. Brian Greene, *The Elegant Universe*, (New York, Random House, 1999) page 280

9   Jesus said that most people will miss the entrance to heaven, perhaps because most people are not even looking for it.

Matthew 7:14 "But small is the gate and narrow the road that leads to life, and only a few find it."

10 Colossians 2:15 "And having disarmed the powers and authorities, he made a public spectacle of them, triumphing over them by the cross."

11 In the womb, blood from the mother never comes in contact with the baby, thanks to the placenta, also known as "the blood barrier." See note 8, page 262.

12 Lucifer and his rebel forces did not know the plan of God in advance. It would be broadcast later, by the church.

Ephesians 3:10   "...through the church, the manifold wisdom of God might now be made known to the rulers and authorities in the heavenly places."

Appendix 2: Endnotes

[13] Jesus had told the thief that "Today you will be with me in paradise," referring to the comfortable part of Hades. See note 6, page 295 about the thief and note 4, page 253 about paradise and Hades.

Pages 151 to 154   23: Legal Matters

[1] John 15:15 "I no longer call you servants, because a servant does not know his master's business. Instead, I have called you friends"

[2] After his crucifixion, Jesus visited the prison reserved for Lucifer's rebels who had assaulted human women.

Jude 6 "And the angels who did not keep their positions of authority but abandoned their proper dwelling—these he has kept in darkness, bound with everlasting chains for judgment on the great Day."

1 Peter 3:18b-20 "He [Jesus] was put to death in the body but made alive by the Spirit, through whom also he went and preached to the spirits in prison* who disobeyed long ago when God waited patiently in the days of Noah while the ark was being built."

* *Passport Please* takes the position that these "spirits in prison" are Lucifer's rebels who intermarried with women on the earth before the time of the flood, in the days of Noah. See note 2 on page 257. These disobedient rebels are held in a dark prison until they face judgment.

2 Peter 2:4 "God did not spare angels when they sinned, but sent them to hell, putting them into gloomy dungeons to be held for judgment"

"Hell" in 2 Peter 2:4 is actually the Greek word "Tartarus." Used only this once in the Bible, the word Tartarus was mentioned in Homer's *Iliad* (c. 700 BC) as being, "As far beneath Hades as heaven is above the earth."

3. Philippians 2:9-10 "Therefore God exalted him to the highest place and gave him the name that is above every name, that at the name of Jesus every knee should bow, in heaven and on earth and under the earth."

Psalm 22:29 "all who go down to the dust will kneel before him – those who cannot keep themselves alive."

4. 1 Corinthians 6:3 [Paul writes] "Do you not know that we will judge angels?

Isaiah 24:21-22 In that day the Lord will punish the powers in the heavens above and the kings on the earth below. They will be herded together like prisoners bound in a dungeon; they will be shut up in prison and be punished after many days.

5. John 20:17 "Jesus said [to Mary], 'Do not hold on* to me, for I have not yet returned to the Father. Go instead to my brothers and tell them, 'I am returning to my Father and your Father, to my God and your God.'"

* The original Greek (and the King James Version) say, "do not touch me." The issue was not one of Mary restraining Jesus from his journey, but rather defiling the Chief Justice on his way into the presence of the King. Mary had recently touched Jesus' dead body, making her "unclean," according to the law. Also according to the law, Jesus could not let an "unclean" person touch him until he had completely fulfilled his mission.

Numbers 19:11 "Whoever touches the dead body of anyone will be unclean for seven days."

Appendix 2: Endnotes

6   Hebrews 9:11-12, 24 "But when Christ came as high priest of the good things that are now already here, he went through the greater and more perfect tabernacle that is not made with human hands, that is to say, is not a part of this creation. He did not enter by means of the blood of goats and calves; but he entered the Most Holy Place once for all by his own blood, thus obtaining eternal redemption ... For Christ did not enter a sanctuary made with human hands that was only a copy of the true one; he entered heaven itself, now to appear for us in God's presence."

7   Daniel was given a view of future court proceedings in heaven, when all power and authority in heaven and earth would return to Jesus.

Daniel 7:9,10,13-14 "As I [Daniel] looked, thrones were placed, and the Ancient of Days [God] took his seat... the court sat in judgment... and behold, with the clouds of heaven there came one like a son of man [Jesus], and he came to the Ancient of Days and was presented before him. And to him was given dominion and glory and a kingdom, that all peoples, nations, and languages should serve him; his dominion is an everlasting dominion, which shall not pass away, and his kingdom one that shall not be destroyed."

8   Daniel was also shown how Jesus would turn over all his power and authority to his human followers...

Daniel 7:27 "And the kingdom and the dominion and the greatness of the kingdoms under the whole heaven shall be given to the people of the saints of the Most High; his [Jesus'] kingdom shall be an everlasting kingdom, and all dominions shall serve and obey him."

Pages 155 to 160   24: Transfer of Authority

1. A very short time later, when Jesus had completed his work at the altar in heaven, it was no problem for Mary to touch and hug him.

   Matthew 28:8-9 "So the women hurried away from the tomb, afraid yet filled with joy, and ran to tell his disciples. Suddenly Jesus met them. 'Greetings,' he said. They came to him, clasped his feet and worshiped him."

2. 1 Corinthians 15:40 "There are also heavenly bodies and there are earthly bodies; but the splendor of the heavenly bodies is one kind, and the splendor of the earthly bodies is another."

3. Luke 24:31 "Then their eyes were opened and they recognized him, and he disappeared from their sight."

   See note 2 on page 246 and note 3 on page 308.

4. Luke 24:37-39 "They were startled and frightened, thinking they saw a ghost. He said to them, "Why are you troubled, and why do doubts rise in your minds? Look at my hands and my feet. It is I myself! Touch me and see; a ghost does not have flesh and bones, as you see I have."

5. John 20:22 "And with that he breathed on them and said, 'Receive the Holy Spirit.'"

6. The Prime Minister of the kingdom lives inside human members of the Royal family. He is, among other things, their passport.

   John 14:16-17 "I [Jesus] will ask the Father, and he will give you another Counselor to be with you forever—the Spirit of truth. The world cannot accept him, because it neither sees him nor knows him. But you know him, for he lives with you and will be in you."

Appendix 2: Endnotes

> Ephesians 1:13b "Having believed, you were marked in him with a seal, the promised Holy Spirit"

7   2 Corinthians 10:4 "The weapons we fight with are not the weapons of the world. On the contrary, they have divine power to demolish strongholds."

> Ephesians 6:12 "For our struggle is not against flesh and blood, but against the rulers, against the authorities, against the powers of this dark world and against the spiritual forces of evil in the heavenly realms."

> John 16:2 "They will put you out of the synagogue; in fact, the time is coming when anyone who kills you will think they are offering a service to God."

> James 4:7b "Resist the devil, and he will flee from you."

8   Luke 24:49 "I am going to send you what my father has promised; but stay in the city until you have been clothed with power from on high."

9   Global deployment awaits those in kingdom service.

> Acts 1:8a "you will be my witnesses in Jerusalem, and in all Judea and Samaria, and to the ends of the earth."

10   Matthew 28:18 "All authority in heaven and on earth has been given to me [Jesus]."

> As Daniel foresaw (see note 8, page 299), the Prince gave that authority to his followers..

> Acts 1:8b "you will receive power when the Holy Spirit comes on you"

> Mark 11:22-24 [Jesus, alone with his disciples, said] "'Truly I tell you, if anyone says to this mountain, 'Go, throw yourself into the sea, and does not doubt in their heart but believes that what they say will happen, it will be done for them.

Therefore I tell you, whatever you ask for in prayer, believe that you have received it, and it will be yours.'"

11. John 12:31 "Now is the time for judgment on this world; now the prince of this world will be driven out."

12. Matthew 13:40-43 "As the weeds are pulled up and burned in the fire, so it will be at the end of the age. The Son of Man will send out his angels, and they will weed out of his kingdom everything that causes sin and all who do evil. They will throw them into the fiery furnace, where there will be weeping and gnashing of teeth. Then the righteous will shine like the sun in the kingdom of their Father. He who has ears, let him hear."

Matthew 25:31-46 tells more on the "weeding" process. "he will separate the people one from another as a shepherd separates the sheep from the goats"

Passport Please takes the position that before the Royal family returns to the royal garden of earth, they will weed it, removing everything that is not authorized to be there.

13. Matthew 28:19-20 "Therefore go and make disciples of all nations, baptizing them in the name of the Father and of the Son and of the Holy Spirit, and teaching them to obey everything I have commanded you. And surely I am with you always, to the very end of the age."

14. John 3:3 "In reply, Jesus declared, "I tell you the truth, no one can see the kingdom of God unless he is born again."

Citizenship in the kingdom is free.

1 Corinthians 2:12 "We have not received the spirit of the world but the Spirit who is from God, that we may understand what God has freely given us."

Appendix 2: Endnotes

15   Matthew 10:22 "All men will hate you because of me, but he who stands firm to the end will be saved."

John 17:14 "the world has hated them [Jesus' disciples], for they are not of the world any more than I [Jesus] am of the world."

16   Kingdom Ambassadors are well-armed by the Prime Minister. See note 7 on page 301.

17   Trouble comes when one gets distracted from their mission. Peter found that out when Jesus beckoned him to walk on the water.

Matthew 14:30 "But when he saw the wind, he was afraid and, beginning to sink, he cried out, 'Lord save me!'"

18   John 10:28b [Jesus said of those who commit to him] "no one can snatch them out of my hand."

Romans 8:38-39 "For I am convinced that neither death nor life, neither angels nor demons, neither the present nor the future, nor any powers, neither height nor depth, nor anything else in all creation, will be able to separate us from the love of God that is in Christ Jesus our Lord."

Pages 161 to 164   *25: Free Will*

1   The US Supreme Court decided in 1833 that the government has no power to force anyone to accept a pardon. To be effective, a pardon must be willingly accepted.

George Wilson had been sentenced to hang for his part in the death of a driver, during a stagecoach robbery. He was granted a pardon by President Andrew Jackson, but Wilson refused to accept it.

The Supreme Court sided with Wilson, and he was hanged. As part of the majority opinion of UNITED STATES v. GEORGE WILSON. U.S. 150 (1833), 32, Chief Justice John Marshall wrote:

"A pardon is an act of grace, proceeding from the power entrusted with the execution of the laws, which exempts the individual on whom it is bestowed from the punishment the law inflicts for a crime he has committed ... A pardon is a deed, to the validity of which delivery is essential, and delivery is not complete without acceptance. It may then be rejected by the person to whom it is tendered; and if it is rejected, we have discovered no power in a court to force it on him."

In the same opinion, Justice Marshall acknowledges that some may choose to refuse a pardon because the conditions attached to it are more than the recipient is willing to bear.

"A pardon may be conditional; and the condition may be more objectionable than the punishment inflicted by the judgment ..."

Passport Please takes the position that the conditions attached to the Royal pardon for humans are; renunciation of all allegiance to Lucifer, admitting the need for a pardon, requesting a pardon and following the Prince to the best of one's ability. Many have decided that this price is more than they are willing to pay.

[2] Acts 2:1-4 "When the day of Pentecost came, they were all together in one place. Suddenly a sound like the blowing of a violent wind came from heaven and filled the whole house where they were sitting. They saw what seemed to be tongues of fire that separated and came to rest on each of them.

Appendix 2: Endnotes

All of them were filled with the Holy Spirit and began to speak in other tongues as the Spirit enabled them."

[3] Acts 2:6-11 "...each one heard their own language being spoken. Utterly amazed, they asked: "Aren't all these who are speaking Galileans? Then how is it that each of us hears them in our native language? Parthians, Medes and Elamites; residents of Mesopotamia, Judea and Cappadocia, Pontus and Asia, Phrygia and Pamphylia, Egypt and the parts of Libya near Cyrene; visitors from Rome (both Jews and converts to Judaism); Cretans and Arabs – we hear them declaring the wonders of God in our own tongues!"

[4] 1 Corinthians 14:2 "For anyone who speaks in a tongue does not speak to men but to God. Indeed, no one understands him; he utters mysteries with his spirit."

1 Corinthians 13:1 [Paul, making a point, says] "If I speak in the tongues of men and of angels..."

Romans 8:26 "the Spirit himself intercedes for us with groans that words cannot express."

Passport Please takes the position that "speaking in a tongue" is the Prime Minister speaking through a human in another language. If the message is intended for the Prince or King, the language may be "tongues of angels," which is only understood in the Kingdom, sounding like 'gibberish' to humans. Throughout history, ambassadors have been equipped with systems enabling encrypted messaging capabilities to keep their messages secret.

[5] John 21:25 "Jesus did many other things as well. If every one of them were written down, I suppose that even the whole world would not have room for the books that would be written."

Pages 165 to 170   26: Competing Offers

1. Acts 2:36-38 [Peter addressing the crowd] "'Let all Israel be assured of this: God has made this Jesus whom you crucified, both Lord and Messiah.' Now when they heard this they were cut to the heart, and said to Peter and the rest of the apostles 'Brothers, what shall we do?' And Peter said to them, 'Repent and be baptized every one of you in the name of Jesus Christ for the forgiveness of your sins, and you will receive the gift of the Holy Spirit.'"

2. John 11:25b "He who believes in me will live, even though he dies; and whoever lives and believes in me will never die."

3. Acts 2:41 "Those who accepted his message were baptized, and about three thousand were added to their number that day."

4. Philippians 3:20a [Peter shouted] "Our citizenship is in heaven"

5. Acts 3:6-10 "Then Peter said, 'Silver or gold I do not have, but what I do have I give you. In the name of Jesus Christ of Nazareth, walk.' Taking him [the crippled man] by the right hand, he helped him up, and instantly the man's feet and ankles became strong. He jumped to his feet and began to walk. Then he went with them into the temple courts, walking and jumping, and praising God. When all the people saw him walking and praising God, they recognized him as the same man who used to sit begging at the temple gate called Beautiful, and they were filled with wonder and amazement at what had happened to him."

Appendix 2: Endnotes

6   Jesus was not murdered or killed. He willingly gave up his life. See note 8 on page 290.

7   Acts 4:4 "But many who heard the message believed and the number of men grew to about five thousand."

8   Acts 4:3 "They seized Peter and John, and because it was evening, they put them in jail until the next day."

9   Peter is an ambassador, speaking boldly, with all the authority of the kingdom of heaven.

2 Corinthians 5:20 "We are therefore Christ's ambassadors ..."

Acts 4:8-12 "Then Peter, filled with the Holy Spirit, said to them: 'Rulers and elders of the people! If we are being called to account today for an act of kindness shown to a cripple and are asked how he was healed, then know this, you and all the people of Israel: It is by the name of Jesus Christ of Nazareth, whom you crucified but whom God raised from the dead, that this man stands before you healed. He is 'the stone you builders rejected, which has become the capstone.' [see 2nd note 2, page 331] Salvation is found in no one else, for there is no other name under heaven given to men by which we must be saved.'"

Acts 5:31 "God exalted him to his own right hand as Prince and Savior that he might give repentance and forgiveness of sins to Israel."

Pages 171 to 178   *27: Punch-Counterpunch*

1   Acts 4:13-17 "When they saw the courage of Peter and John and realized that they were unschooled, ordinary men, they were astonished and they took note that these men had been with Jesus.

But since they could see the man who had been healed standing there with them, there was nothing they could say. So they ordered them to withdraw from the Sanhedrin and then conferred together. 'What are we going to do with these men?' they asked. 'Everybody living in Jerusalem knows they have done an outstanding miracle, and we cannot deny it. But to stop this thing from spreading any further among the people, we must warn these men to speak no longer to anyone in this name.'"

2. Acts 5:12b-13a "all the believers used to meet together in Solomon's Colonnade. No one else dared join them"

3. Acts 9:3-6 "As he neared Damascus on his journey, suddenly a light from heaven flashed around him. He fell to the ground and heard a voice say to him, 'Saul, Saul, why do you persecute me?' 'Who are you, Lord?' Saul asked. 'I am Jesus, whom you are persecuting," he replied. 'Now get up and go into the city, and you will be told what you must do.'"

4. Healing the sick will always gather a crowd.

    Luke 9:2 "he [Jesus] sent them [the Apostles] out to proclaim the kingdom of God and to heal the sick."

    Acts 5:16 "Crowds gathered also from the towns around Jerusalem, their sick and those tormented by impure spirits, and all of them were healed [by the Apostles]."

5. Matthew 5:17 "Do not think that I [Jesus] have come to abolish the Law or the Prophets; I have not come to abolish them but to fulfill them."

    John 11:25 "Jesus said to her [Martha, sister of his friend Lazarus], "I am the resurrection and the life. The one who believes in me will live, even though they die"

Appendix 2: Endnotes

6. Romans 10:9 "if you confess with your mouth, 'Jesus is Lord,' and believe in your heart that God raised him from the dead, you will be saved."

7. Philippians 3:21 "[Jesus] who, by the power that enables him to bring everything under his control, will transform our lowly bodies so that they will be like his glorious body."

   1 John 3:2 "Dear friends, now we are children of God, and what we will be has not yet been made known. But we know that when he appears, we shall be like him, for we shall see him as he is."

8. John 14:6 "I am the way and the truth and the life. No one comes to the Father except through me."

   Passport Please takes the position that if there truly is any other way into the kingdom, and Jesus taught that following him is the only way, then Jesus is either foolish or deluded or evil - and clearly not a "good teacher." Also, he could have avoided a senseless, gruesome death by simply pointing people to one of the other ways.

9. Luke 9:26 "If anyone is ashamed of me and my words, the Son of Man will be ashamed of him when he comes in his glory and in the glory of the Father and of the holy angels."

   Luke 12:9 "But he who disowns me before men will be disowned before the angels of God."

   2 Peter 2:21 "It would have been better for them not to have known the way of righteousness, than to have known it and then to turn their backs on the sacred command that was passed on to them."

   Luke 10:16 "he who rejects me [Jesus] rejects him who sent me."

Passport Please takes the position that ignoring the requirements for entry into the Kingdom will have negative consequences at the kingdom border crossing.

10 Matthew 6:33 "But seek first his kingdom and his righteousness, and all these things will be given to you as well."

Luke 12:34 "For where your treasure is, there your heart will be also."

11 John 14:21 "Whoever has my commands and obeys them, he is the one who loves me. He who loves me will be loved by my Father, and I too will love him and show myself to him."

John 14:23-24 "Jesus replied, 'Anyone who loves me will obey my teaching. My Father will love them, and we will come to them and make our home with them. Anyone who does not love me will not obey my teaching. These words you hear are not my own; they belong to the Father who sent me.'"

12 If one does not actually accept the pardon which is offered to them, the pardon has no value. See note 1 on page 303.

13 Today is the only day we have. No one is promised tomorrow...

1 Chronicles 29:5 "Now, who is willing to consecrate himself today to the Lord?"

Luke 12:19-20 (the rich man said) "And I'll say to myself, 'You have plenty of good things laid up for many years. Take life easy; eat, drink and be merry.' But God said to him, 'You fool! This very night your life will be demanded from you.'"

Appendix 2: Endnotes

Matthew 6:24 "No one can serve two masters. Either he will hate the one and love the other, or he will be devoted to the one and despise the other."

Revelation 3:16 "So, because you are lukewarm—neither hot nor cold—I am about to spit you out of my mouth."

Pages 179 to 182 *28: Media Blitz*

[1] A civilized nation which is about to invade another will often drop leaflets as a warning to the general population as well as enemy combatants, regarding the invasion to come and instructions on how to find safety.

In 2006, Israel dropped huge numbers of leaflets on southern Lebanon prior to initiating a military response.

These leaflets provided warnings regarding the enemy:

> "*Terrorists are operating in your area, and you are being exploited as 'human shields'*"

About Israel's plans:

> "*The Israel Defense Force will intensify its activities and will heavily bomb the entire area from which rockets are being launched*"

About what behavior will put one in danger:

> "*anyone traveling in a pickup truck or truck is endangering his life*"

And instructions on how to find safety:

> "*evacuate your villages and move north of the Litani River*"

From www.mfa.gov.il, Israel Ministry of Foreign Affairs

Passport Please takes the position that the Bible serves as a leaflet, disclosing to everyone, the nature and identity of the enemy, the intentions of the Kingdom of Heaven and its rulers, the behaviors which will put one in danger, and instructions on how to find safety.

2   Johann Gutenberg (1400-1468) invented the mechanical printing press. The first book printed was 180 copies of the Bible. The most widely distributed and translated book on the planet, by the end of the 20th century the number of Bibles sold exceeded one billion, in over 2,000 languages. *The New Evidence that Demands a Verdict,* Josh McDowell (1999) page 8

3   The earth has a bloody history and the carnage is accelerating... In the 20th century, over 203,000,000 persons killed by war and government actions. This is more than a 20% increase in the estimated number from *all* prior recorded history combined. R.J. Rummel, Death by Government (New Brunswick, NJ, Transaction Publishers, 1994), Chapters 1-3

Pages 183 to 188   29: *Out of Harm's Way*

1   Mark 13:32-33 "...about that day or hour no one knows, not even the angels in heaven, nor the Son, but only the Father. Be on guard! Be alert! You do not know when that time will come."

2   1 Thessalonians 4:16 "For the Lord himself will come down from heaven, with a loud command, with the voice of the archangel and with the trumpet call of God, and the dead in Christ* will rise first."

* Passport Please takes the position that this exit from the KAL is only for "the dead in Christ," those who had received the Prince's pardon and were kingdom citizens.

Appendix 2: Endnotes

Those in the KAL who committed to the kingdom before the Royal pardon was issued are honorary kingdom citizens. They will remain in the lounge for a while longer and will join the Royal family later. Abraham, who was in the Kingdom Arrival Lounge with Lazarus, is an example of such a person. See note 4 on page 253.

3   Before a nation launches a major attack, it will evacuate its own diplomats and citizens, out of harms way.

1 Thessalonians 4:17 "After that, we who are still alive and are left will be caught up together with them in the clouds to meet the Lord in the air. And so we will be with the Lord forever."

Matthew 24:40-41 "Two men will be in the field; one will be taken and the other left. Two women will be grinding with a hand mill; one will be taken and the other left."

Isaiah 57:1 "The righteous perish, and no one ponders it in his heart; devout men are taken away, and no one understands that the righteous are taken away to be spared from evil."

Passport Please takes the position that a sudden unexplainable disappearance of kingdom citizens and ambassadors from the earth into the safe zone in a higher dimension, happens just prior to the kingdom's onslaught. (referred to by many as the "rapture" of kingdom citizens – a term not found in the Bible)

The Bible records an earlier sudden disappearance of a kingdom-minded person. Enoch was evacuated from earth before a flood destroyed the earth, much like kingdom citizens disappearing before the attack on earth.

Genesis 5:24 "Enoch walked with God; then he was no more, because God took him away."

Hebrews 11:5 "By faith Enoch was taken from this life, so that he did not experience death; he could not be found, because God had taken him away. For before he was taken, he was commended as one who pleased God."

4 Revelation 21:4 "He will wipe every tear from their eyes. There will be no more death or mourning or crying or pain, for the old order of things has passed away."

1 Corinthians 15:54-55 "When the perishable has been clothed with the imperishable, and the mortal with immortality, then the saying that is written will come true: 'Death has been swallowed up in victory. Where, O death, is your victory? Where, O death, is your sting?'"

5 John 14:3 "And if I [Jesus] go and prepare a place for you, I will come back and take you to be with me that you also may be where I am."

Passport Please takes the position that this crossing into the kingdom proper is for citizens evacuated from earth and for those in the KAL, who committed to the Prince before they died. "Honorary citizens" still wait in the KAL. See (2nd) note 2 on page 312 and note 5 on 328.

The popular song *When the Saints Go Marching In*, is taken from the Bible. It is a word-picture of kingdom citizens entering heaven from the KAL, all at the same time, after multiple cosmic disasters have befallen the earth. Over the years, popular artists have changed the words, to make the song less scary. The original lyrics are...

Appendix 2: Endnotes

"Oh, when the saints go marching in,
Oh, when the saints go marching in,
Lord how I want to be in that number, when the...

...saints go marching in.   *1 Thessalonians 4:17*

Lord, how I want to be in that number,
when the saints go marching in."

Oh when the...
...trumpet sounds its call,   *1 Thessalonians 4:16*
...sun refuse to shine,   *2 Peter 3:10*
...moon turns red with blood,   *Joel 2:31*

Lord, how I want to be in that number,
when the saints go marching in."

Traditional American gospel song, author unknown.

[6] Isaiah 25:6 "On this mountain the Lord Almighty will prepare a feast of rich food for all peoples, a banquet of aged wine—the best of meats and the finest of wines."

Revelation 19:9 "Blessed are those who are invited to the wedding supper of the Lamb!" [John the Baptist referred to Jesus as "the Lamb of God" John 1:29]

Passport Please takes the position that this banquet is a wedding feast, where the Prince celebrates his marriage to the church. His father the King already has his bride, now waiting for him in the KAL. See note 5, page 269.

Ephesians 5:25 "Husbands love your wives, just as Christ loved the church and gave himself up for her."

[7] Revelation 15:2b "standing beside the sea, those who had been victorious over the beast and its image and over the number of its name. They held harps given them by God"

[8] Isaiah 13:4b-5 "The Lord Almighty is mustering an army for war. They come from faraway lands, from the ends

of the heavens—the Lord and the weapons of his wrath—to destroy the whole country."

⁹ Revelation 6:9-10 "I saw under the altar the souls of those who had been slain because of the word of God and the testimony they had maintained. They called out in a loud voice, "How long, Sovereign Lord, holy and true, until you judge the inhabitants of the earth and avenge our blood?"

Passport Please takes the position that after the evacuation from earth, humans can still apply for kingdom citizenship. Many who do so are killed for it, but they then find refuge in a special section of the KAL.

¹⁰ Rev 20:4b "And I saw the souls of those who had been beheaded because of their testimony about Jesus and because of the word of God. They had not worshiped the beast or its image and had not received its mark on their foreheads or their hands. They came to life and reigned with Christ a thousand years."

Pages 189 to 196   30: *Commence Firing*

¹ The deal with Lucifer for the earth had a buyback clause. Adam was the Royal human who had lost the earth, so a relative of his (a Royal human) has the right to buy back the land. See note 1 on page 249 on the "kinsman redeemer." The Royals bought back the earth with the death of Jesus, but Lucifer did not yield. He was now in default on the agreement and must suffer the penalties.

² Revelation 6 tells of the opening of the first four seals on the scroll, with instructions for the "four horsemen of the Apocalypse," to bring destruction on the earth.

Appendix 2: Endnotes

Revelation 6:1-2 "I watched as the Lamb opened the first of the seven seals. Then I heard one of the four living creatures say in a voice like thunder, "Come!" I looked, and there before me was a white horse! Its rider held a bow, and he was given a crown, and he rode out as a conqueror bent on conquest."

Revelation 6:7-8 "When the Lamb opened the fourth seal, I heard the voice of the fourth living creature say, 'Come!' I looked, and there before me was a pale horse! Its rider was named Death, and Hades was following close behind him. They were given power over a fourth of the earth to kill by sword, famine and plague, and by the wild beasts of the earth."

Joel 1:15 "For the day of the Lord is near, and as destruction from the almighty, it comes."

[3] Revelation 6:9-11 "When he opened the fifth seal, I saw under the altar the souls of those who had been slain because of the word of God and the testimony they had maintained. They called out in a loud voice, 'How long... until you judge the inhabitants of the earth and avenge our blood?' ... They were told to wait a little longer, until the full number of... their brothers and sisters, were killed just as they had been."

[4] Revelation 6:12 "as he opened the sixth seal... the sun turned black like sackcloth..."

Revelation 6:14 "The heavens receded like a scroll being rolled up, and every mountain and island was removed from its place."

Joel 2:10-11 "Before them the earth shakes, the heavens tremble, the sun and moon are darkened, and the stars no longer shine. The Lord thunders at the head of his army;

his forces are beyond number, and mighty is the army that obeys his command. The day of the Lord is great; it is dreadful. Who can endure it?"

5. Revelation 8:1 "When he opened the seventh seal, there was silence in heaven for about half an hour."

6. Revelation 8:5 "the angel took the censer, filled it with fire from the altar, and hurled it on the earth; and there came peals of thunder, rumblings, flashes of lightning and an earthquake."

7. Worldwide destruction...

A volcano-induced tsunami? Revelation 8:8 "The second angel sounded his trumpet, and something like a huge mountain, all ablaze, was thrown into the sea."

A collapse of Cumbre Vieja, the most active volcano in the Canary Islands, would generate a dome of water nearly 3,000 ft. high, which would speed across the Atlantic, hitting coastlines from Maine to Brazil with waves over 100 feet high. From *Cumbre Vieja Volcano – Potential Collapse and Tsunami at La Palma, Canary Islands*, (2001) by Steven Ward, University of California Institute of Geophysics and Planetary Physics and Simon Day, University College (UK) Department of Geological Sciences. Information from this paper was reprinted by CNN, Popular Mechanics, and other media outlets.

Nuclear contamination? Revelation 8:10 "The third angel sounded his trumpet, and a great star, blazing like a torch, fell from the sky on a third of the rivers and on the springs of water - the name of the star is Wormwood.* A third of the waters turned bitter, and many people died from the waters that had become bitter."

Appendix 2: Endnotes

>*A web search will quickly reveal much Bible-centered discussion based on the fact that "Chernobyl" is the Ukrainian word for "Wormwood." Chernobyl is a city in Ukraine, the site of the 1986 nuclear disaster, which spread radiation over Russia and Europe.

[8] Revelation 7:4 "Then I heard the number of those who were sealed: 144,000 from all the tribes of Israel."

Revelation 14:1 "Then I looked, and there before me was the Lamb, standing on Mount Zion, and with him 144,000 who had his name and his Father's name written on their foreheads."

Passport Please takes the position that many from Israel will recognize the Prince and join him. The concept of Israel going through great trials and coming to acknowledge the Prince is reminiscent of the story of Joseph. His brothers, "the sons of Israel," went through many difficulties after trying to kill their brother. Finally, when Joseph revealed himself, they bowed to their brother, who ultimately turned out to be their deliverer. See note 4 on page 264.

[9] It is clear that the kingdom is behind the attacks.

Revelation 6:15-16 "Then the kings of the earth, the Princes, the generals, the rich, the mighty, and every slave and every free man hid in caves and among the rocks of the mountains. They called to the mountains and the rocks, 'Fall on us and hide us from the face of him who sits on the throne and from the wrath of the Lamb!'"

Revelation 20:4 "And I saw the souls of those who had been beheaded because of their testimony for Jesus and because of the word of God."

10. Luke 12:4-5 "I [Jesus] tell you, my friends, do not be afraid of those who kill the body and after that can do no more. But I will show you whom you should fear: Fear him who, after your body has been killed, has authority to throw you into hell. Yes, I tell you, fear him."

11. Revelation 7:16 "Never again will they hunger; never again will they thirst."

12. Revelation 9:20 "The rest of mankind that were not killed by these plagues still did not repent... they did not stop worshiping demons, and idols of gold, silver, bronze, stone and wood—idols that cannot see or hear or walk. Nor did they repent of their murders, their magic arts, their sexual immorality or their thefts."

13. A world leader emerges onto the scene (Darta, in the novel). He is the "beast" (AKA "the anti-Christ"). He is followed by a second beast (Runson, in the novel).

    Revelation 13:1-10 "It [the Beast] was given authority over every tribe, people, language and nation. All inhabitants of the earth will worship the beast."

    Revelation 13:11-17, [the second beast] "exercised all the authority of the first beast on its behalf, and made the earth and its inhabitants worship the first beast"

    In Revelation 16:13, that second beast is known as the "false prophet." *Passport Please* takes the position that these two beasts are the anti-Prince and the anti-Prime Minister. Together with Lucifer (the anti-King), they are the "unholy trinity."

14. Revelation 13:7 "He [the anti-Christ] was given power to make war against the saints and to conquer them."

Appendix 2: Endnotes

John 16:2 "a time is coming when anyone who kills you will think they are offering a service to God."

[15] The blockchain is a 21st century global electronic, encrypted system designed to prevent "tampering with the books." Crypto-currencies use this technology to maintain accurate accounts and to prevent fraud.

[16] Every human will be required to receive "the mark," without which, buying or selling will be impossible.

Revelation 13:16-18 "It also forced all people, great and small, rich and poor, free and slave, to receive a mark on their right hands or on their foreheads, so that they could not buy or sell unless they had the mark, which is the name of the beast or the number of its name. This calls for wisdom. Let the person who has insight calculate the number of the beast, for it is the number of a man. That number is 666."

[17] The world leader survives an apparently fatal wound.

Revelation 13:3 "One of the heads of the beast seemed to have had a fatal wound, but the fatal wound had been healed. The whole world was astonished and followed the beast."

[18] Darta will be in power for 3½ years.

Revelation 13:5 "The beast was given a mouth to utter proud words and blasphemies and to exercise its authority for forty-two months."

Pages 197 to 202   31: *The Take-Down*

[1] The kingdom army storms the earth.

Revelation 19:14 "The armies of heaven were following him, riding on white horses and dressed in fine linen, white and clean."

Kingdom citizens just arrived from earth may be part of that army. They had similar uniforms – white robes.

Revelation 7:9 "I looked, and there before me was a great multitude that no one could count, from every nation, tribe, people and language, standing before the throne and before the Lamb [Jesus]. They were wearing white robes and were holding palm branches in their hands."

2. Revelation 19:20 "But the beast was captured and with him the false prophet … The two of them were thrown alive into the fiery lake of burning sulfur."

3. Lucifer is imprisoned in a pit for 1,000 years

Revelation 20:1-3 "And I saw an angel coming down out of heaven, having the key to the Abyss and holding in his hand a great chain. He seized the dragon, that ancient serpent, who is the devil, or Satan [Lucifer], and bound him for a thousand years. He threw him into the Abyss, and locked and sealed it over him, to keep him from deceiving the nations anymore until the thousand years were ended. After that, he must be set free for a short time."

Revelation 9:2-3a, 10-11 "When he [an angel] opened the Abyss, smoke rose from it like the smoke from a gigantic furnace. The sun and sky were darkened by the smoke from the Abyss. And out of the smoke locusts came down on the earth … They had tails with stingers, like scorpions, and in their tails they had power to torment people for five months. They had as king over them the angel of the Abyss, whose name in Hebrew is Abaddon and in Greek is Apollyon (that is, Destroyer)."

Luke 8:31 "And they [the demons] begged Jesus repeatedly not to order them to go into the Abyss."

Appendix 2: Endnotes

[4] Revelation 11:15 "The seventh angel sounded his trumpet, and there were loud voices in heaven, which said: "The kingdom of the world has become the kingdom of our Lord and of his Messiah, and he will reign for ever and ever."

[5] Many on earth who committed publicly to the Prince after the evacuation of kingdom citizens, were executed for making that commitment. Later, they will rule the earth with the Prince for 1,000 years. During that time of the Prince's 1,000 year reign on earth, Jews will be known for their special relationship with the Prince.

Revelation 20:4b, 6 "And I saw the souls of those who had been beheaded because of their testimony for Jesus and because of the word of God. They had not worshiped the beast or his image and had not received his mark on their foreheads or their hands. They came to life and reigned with Christ a thousand years ... Blessed and holy are those who have part in the first resurrection. The second death has no power over them, but they will be priests of God and of Christ and will reign with him for a thousand years."

Zechariah 8:3, 7b-8, 23 "I [the Lord] will return to Zion and dwell in Jerusalem... I will save my people from the countries of the east and the west. I will bring them back to live in Jerusalem; they will be my people, and I will be faithful and righteous to them as their God... In those days ten people from all languages and nations will take firm hold of one Jew by the hem of his robe and say, 'Let us go with you, because we have heard that God is with you.'"

6   The Prince rules over a bountiful earth where sickness and death is rare, and long life is common.

Isaiah 65:20-23 "Never again will there be in it an infant who lives but a few days, or an old man who does not live out his years; he who dies at a hundred will be thought a mere youth; he who fails to reach a hundred will be considered accursed. They will build houses and dwell in them; they will plant vineyards and eat their fruit. No longer will they build houses and others live in them, or plant and others eat. For as the days of a tree, so will be the days of my people; my chosen ones will long enjoy the works of their hands. They will not toil in vain or bear children doomed to misfortune; for they will be a people blessed by the Lord, they and their descendants with them."

Pages 203 to 208 *32: Last Gasp*

1   John 10:9 "I [Jesus] am the gate; whoever enters through me will be saved."

John 14:6 "Jesus answered, "I am the way and the truth and the life. No one comes to the Father except through me."

2   Ezekiel 38:2 "Son of man, set your face against Gog, of the land of Magog, the chief Prince of Meshech and Tubal; prophesy against him"

3   Lucifer picks up where he left off, fomenting rebellion...

Revelation 20:7-8 "When the thousand years are over, Satan will be released from his prison and will go out to deceive the nations in the four corners of the earth—Gog and Magog—to gather them for battle. In number they are like the sand on the seashore."

Appendix 2: Endnotes

4   Gog was convinced to plunder but his attack was not a surprise to the King...

Ezekiel 38:10-12 "thoughts will come into your mind and you [Gog] will devise an evil scheme. You will say, 'I will invade a land of unwalled villages; I will attack a peaceful and unsuspecting people.'"

Ezekiel 38:15-16 "You [Gog] will come from your place in the far north, you and many nations with you, all of them riding on horses, a great horde, a mighty army. You will advance against my people Israel like a cloud that covers the land. In days to come, Gog, I will bring you against my land, so that the nations may know me when I am proved holy through you before their eyes."

5   After Noah's flood, God promised he would never destroy the earth again by water, so this time, it's fire...

Genesis 9:11 "Never again will all life be destroyed by the waters of a flood; never again will there be a flood to destroy the earth."

2 Peter 3:7 "the present heavens and earth are reserved for fire, being kept for the day of judgment and destruction of the ungodly."

6   Ezekiel 38:21-33 "I will execute judgment on him [Gog] with plague and bloodshed; I will pour down torrents of rain, hailstones and burning sulfur on him and on his troops and on the many nations with him. And so I will show my greatness and my holiness, and I will make myself known in the sight of many nations. Then they will know that I am the Lord."

Isaiah 66:15-16 "See, the Lord is coming with fire, and his chariots are like a whirlwind; he will bring down his anger with fury, and his rebuke with flames of fire. For with fire and with his sword the Lord will execute judgment on all people, and many will be those slain by the Lord."

7. Revelation 20:10 "And the devil, who deceived them, was thrown into the lake of burning sulfur, where the beast and the false prophet had been thrown. They will be tormented day and night for ever and ever."

8. Revelation 20:9 "They marched across the breadth of the earth and surrounded the camp of God's people, the city he loves. But fire came down from heaven and devoured them."

Isaiah 66:24 "they will go out and look on the dead bodies of those who rebelled against me; the worms that eat them will not die, the fire that burns them will not be quenched, and they will be loathsome to all mankind."

Revelation 14:20 "They were trampled in the winepress outside the city, and blood flowed out of the press, rising as high as the horses' bridles for a distance of 1,600 stadia [180 miles]"

9. 2 Peter 3:10-13 "The heavens will disappear with a roar... That day will bring about the destruction of the heavens by fire and the elements will melt in the heat."

10. Revelation 20:11-12 "I saw a great white throne and him who was seated on it. The earth and the heavens fled from his presence, and there was no place for them. And I saw the dead*, great and small, standing before the throne [*see note 1 on page 327] and books were opened. Another book was opened, which is the book of life. The dead were judged according to what they had done as recorded in the books."

Appendix 2: Endnotes

Pages 209 to 214   33: Immigration Hearing

[1] Only "the dead" will stand before the judge to determine if they may stay in Heaven. This is not for people who, during their lives, committed their lives to the Kingdom, because they, as kingdom citizens, had already been raised back to life. See note 5 on page 314.

Paul clarifies how Kingdom citizens will be judged...

2 Corinthians 5:10 "we [believers] must all appear before the judgment seat* of Christ."

* "Judgment seat" is the Greek word "bema," which is the platform on which Olympic athletes stand when they receive awards from the judges. It is not a court of law. Paul focused on the post-life awards ceremony, and ran his life on earth like an athlete running a race...

Acts 20:24 "my only aim is to finish the race and complete the task the Lord Jesus has given me..."

[2] The new capital city will be free of evil and corruption.

Revelation 21:27 "Nothing impure will ever enter it, nor will anyone who does what is shameful or deceitful, but only those whose names are written in the Lamb's book of life."

[3] Immigration detention is where unauthorized immigrants are held until a decision is made to either allow them into the country, send them back where they came from, or deport them elsewhere.

[4] Psalm 50:4 "He summons the heavens above, and the earth, that he may judge his people"

Daniel 12:2 "Multitudes who sleep in the dust of the earth will awake: some to everlasting life, others to shame and everlasting contempt."

Joel 3:2 "I will gather all nations and bring them down to the Valley of Jehoshaphat. There I will put them on trial for what they did to my inheritance, my people Israel, because they scattered my people among the nations and divided up my land."

5   Many were admitted to the kingdom, who, during their lives, never actually met or even heard of the Prince, and/or who were not aware of the kingdom pardon offered by the Prince. However, by their actions, they demonstrated that their allegiance was with the King.

Hebrews 11 calls out a number of them, including Abel, Noah, Abraham, Sarah, Isaac, Jacob and more.

Passport Please refers to these people as honorary kingdom citizens. See the 2nd note 2 on page 312.

6   James 5:9b "The Judge is standing at the door!"

7   *Passport Please* takes the position that all humans who want to enter heaven, but chose not to accept a kingdom pardon while living on earth, will stand before the judge at the immigration hearing. See note 1 on page 303.

8   Isaiah 3:13 "The Lord takes his place in court; he rises to judge the people."

Acts 17:31 "For he has set a day when he will judge the world with justice by the man he has appointed. He has given proof of this to everyone by raising him from the dead."

9   John 5:22 "Moreover, the Father judges no one, but has entrusted all judgment to the Son"

10   Matthew 7:22-24 "Many will say to me on that day, 'Lord, Lord, did we not prophesy in your name, and in your name drive out demons and perform many

Appendix 2: Endnotes

miracles?' Then I will tell them plainly, 'I never knew you. Away from me, you evildoers!'"

Romans 3:20a "Therefore, no one will be declared righteous in his [God's] sight by observing the law"

Passport Please takes the position that a long list of good deeds or extensive religious knowledge, by themselves, is insufficient to gain access to the kingdom.

11. The law is not up for debate.

    Job 40:6-8 "Then the Lord spoke to Job out of the storm: 'Brace yourself like a man; I will question you, and you shall answer me. Would you discredit my justice? Would you condemn me to justify yourself?'"

12. The King respects anyone's right to reject him.

    Luke 12:8-9 "I tell you, whoever acknowledges me before men, the Son of Man will also acknowledge him before the angels of God. But he who disowns me before men will be disowned before the angels of God."

13. 2 Thessalonians 1:8-9 "He will punish those who do not know God and do not obey the gospel of our Lord Jesus. They will be punished with everlasting destruction and shut out from the presence of the Lord and from the majesty of his power"

14. Leniency is allowed, as long as it is consistent with the law.

    Romans 2:12 "All who sin apart from the law will also perish apart from the law, and all who sin under the law will be judged by the law."

    Romans 4:15 "law brings wrath. And where there is no law there is no transgression."

Luke 12:48 "But the one who does not know and does things deserving punishment will be beaten with few blows. From everyone who has been given much, much will be demanded; and from the one who has been entrusted with much, much more will be asked."

15 Galatians 6:7 "Do not be deceived: God cannot be mocked. A man reaps what he sows."

16 All the evidence is available to the judge.

Revelation 20:12b "The dead were judged according to what they had done as recorded in the books."

Matthew 12:37 "For by your words you will be acquitted, and by your words you will be condemned."

Psalm 90:8 "You have set our iniquities before you, our secret sins in the light of your presence."

Romans 2:5 "But because of your stubbornness and your unrepentant heart, you are storing up wrath against yourself for the day of God's wrath, when his righteous judgment will be revealed."

17 Revelation 20:15 "If anyone's name was not found written in the book of life, he was thrown into the lake of fire."

Daniel 12:1 "at that time your people—everyone whose name is found written in the book—will be delivered."

18 Revelation 20:14 "Then death and Hades were thrown into the lake of fire."

Resurrection, even of the earth, is a recurring theme in the Bible. See note 1, page 240.

Appendix 2: Endnotes

Pages 215 to 218   *34: Moving Day*

1. John 15:13 "Greater love has no one than this, that he lay down his life for his friends."

2. 1 John 4:19 "We love because he [God] first loved us."

   John 3:16 "For God so loved the world that he gave his one and only Son, that whoever believes in him shall not perish but have eternal life."

3. John 14:16-17 "And I [Jesus] will ask the Father, and he will give you another Counselor to be with you forever—the Spirit of truth. The world cannot accept him, because it neither sees him nor knows him. But you know him, for he lives with you and will be in you."

4. 1 Corinthians 2:9 "...what no eye has seen, what no ear has heard, and what no human mind has conceived' the things God has prepared for those who love him" [here Paul is quoting from Isaiah 64:4]

5. Revelation 21:3 "And I heard a loud voice from the throne saying, 'Now the dwelling of God is with men, and he will live with them. They will be his people, and God himself will be with them and be their God.'"

Pages 219 to 220   *35: Another Age Begins*

1. Revelation 21:5 "He who is seated on the throne said, 'I am making everything new!'"

2. John the Apostle was shown what the capital city of the kingdom of heaven on earth would look like...

   Revelation 21:16-17 "He [an angel] measured the city with the rod and found it to be 12,000 stadia in length, and as wide and high as it is long. [1400 x 1400 miles]

He measured its wall and it was 144 cubits thick [200 ft], by man's measurement, which the angel was using."

To be "as wide and high as it is long" *Passport Please* takes the position that the new city has an unmistakable pyramid shape, just like the ancient "witness to the Lord Almighty" in Egypt.

Isaiah 19:19-20a "In that day there will be an altar to the Lord in the heart of Egypt, and a monument to the Lord at its border. It will be a sign and witness to the Lord Almighty in the land of Egypt."

The great pyramid of Giza is that witness. The great Pyramid is located in the geographical heart of Egypt, and it also lies on Egypt's border. Giza lies on the ancient border between "lower Egypt" and "upper Egypt," between the broad and fertile Nile delta region and the higher sources of the Nile. It also lies on the border of Egypt and the land promised to Israel. See the map on page 105.

A pyramid has five corners. The final stone to be put in place to complete a pyramid is the top cornerstone, or capstone. It should be noted that the great pyramid of Giza has a 30' by 30' flat top and does not (yet) have a top cornerstone. There is no evidence that it ever had one. Interestingly, the back of the US one-dollar bill depicts a capstone descending onto a pyramid from above.

Psalm 118:22 "The stone the builders rejected has become the cornerstone."

Ephesians 6:19-21 "you are no longer foreigners and strangers, but fellow citizens with God's people and also members of his household, built on the foundation of the apostles and prophets, with Christ Jesus himself as the chief cornerstone."

Appendix 2: Endnotes

Passport Please takes the position that in this new city, the Prince occupies the highest "corner office" which overlooks his reclaimed earth, and his family is with him.

Ephesians 2:6 [Paul wrote to faithful followers of Jesus, saying] "God raised us up with Christ and seated us with him in the heavenly realms in Christ Jesus."

[3] Revelation 21:1 "Then I saw a new heaven and a new earth, for the first heaven and the first earth had passed away, and there was no longer any sea."

Passport Please takes the position that since the old earth had already been burned up, it was the Crystal Sea above that disappeared. Lucifer was gone, so a moat was no longer needed. See note 3, page 241.

[4] Revelation 21:2 "I saw the Holy City, the new Jerusalem, coming down out of heaven from God, prepared as a bride beautifully dressed for her husband."

Amos 9:6 "he builds his lofty palace in the heavens and sets its foundation on the earth; he calls for the waters of the sea and pours them out over the face of the land—the Lord is his name."

[5] Ezra 3:12-13 "But many of the older priests and Levites and family heads, who had seen the former temple, wept aloud when they saw the foundation of this temple being laid, while many others shouted for joy. No one could distinguish the sound of the shouts of joy from the sound of weeping, because the people made so much noise. And the sound was heard far away."

[6] Revelation 21:18-21 "The wall was made of jasper, and the city of pure gold, as pure as glass. The foundations of the city walls were decorated with every kind of precious stone. The first foundation was jasper, the second

sapphire, the third chalcedony, the fourth emerald, the fifth sardonyx, the sixth carnelian, the seventh chrysolite, the eighth beryl, the ninth topaz, the tenth chrysoprase, the eleventh jacinth, and the twelfth amethyst. The twelve gates were twelve pearls, each gate made of a single pearl [*the pearly gates*]. The great street of the city was of pure gold, like transparent glass."

7   Jesus prepared this place for his human family.

John 14:3 "And if I [Jesus] go and prepare a place for you, I will come back and take you to be with me that you also may be where I am."

8   Revelation 22:1-2 "Then the angel showed me the river of the water of life, as clear as crystal, flowing from the throne of God and of the Lamb down the middle of the great street of the city. On each side of the river stood the tree of life, bearing twelve crops of fruit, yielding its fruit every month."

Passport Please takes the position that one tree on two sides of the river implies that the additional, higher dimensions of the kingdom are now in play for humans.

9   *Passport Please* takes the position that if one sticks with the Prince, the adventure will continue in the ages to come...

John 1:39 "They said [to Jesus] 'Rabbi, where are you staying?' 'Come,' he replied, 'and you will see.'"

Appendix 2: Endnotes

Passport Please - Epic of the Kingdom III

KINGDOM OF HEAVEN
DEPARTMENT OF IMMIGRATION

"You have enlarged the nation, Lord;
you have enlarged the nation.
You have gained glory for yourself;
You have extended all the borders of the land."

Isaiah 26:15

For more information on this book and
on the upcoming movie adaptation
of *Passport Please*, visit:

www.epicofthekingdom.com